HIERO THE TYRANT
AND OTHER TREATISES

XENOPHON was an Athenian country gentleman born in the early 420s BC. He may have helped to publish Thucydides' *History* and certainly wrote his own *Hellenica*, also known as *A History of My Times*, as a continuation of it. By his own (probably reliable) account he was a fine officer and outstanding leader, but his admiration for Sparta and devotion to Socrates led to his banishment. He was given an estate at Scillous, near Olympia, and settled down to enjoy the life of a landed aristocrat under Spartan protection, and it was during this period that he began to write histories, biographies, memoirs and specialist treatises. Events forced him to move to Corinth in 371, but he was allowed to return to Athens in 365, where he lived until his death in the late 350s.

ROBIN WATERFIELD was born in 1952. He graduated from Manchester University in 1974 and went on to research ancient Greek philosophy at King's College, Cambridge. He has been a university lecturer (at Newcastle upon Tyne and St Andrews) and both copy-editor and commissioning editor for Penguin Books. He now makes a living as a self-employed writer and consultant editor. His publications range from academic articles to children's fiction, and he has translated various Greek philosophical texts, including (for Penguin Classics) Xenophon's *Conversations of Socrates*, Plutarch's *Essays*, Plato's *Philebus* and *Theaetetus* and (in Plato's *Early Socratic Dialogues*) *Hippias Major*, *Hippias Minor* and *Euthydemus*. He also edited *The Voice of Kahlil Gibran* for Penguin Arkana.

PAUL CARTLEDGE was born in 1947. He was an undergraduate and junior research fellow at Oxford, where he took his D.Phil. in early Spartan archaeology and history under Sir John Boardman. He has taught since 1979 at the University of Cambridge, where he is *ad hominem* Reader in Greek History and a Fellow of Clare College. His publications include *Agesilaos and the Crisis of Sparta* (Duckworth and Johns Hopkins University Press, 1987), *Nomos: Essays in Athenian Law, Politics and Society* (Cambridge University Press, 1990) and *The Greeks: A Portrait of Self and*

Others (Oxford University Press; revised edition, 1997), and forthcoming are *Political Thought in Ancient Greece* and *The Cambridge Illustrated History of Ancient Greece*, both to be published by Cambridge University Press.

XENOPHON

HIERO THE TYRANT
AND OTHER TREATISES

Translated by ROBIN WATERFIELD
With introductions and notes by
PAUL CARTLEDGE

PENGUIN BOOKS

PENGUIN BOOKS

Published by the Penguin Group
Penguin Books Ltd, 27 Wrights Lane, London w8 5tz, England
Penguin Books USA Inc., 375 Hudson Street, New York, New York 10014, USA
Penguin Books Australia Ltd, Ringwood, Victoria, Australia
Penguin Books Canada Ltd, 10 Alcorn Avenue, Toronto, Ontario, Canada m4v 3b2
Penguin Books (NZ) Ltd, 182–190 Wairau Road, Auckland 10, New Zealand

Penguin Books Ltd, Registered Offices: Harmondsworth, Middlesex, England

Published in Penguin Classics 1997
1 3 5 7 9 10 8 6 4 2

Maps and figure by Nigel Andrews

Set in 10/12.5pt Postscript Monotype Bembo
Typeset by Rowland Phototypesetting Ltd, Bury St Edmunds, Suffolk
Printed in England by Clays Ltd, St Ives plc

CONTENTS

ON HUNTING
(*Cynegeticus*)

WAYS AND MEANS
(*Poroi*)

INTRODUCTION

A brief life

Xenophon of Athens is an elusive and seemingly self-effacing writer. Unlike his historian predecessors, Herodotus and Thucydides, he does not begin his most general Greek history, the *Hellenica* (in Penguin *A History of My Times*), with a formal autobiographical preface. Unlike Plato, he does not include members of his own family as characters in his philosophical recollections of their common mentor Socrates, the *Memorabilia* (Penguin *Memoirs of Socrates*). Xenophon's only explicitly autobiographical work is the *Anabasis* (Penguin *The Persian Expedition*), an account chiefly of his experiences as a mercenary commander between 401 and 399; yet at *History of My Times* 3.1.2 he states poker-faced that 'the story of that campaign' has been recorded, not by 'Xenophon of Athens', but by the otherwise unknown 'Themistogenes of Syracuse', who is generally presumed to be an autobiographical pseudonym of Xenophon himself. This reticence should not necessarily be confused with modesty. Xenophon was surely as self-consciously proud of his authorial skills, and as competitively present in his multifarious and often innovatory works, as any of his contemporaries – and rivals. For example, the Penguin title 'A History of My Times' catches very well the personalized, memoirist and apologetic character of that supposedly general history of Greek affairs between 411 and 362.[1]

A significant proportion of the *œuvre* that has been transmitted to us under Xenophon's name is bedevilled by the problem of authenticity. In the six treatises translated here there is just one extended authorial self-reference, in the final chapter of *On Hunting* (*Cynegeticus*). But that chapter, if not the whole treatise, is widely believed to be by another hand. Straightforwardly inauthentic is the political pamphlet formally entitled *Athenaion Politeia*, or *Athenian Constitution*, often familiarly referred to in the English-speaking world as 'The Old Oligarch'. This was composed probably in the third quarter of the fifth century, possibly even before Xenophon was born, and is very likely therefore to be the earliest extant piece of Attic (Athenian) prose writing. The misattribution was due to carelessness on the part of some ancient copyist or librarian; and Xenophon himself, although he was also firmly of an oligarchic persuasion, would doubtless have been mortified at being credited with a work suffused with the sophistry that both he himself in the *Memoirs of Socrates* and the author of chapter 13 of *On Hunting* (if that was not also Xenophon) likewise roundly condemned.[2] All or parts of several other works in the attributed Xenophontic corpus, including some in the present selection, are of either disputed or disputable authenticity: for example, *Spartan Society* (which the editor of the Penguin *Plutarch on Sparta* would condemn *in toto*) and the treatise *On Horsemanship*, which – despite a cross reference to the less contentiously authentic *How to Be a Good Cavalry Commander* – has often been judged on linguistic grounds to have been composed much later. The editors of the present volume, however, would robustly defend its (and the other treatises') presence here on the grounds of intrinsic interest as well as authentically Xenophontic allure.[3] Resolving problems of authenticity is not aided by our desperate dearth of reliable biographical information on Xenophon, which is due in part to the fact that biography itself was not yet an established literary genre in his day (see further the Introduction to *Agesilaus*). The following 'brief life' aims therefore to err severely on the side of caution.[4]

Xenophon was born if not quite into the purple at any rate into an elite and propertied Athenian family in the early 420s. His unusual name – a compound of the Greek words for foreigner or special foreign friend (*xenos*) and voice (*phone*) – was intended to call attention to his family's foreign connections, a sure mark of aristocratic pedigree. By economic circumstance and military choice Xenophon was a Hippeus, or Cavalryman. He belonged, that is, to the highest but one of the four official Athenian census- or property-classes, membership of which conferred distinctive political entitlements. On coming of age, he chose to serve with the Athenian cavalry – militarily speaking, a largely ineffectual body of a few hundred men with strongly marked social overtones of old-fashioned exclusivity in a professedly egalitarian political community. Here was suitable grist for Aristophanes' comic mill in the play he named after them, the *Knights*, which was produced at the lesser of the two annual Athenian play-festivals in 424, just a few years after Xenophon's birth.[5]

To Xenophon's elite birth and exceptional wealth was added an inegalitarian, oligarchic political disposition, which will not have been softened by his encounter with the teaching of Socrates. The master's own political outlook has been the subject of much dispute among modern scholars, but most of his Athenian contemporaries were in little doubt that Socrates' ideological sympathies did not lie primarily with Athens' form of democratic self-government, and it was largely because of this that a democratic jury condemned him to death in 399. That verdict (which Socrates' conduct at his trial did nothing to avert or mitigate) engendered a furious pamphleteering war among the philosophically minded literati of Athens. Xenophon contributed both a reconstruction of Socrates' defence speech, the *Apology* (far more intrinsically plausible as a reconstruction than the more famous *Apology* of his fellow former pupil Plato),[6] and a set of moral-philosophical homilies featuring Socrates as principal interlocutor, the *Memoirs of Socrates*.

At the time of the trial, however, in 399, Xenophon had other things on his mind, and was anyway far from Athens, campaigning in Asia Minor as a mercenary captain. His presence there can be traced ultimately to the circumstances in which Athens had finally been defeated by Sparta in the Peloponnesian War, thanks crucially to massive foreign aid from Persia, in 404. The peace terms enforced on Athens by Sparta included not merely military and economic sanctions, but what the majority of the defeated considered to be their political 'enslavement', a term that carried a specially emotive charge in a society with thousands of actual slaves. Instead of rule by the People, there was now for Athens rule by a *dunasteia* or junta of thirty extreme oligarchs, abetted by the ten adjutant governors, placed in charge of the economically as well as militarily vital Athenian port city of

Peiraeus. But those forty Athenians could hardly have ruled alone. Lacking the consent of the now even more fiercely democratic majority of Athenian citizens, they secured the services of a Spartan garrison of 700. But it was the use they made of the doubtless not unwilling Athenian cavalry in order to police the resistant masses that was to seal Xenophon's fate when the restoration of independence and democracy came − as it did, unexpectedly quickly and relatively smoothly, in 403. Tainted by his oligarchic past, Xenophon was only too glad to escape Athens − with the blessing of the Delphic oracle, as recommended to him by Socrates, allegedly − in 401.[7]

Together with a Theban family friend (*xenos*) called Proxenus, Xenophon signed up as a mercenary officer under the banner of the Persian pretender, Cyrus the Younger, who eventually raised a huge force of some 13,000 Greek mercenaries. Here was practical soldiering with a vengeance, but far more than that, it provided for the adult Xenophon (by then in his late twenties) a properly political education, a sort of finishing school. Despite the prowess of his mercenaries, Cyrus lost the decisive pitched battle of Cunaxa against the reigning Great King, his elder brother Artaxerxes II (reigned *c*. 404−359). The Greeks now found themselves thrown back on their own resources, marooned far inland at the heart of the Persian empire and immensely vulnerable to attack from both Artaxerxes' chief lieutenant, the satrap (viceroy) Tissaphernes, and the variety of native peoples who stood between the Greeks and their much desired return to their Mediterranean homelands.

The vast majority of mercenaries did, nevertheless, manage to extricate themselves safely. Most conspicuously, Xenophon himself lived to tell the tale − or rather his version of it, since it seems that he was in part writing against an earlier account that gave him less personal credit, at any rate less than he felt was his due. In the early 390s, however, his own personal situation and the general geopolitical situation precluded an immediate return to Athens. Xenophon may indeed have been formally exiled already for having collaborated with Cyrus, an enemy of Athens; but if not, he soon was to be for co-operating with, that is serving under, Sparta. For Xenophon enlisted the remnant of Cyrus's mercenaries under the Spartans' banner in 399 to fight, officially, for the liberation of the Greeks of Asia from Persian rule. To most Athenian eyes, however, that would have looked uncomfortably like supporting Sparta in its imperial and therefore anti-Athenian ambitions, and the implied logic of Xenophon's position became unambiguously explicit in 394, when with the 'Cyreians', as they were still known, he fought on the side of Sparta against his own native Athens at Coroneia in Boeotia.

Key to this unquestionably flagrant act of high treason was the close personal relationship Xenophon had struck up since 396 with Agesilaus, that is King Agesilaus II of Sparta, a remarkable figure whose exceptional character may be gathered initially from the fact that he was the first Spartan king to campaign on the Asiatic mainland. Like many upper-class, anti-democratic Athenians, Xenophon will have been predisposed in his favour because of the Spartans' traditional policy of supporting conservative oligarchic regimes both within and outside their alliance. But in Agesilaus Xenophon believed he had discovered more than that, indeed an exemplar of 'perfect goodness', as he was to put it a touch enthusiastically in the exordium of his laudatory biography (1.1). His Agesilaus was the living embodiment of the sort of moral virtues that Xenophon himself vigorously espoused and through his writings no less vigorously promulgated. It did nothing to diminish the exiled Athenian's respect, affection and loyalty that from 394 Xenophon was also deeply in Agesilaus' debt, for his life-style as well as his life.

Barred from Athens, no longer attracted by the notion of founding a new Greek settlement on the southern shore of the Black Sea, in sympathy with the Spartan regime at home and with most of its representatives and supporters abroad, Xenophon – like Cimon, a conservative Athenian of an earlier generation – quickly came to identify himself as 'Peloponnesian' in spirit, as one of those Greeks who in his own words 'had the best interests of the Peloponnese at heart'.[8] To enable him to live a truly Peloponnesian life-style, Agesilaus was instrumental in securing him a large country estate at Scillous not far from Olympia. Control of this land, however, was fiercely contested by Elis, a volatile and recently disaffected ally of Sparta. Traditionally, Elis ran the Olympic Games, and had flagrantly exploited its position to ban Spartans from competing there in 420 (there is nothing new in making political capital out of the Olympics . . .). The final action of Agesilaus' older half-brother Agis II in the late 400s was a campaign to discipline Elis. A friendly presence at nearby Scillous would therefore suit Agesilaus and Sparta very well. The personal connection between Xenophon and Agesilaus was reportedly reinforced by Xenophon's agreeing to send his two sons to be educated at Sparta. There they joined other sons of pro-Spartan foreigners who wished their children to experience the noble qualities of the famously rigorous Spartan educational regimen.[9]

In 371, however, Sparta's foreign policy of supporting friendly oligarchies, with force if necessary, came apart at the seams on the battlefield of Leuctra in Boeotia. Agesilaus, by then a veteran in his mid-70s, was not actually in command of the Spartan and allied force that was routed by the larger and more up-to-date army trained, inspired and led by the Thebans Epameinondas and Pelopidas. But the responsibility for the disaster was squarely his. The knock-on effect of Sparta's loss of the hegemony of the Peloponnese on Agesilaus' clients including Xenophon was almost immediate and palpably material. With his Scillous base rendered unviable, Xenophon retired, it is usually thought, to Corinth, where he lived possibly until his death in the late 350s. Or possibly not: another school of thought maintains that after 371, perhaps sooner rather than later since Athens was now allied with the old enemy Sparta against the common threat of a newly surgent Thebes, Xenophon returned as an elder statesman to his native city. Hence, so it is argued, the specifically Athenian character of at least some of his putatively late works, including notably two of those included here, *Cavalry Commander* and *Ways and Means*.

That raises, finally, the questions of when and where, rather than why (to which we shall return below), he wrote his various works. Certainty, be it stated straightaway, is impossible; even probability is usually well beyond our grasp. One extreme, 'unitarian' view would place all his works – or, to be more specific, the whole of all his works – in the post-Leuctra 360s and 350s. At the other extreme, there are those who argue that at least all *The Persian Expedition* and the relevant

portions of *A History of My Times* and *Agesilaus*, and perhaps also the
Memoirs of Socrates, were composed at Scillous and also published close
to the time of the events and situations they describe or presuppose.
Even an extreme 'analyst' view, however, would still have to assign
a large proportion, if not the bulk, of the *œuvre* in its final, published
form to the post-Leuctra period. My own impression is that Xenophon, like many another ex-politician compelled to fill a vacuum of
unwanted and unwonted inactivity, devoted himself to the publication
of written work in polished form only in his final decade or decade
and a half. It would not surprise me, either, though I could not
consider it anything remotely approaching a racing certainty, if their
publication had been crucially stimulated by the author's restoration to
the vibrant intellectual atmosphere of Athens, to what Plato (*Protagoras*
337d) once styled the 'city hall' (*prutaneion*) of *sophia*.[10]

In the city hall of wisdom

The conventional translation of *sophia* as 'wisdom' suits well a straight
rendering of *philosophia* (literally, 'love of *sophia*') as 'philosophy'. But
ancient Greek *sophia*, although it included knowing-that as well as
knowing-how, was more than the wisdom of the philosopher as we
might understand it. It connoted also the idea of professionalism, the
possession of a relevant skill, knack or technique in any particular area
– be it medicine, or politics, or shipbuilding, or whatever. To meet
the growing complexity of public life in the developing Athenian
democracy, there was a correspondingly increased demand for professional instruction in relevant skills and techniques. The sophists,
though definitely not constituting a school, and perhaps only second-
arily linked together as part of a single intellectual movement, offered
themselves as teachers of useful knowledge and usable skills.[11]

Since they charged high fees affordable only by the seriously wealthy,
they pitched their appeal especially to the adolescent and young adult
sons of the propertied leisure class. This was a section of society
that in democratic Athens was finding itself increasingly out of
sympathy with the shift in the balance of power from the elite few to
the – as the elite saw them – untutored and unwashed masses. The

pseudo-Xenophontic 'Old Oligarch' neatly reflects both the anti-democratic outlook of this elite and the consequences of sophistic teaching. The sophists themselves, however, were by no means all necessarily anti-democratic. The instruction they provided in the arts of persuasive rhetoric could have been as well deployed on the democratic side of an argument. For it was argument, one of the several meanings of the Greek word *logos*, that their teaching was principally about, in both theory and practice.

One of their main pedagogical gambits was to ask a pupil to distinguish between ideas or practices that were traditional and yet intellectually respectable and those that were merely conventional but rationally indefensible. It was not difficult therefore for conservatives to paint the sophists as dangerous radicals undermining the traditional foundations of social solidarity. This was how Aristophanes comically represented Socrates and his 'Thinkery' in his *Clouds* of 423. But that was not at all how Socrates' own pupils saw him. Indeed, it was they who in their all too successful efforts to distinguish their revered mentor as sharply as possible from the sophists gave them their bad name (and us the negative term 'sophistical'). What Plato seems to have objected to most about the sophists was their claim both to know and to be able to teach wisdom, when really they were merely clever-clever tinkerers with words and ignorant of what true wisdom was. What Xenophon, however, seems to have principally feared was that their teaching would legitimize and foster the irreligion that he saw as in any case steeply on the increase, thanks to an unholy combination of factors fostered by the morally debilitating circum-stances of the Peloponnesian War. In this regard, as in many others, Xenophon's outlook was far more conventional and traditional than that of Plato.[12]

In one respect, however, Xenophon was very much a child of his progressive times. Although he spent almost half of his life, and perhaps as much as three-quarters of his adulthood, in exile, he had been born and raised at the epicentre of the panhellenic intellectual ferment associated with the 'sophists'. He thus became willy-nilly part of the revolution in intellectual discourse that these newfangled thinkers set in train. A subsidiary but vital part of this revolution was the transformation of a broadly oral intellectual culture into a broadly written one. Strictly, Greek had no word for a 'reader'. The word that did service for it, *akroates*, meant literally a 'hearer'. Likewise, one of the Greek verbs used to mean 'to read', *anagignoskein*, meant literally 'to recognize again', that is recognize again in their concretized, written form the sounds of words that one had first heard. Most Greeks most of the time would primarily hear words rather than read texts. But from the second half of the fifth century onwards, intellectual interchange increasingly relied on the written word. It is not therefore accidental that Xenophon's work should contain some of the earliest known references to the ownership of books. In *The Persian Expedition* (7.5.14), for example, we are told that among the items carried on a trading ship wrecked off Salmydessus in the northern Aegean would be found 'numbers of written books [*bibloi*, papyrus book-rolls] and a lot of other things of the sort that sea-captains carry in their wooden chests'; and in *Memoirs of Socrates* 4.2.1 Socrates is said to have 'discovered that the handsome Euthydemus had collected a great many writings (*grammata*) of the best-known poets and sages'. A little later in that same vignette (4.2.8), however, a characteristically Socratic note of doubt is sounded: 'Is it true what I hear', Socrates enquires of Euthydemus, 'that you have collected a large number of books (*grammata*) by reputed experts (*sophoi*)?' The key word here, of course, is 'reputed': the reference is to the writings of sophists. Socrates, born in about 470, apparently never wrote a word of his teaching, whereas the sophists, some of whom were older than he, more flexibly employed both oral and written means. Socrates, it seems, distrusted the medium as well as the message of these pseudo-experts. Xenophon, born over forty years after Socrates, fully shared his master's distrust of sophistic doctrine but did not shun the use of the written word.

Not that the traditional methods of education and instruction through face-to-face dialogue and practical demonstration were entirely superseded by any means. Apart from anything else, written texts, if they were to be made available in any numbers, had to be laboriously transcribed on valuable Egyptian papyrus by specially trained slaves, and so were in Xenophon's day fairly rare and expensive commodities. Their target audiences, which included the intended readerships of these treatises, must therefore normally be sought among only the highest socio-economic echelons of Greek and Athenian society.[13]

Xenophon the pedagogue

Xenophon's range of publications in terms of their genre and subject matter was quite exceptionally wide: from history, personal memoirs and biography, through philosophical dialogues and a philosophical novel, to technical treatises. In more than one field, moreover, he was a pioneer working at the intellectual and literary cutting edge. The quality of his intellect is a separate issue. It is perhaps doubtful, for example, whether Xenophon can be shown to be a penetrating or even consistent philosophical theorist.[14] On the other hand, there can be no doubting that all his *œuvre*, not only the more overtly philosophical works, was intended as a teaching of practical philosophy by examples. It was informed throughout by a high moral and especially religious purpose.

Thus Xenophon's account of the civil war at Athens in 404–403 has little or nothing in common with Thucydides' famously pragmatic analysis of the civil war on Corcyra (modern Corfu), in 427 (3.82–3). Its essential theme is rather friendship, and its betrayal, and how breaches of friendship can and should be overcome by ritually negotiated reconciliation. Friendship recurs prominently at *Memoirs of Socrates* 1.2.8, where Xenophon's Socrates is credited with locating the main profit to be gained from his philosophy in the fact that it rendered his associates good friends to each other (compare 2.4–10). The theme that dominates all others, however, is religion or rather piety. Again and again, conventional piety is recommended and impiety condemned, usually in a simple or even simplistic way. Being pious is indeed represented by Xenophon uncomplicatedly (rather than critically defined, in the Platonic manner) as a matter of fulfilling the conventionally practised rituals, and conforming to the traditional articles of belief, regarding the gods (or 'the god', 'the divine'). Religious nonconformity, in Xenophon's unswerving view, deservedly brought disaster to both individuals and communities. 'Many examples could be given from both Greek and foreign history to show that the gods are not indifferent to irreligion or to evil doing' is how Xenophon, commenting on an admittedly egregious instance of sacrilege, introduces and explains the major public political process of the Greek world in his day, Sparta's downfall as a great Greek power (*History of My Times* 5.4.1). Xenophon's underlying framework for the explanation and evaluation of human affairs was, in short, profoundly but somewhat naively theological.

His other major preoccupation besides proper piety towards the gods was the leadership of men. Three of the six treatises translated here, *Hiero*, *Agesilaus* and *Cavalry Commander*, are explicitly and centrally about leadership in its various forms, on and off the battlefield, within a city and on the international stage. The theme also reappears importantly in the possibly not (entirely) authentic treatises on horsemanship and hunting. Successful leadership, Xenophon predictably argued, was crucially dependent on the leader's showing true piety. Apart from piety in the leader, what the disciplinarian author primarily looked for and inculcated was unquestioning obedience in the subordinate. Xenophon's 'devotion to the principle of order', which he ranked well above the value of freedom, is perspicuous throughout his writings.[15]

Reception

Taken at face value, therefore, Xenophon looks like a classic exponent of conservatism and counter-enlightenment. One distinguished contemporary specialist in ancient philosophy, indeed, once dismissed him as 'quite closely resembl[ing] a familiar British figure – the retired general, staunch Tory and Anglican, firm defender of the Establishment in Church and State'.[16] But it is only fair to Xenophon to add that there are the glimmerings of new readings in sight. One reviewer of a commentary on *The Estate-manager*, for example, wrote that 'The distinct possibility exists that to take at face value the words of Xenophon's characters may mean that we in turn fail to understand the point of the [work].'[17]

Such new readings are part of the ongoing process of competitive reception that characterizes all writers deemed worthy of inclusion in a literary canon. Xenophon himself was full of self-righteous ambition to be so included. He seems to have written *The Persian Expedition*, for example, in response to a less pro-Xenophon version, and to have published the *Agesilaus* as a pre-emptive strike in an anticipated posthumous pamphlet war over Agesilaus' legacy. He would therefore have expected his work to be at least controversial and controverted. On the whole, though, the judgement of antiquity proved favourable: 'most learned' was how the second century BC historian Polybius (6.45.1) found him; and 'the sweetest and most graceful Xenophon' was the opinion of Athenaeus of Naucratis in Egypt, the voraciously learned compiler in about AD 200 of a prodigiously extended bout of invented literary table talk (Athen. 504c). One Greek writer of the second century AD, Flavius Arrianus, actually identified himself quite literally as the new Xenophon and modelled his history of Alexander the Great on Xenophon's *Persian Expedition* in both its name and its seven-book structure.[18] It was such approbation, coupled with Xenophon's good Attic Greek, that ensured the continued manuscript copying of his texts throughout antiquity and the Middle Ages on papyrus and vellum and thence his survival into the age of printing.[19]

The modern reception of Xenophon, however, has been considerably more chequered. The third Earl of Shaftesbury, in his *Characteristics of Men, Manners, Opinions, and Times* (1711), praised Xenophon fulsomely as the author of 'an original system of works, the politest, wisest, usefullest, and (to those who can understand the divineness of a just simplicity) the most amiable and even the most elevating and exalting of all uninspired and merely human authors'. Towards the end of the eighteenth century Edward Gibbon rated highly the lively narrative prose of the supposedly veristic *Persian Expedition*, but found the fictional *Cyropaedia* (*Education of Cyrus*, an invented biography of the founder of the Persian empire) correspondingly tedious. The appreciably lower current estimate of the quality of Xenophon's mind (though not of his prose) seems to have set in first in early to mid nineteenth-century Germany, whence it passed to Britain and points further west. The main reason for this negative rating, I suspect, is unfavourable comparison of Xenophon with other writers in the many genres he attempted, most conspicuously with Plato in philosophy, and with Thucydides in history. But that depreciation has probably also been aggravated by failure to appreciate duly the nature of Xenophon's rhetoric – an aspect of ancient (as of modern) writers to which a great deal of attention is now belatedly being paid. It remains to be seen whether as a result of such fresh reassessments of his style Xenophon's stock will continue to rise significantly on the scholarly market. The present collection will, it is hoped, help to make any re-evaluation of Xenophon, if not necessarily wiser, at any rate better informed.

NOTES

1. In Penguin Classics the *Memoirs of Socrates* is translated by H. Tredennick and R. Waterfield in the volume entitled *Conversations of Socrates* (1990); *The Persian Expedition* (1972) and *A History of My Times* (1979) are by R. Warner, with introductions and notes by G. Cawkwell. For these and other bibliographical details and recommendations, see Further Reading.

2. The 'Old Oligarch' is conveniently available in English translation with commentary in J. M. Moore, *Aristotle and Xenophon on Democracy and Oligarchy* (Chatto & Windus and University of California Press, 2nd edn., 1983). On sophistry, see the next section of this Introduction.

3. *Spartan Society* (*Lakedaimonion Politeia*) is translated with commentary in the Penguin *Plutarch on Sparta* (1988), pp. 166–84. Modern scholarship on Xenophon is reviewed in the works by Morrison and Nickel.

4. Further detail, and references to the relevant passages in Xenophon's works, may be found in Cawkwell's excellent introductions to the Penguin *Persian Expedition* and *History of My Times*; it was a particular privilege for the present writer to attend George Cawkwell's Oxford lectures on Xenophon in the early 1970s.

5. For an attempt to situate Aristophanes' plays within their social and political context, see Cartledge, *Aristophanes and His Theatre of the Absurd* (Duckworth, 1995).

6. The *Apology* (as *Socrates' Defence*) is included in the Penguin *Conversations of Socrates*.

7. Xenophon's account of the defeat of Athens and its oligarchic aftermath is given in the first two books of *A History of My Times*; these may usefully be read with the commentary of P. Krentz (Aris & Phillips, 2 vols., 1989–94). See also his *The Thirty at Athens* (Cornell University Press, 1982).

8. *A History of My Times* 7.4.35 (and note), 7.5.1. On Xenophon's exile, see Green.

9. On Spartan education, see Xenophon's *Spartan Society*, in the Penguin *Plutarch on Sparta*. For the career of Agesilaus generally, see Cartledge, *Agesilaos*.

10. The extreme 'unitarian' view is argued or assumed by Higgins; the extreme 'analyst' position by Delebecque, *Essai sur la vie*.

11. On the sophists see Kerferd, Rankin and de Romilly.

12. The view that the sophists caused rather than exploited or contributed to a grave spiritual crisis in Greece, not confined to Athens, is argued by Burkert, *Greek Religion*, pp. 311–17.

13. On changing patterns of literacy and orality in Greece generally and in democratic Athens specifically, see Thomas.

14. See Waterfield's introduction to *Memoirs of Socrates*, but contrast more favourable assessments in Vander Waerdt.

15. The phrase quoted is that of Dillery, *Xenophon and the History*.

16. T. H. Irwin, as quoted in Cartledge, *Agesilaos*, p. 61.

17. Y. L. Too, *Classical Review* 45 (1995), 248 reviewing Pomeroy. See also n. 14.

18. See J. R. Hamilton's Penguin Arrian, *The Campaigns of Alexander* (1971).

19. See L. D. Reynolds and N. G. Wilson, *Scribes and Scholars: A Guide to the Transmission of Greek and Latin Literature*, 3rd edn. (Oxford University Press, 1991).

FURTHER READING

I. GENERAL CONTEXT

a. History of the times

Buckley, T., *Aspects of Greek History 750–323 B.C.: A Source-based Approach* (Routledge, 1996)

The Cambridge Ancient History, 2nd edn., vol. V *The Fifth Century* (Cambridge University Press, 1992), vol. VI *The Fourth Century* (1994)

Cartledge, P., *Agesilaos and the Crisis of Sparta* (Duckworth and Johns Hopkins University Press, 1987)

— (ed.), *The Cambridge Illustrated History of Ancient Greece* (Cambridge University Press, forthcoming)

Davies, J., *Democracy and Classical Greece*, 2nd edn. (Fontana/Harper-Collins, 1993)

Finley, M. I., *Politics in the Ancient World* (Cambridge University Press, 1983)

b. Athenian society and intellectual milieu

Andrewes, A., *Greek Society* (Penguin, 1971)

Davies, *Democracy and Classical Greece*, chapter 12

Irwin, T. H., 'Plato: the intellectual background', in R. Kraut (ed.), *The Cambridge Companion to Plato* (Cambridge University Press, 1992), pp. 51–89

Kerferd, G. B., *The Sophistic Movement* (Cambridge University Press, 1981)

Muir, J. V., 'Religion and the new education: the challenge of the Sophists', in P. Easterling and J. V. Muir (eds.), *Greek Religion and Society* (Cambridge University Press, 1985), pp. 191–218

Rankin, H. D., *Sophists, Socratics and Cynics* (Croom Helm and Barnes & Noble, 1983)

Romilly, J. de, *The Great Sophists in the Age of Pericles* (Oxford University Press, 1992)

Thomas, R., *Literacy and Orality in Ancient Greece* (Cambridge University Press, 1992)

Vander Waerdt, P. (ed.), *The Socratic Movement* (Cornell University Press, 1994)

Wood, N. and E. M., *Class Ideology and Ancient Political Theory* (Blackwell, 1978)

c. Greek religion

Bruit-Zaidman, L., and Schmitt-Pantel, P., *Religion in the Ancient Greek City*, ed. and trans. P. Cartledge (Cambridge University Press, 1992)

Burkert, W., *Greek Religion: Archaic and Classical* (Blackwell, 1985)

Easterling, P., and Muir, J. V. (eds.), *Greek Religion and Society* (Cambridge University Press, 1985)

Mikalson, J. D., *Athenian Popular Religion* (University of North Carolina Press, 1983)

d. General climate of beliefs

Cohen, D., *Law, Sexuality and Society: The Enforcement of Morals in Classical Athens* (Cambridge University Press, 1991)

—, *Law, Violence and Community in Classical Athens* (Cambridge University Press, 1995)

Dover, K. J., *Greek Popular Morality in the Time of Plato and Aristotle* (Blackwell, 1974)

—, *Greek Homosexuality* (Duckworth and Harvard University Press, 1978; rev. edn, 1989)

Fisher, N., *Hybris: A Study in the Values of Honour and Shame in Ancient Greece* (Aris & Phillips, 1992)

II. XENOPHON'S LIFE AND WORK

a. General

Anderson, J. K., *Xenophon* (Duckworth, 1974)

Breitenbach, H. R., 'Xenophon', *Pauly-Wissowa/RE* IXA2 (1967)

Cartledge, P., 'Xenophon's women: a touch of the Other', in H. D. Jocelyn & H. Hurst (eds.), *Tria Lustra: Fest. J. Pinsent* (Liverpool Classical Paper 3, 1993), pp. 163–75

Delebecque, E., *Essai sur la vie de Xénophon* (Klincksieck, 1957)

Dillery, J., *Xenophon and the History of His Times* (Routledge, 1995)

Green, P. M., 'Text and context in the manner of Xenophon's exile', in I. Worthington (ed.), *Ventures into Greek History* (Oxford University Press, 1994), pp. 215–27

Higgins, W. E., *Xenophon the Athenian: The Problem of the Individual and the Society of the Polis* (State University of New York Press, 1977)

Hindley, C., 'Eros and military command in Xenophon', *Classical Quarterly*, 44 (1994), pp. 347–66

Johnstone, S., 'Virtuous toil, vicious work: Xenophon on aristocratic style', *Classical Philology*, 89 (1994), pp. 219–40

Morrison, D. R., *Bibliography of Editions, Translations, and Commentary on Xenophon's Socratic Writings 1600–Present* (Mathesis Publications, Inc., 1988)

Münscher, K., *Xenophon in der griechisch-römischen Literatur* (*Philologus* Supp. 13, 1920)

Nickel, R., *Xenophon* (Wissenschaftliche Buchgesellschaft, 1979)

Rawson, E., *The Spartan Tradition in European Thought* (Oxford University Press, 1969, 1991)

Wood, N., 'Xenophon's theory of leadership', *Classica et Mediaevalia*, 25 (1964), pp. 33–66

b. Particular works

All the treatises in this volume may be found in translation with facing Greek text in E. C. Marchant's Loeb Classical Library edition, 1925.

1. Hiero the Tyrant

Gray, V. J., 'Xenophon's *Hiero* and the meeting of the wise man and the tyrant', *Classical Quarterly*, 36 (1986), pp. 115–23

2. Agesilaus

Cartledge, P., *Agesilaos and the Crisis of Sparta*

Gentili, B., and Cerri, G., *History and Biography in Ancient Thought* (Gieben, 1988)

Momigliano, A. D., *The Development of Greek Biography*, augmented edn. (Harvard University Press, 1993)

Proietti, G., *Xenophon's Sparta* (*Mnemosyne* Supp. 98, 1987)

Talbert, R. (ed.), *Plutarch on Sparta* (Penguin, 1988)

3. How to Be a Good Cavalry Commander
4. On Horsemanship

Anderson, J. K., *Ancient Greek Horsemanship* (University of California Press, 1961)

Bugh, G. R., *The Horsemen of Athens* (Princeton University Press, 1988)

Delebecque, E. (ed.), *De l'art équestre* (Budé, 1978)

— (ed.), *Le commandant de la cavalerie* (Budé, 1973)

Morgan, M. H., *Xenophon: The Art of Horsemanship* (Dent, 1894)

Piggott, S., *Wagon, Chariot and Carriage* (Thames & Hudson, 1992)

Spence, I. G., *The Cavalry of Classical Greece: A Social and Military History with Particular Reference to Athens* (Oxford University Press, 1993)

Worley, L., *Hippeis: The Cavalry of Ancient Greece* (Westview Press, 1994)

5. On Hunting

Anderson, J. K., *Hunting in the Ancient World* (University of California Press, 1985)

Classen, C. J., 'Xenophons Darstellung der Sophistik und der Sophisten', *Hermes*, 112 (1984), pp. 154–67

David, E., 'Hunting in Spartan society and consciousness', *Echos du Monde Classique/Classical Views*, 12 (1993), pp. 393–413

Delebecque, E. (ed.), *Xénophon. L'Art de la Chasse* (Budé, 1970)

Gray, V. J., 'Xenophon's *Cynegeticus*', *Hermes*, 113 (1985), pp. 156–72

Schnapp, A., *Le Chasseur et la cité. Chasse et érotique dans la Grèce ancienne* (Albin Michel, 1997)

6. Ways and Means

Austin, M. M., and Vidal-Naquet, P., *Economic and Social History of Ancient Greece: An Introduction* (Batsford, 1977)

Dillery, J., 'Xenophon's *Poroi* and Athenian imperialism', *Historia*, 42 (1993), pp. 1–11

Finley, M. I., *The Ancient Economy*, 2nd edn. (Hogarth Press and University of California Press, 1985)

Garlan, Y., *Slavery in Ancient Greece* (Cornell University Press, 1988)

—, *Warfare in the Ancient World* (Chatto & Windus, 1975)

Gauthier, Ph., *Une commentaire historique des Poroi de Xénophon* (Droz, 1976)

Hunt, P., *The Spear and the Whip* (Cambridge University Press, forthcoming)

7. Other Works

Bartlett, R. C. (trans.), *Xenophon: The Shorter Socratic Writings* (*Apology of Socrates to the Jury*, *Oeconomicus* and *Symposium*) (Cornell University Press, 1996)

Brown, T. S., 'Echoes from Herodotus in Xenophon's Hellenica', *Ancient World*, 21 (1990), pp. 97–101

Cawkwell, G. L., Introduction and notes to *A History of My Times* (trans. of *Hellenica*), by R. Warner (Penguin, 1979)

—, Introduction and notes to *The Persian Expedition* (trans. of *Anabasis*), by R. Warner (Penguin, 1972)

Connor, W. R., 'Historical writing in the fourth century and in the Hellenistic period', in P. Easterling and B. Knox (eds.), *The Cambridge History of Classical Literature*, vol. I, *Greek Literature* (Cambridge University Press, 1985), pp. 458–71

Due, B., *The Cyropaedia: Xenophon's Aims and Methods* (Aarhus University Press, 1989)

Georges, P., *Barbarian Asia and the Greek Experience: From the Archaic Period to the Age of Xenophon* (Johns Hopkins University Press, 1995)

Gera, D., *Xenophon's Cyropaedia* (Oxford University Press, 1993)

Gray, V. J., *The Character of Xenophon's Hellenica* (Duckworth and Johns Hopkins University Press, 1989)

Henry, W. P., *Greek Historical Writing: A Historiographical Essay Based on Xenophon's Hellenica* (Argonaut Press, 1967)

Hirsch, S. W., *The Friendship of the Barbarians: Xenophon and the Persian Empire* (University Press of New England, 1985)

O'Connor, D., 'The erotic self-sufficiency of Socrates: a reading of Xenophon's Memorabilia', in Vander Waerdt (ed.), *The Socratic Movement*, pp. 151–80

Pomeroy, S. B., *Xenophon's Oeconomicus: A Social and Historical Commentary* (Oxford University Press, 1994)

Sandbach, F. H., 'Plato and the Socratic work of Xenophon', in P. Easterling and B. Knox (eds.), *The Cambridge History of Classical Literature*, vol. I, *Greek Literature* (Cambridge University Press, 1985), pp. 478–97

Tatum, J., *Xenophon's Imperial Fiction: On The Education of Cyrus* (Princeton University Press, 1989)

Tuplin, C. J., *The Failings of Empire: A Reading of Xenophon Hellenica 2.3.11–7.5.27* (Franz Steiner, 1993)

—, 'Xenophon, Sparta and the Cyropaedia', in A. Powell and S. Hodkinson (eds.), *The Shadow of Sparta* (Routledge and University of Wales Press, 1994), pp. 127–81

Waterfield, R., Introduction and notes to *Conversations of Socrates* (trans. of *Apology*, *Memorabilia*, *Symposium*, and *Oeconomicus*), by H. Tredennick and R. Waterfield (Penguin, 1990)

Westlake, H. D., 'Individuals in Xenophon's Hellenica', *Bulletin of the John Rylands Library*, 49 (1966–7), pp. 246–69

A NOTE ON
THE TEXTS

The six treatises translated in this book occur in volume 5 of the Oxford Classical Text of Xenophon, edited by E. C. Marchant (*Xenophontis Opera*, Oxford University Press, 1920), the text of which has been followed except at the places marked with an asterisk, which refers the interested reader to the Textual Notes.

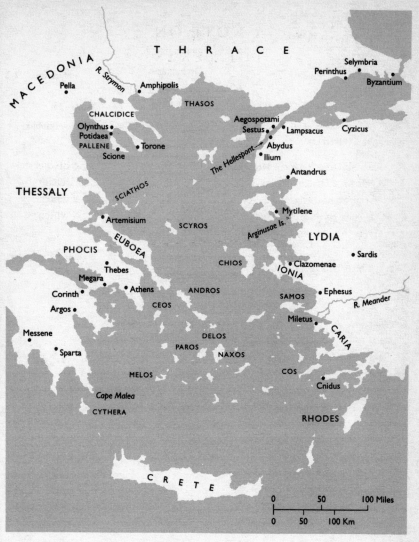

Greece and the Aegean

The Peloponnese showing Xenophon's retreat into exile at Scillons

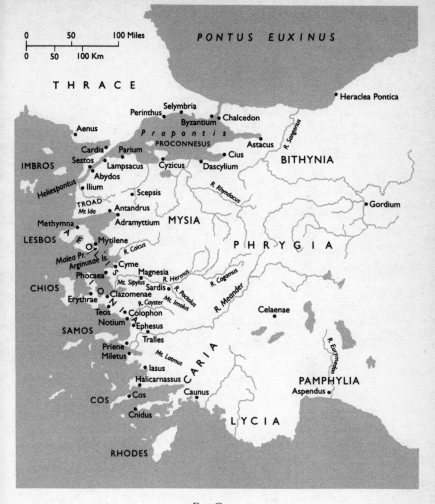

East Greece

HIERO THE TYRANT

INTRODUCTION

At the very end of *The Estate-manager* (*Oeconomicus*), his treatise on
the good management of a large *oikos* or 'household' (including human
as well as real property), Xenophon equates the prospects of a human
tyrant with the torments suffered mythically in Hades by the anti-hero
Tantalus. Tyranny, that is to say, which Xenophon's Socrates defines
in *Memoirs of Socrates* (*Memorabilia*) 4.6.12 as 'authority without consent
and in accordance not with the laws but with the whim of the ruler',
is here represented as a living hell, for the tyrant as well as the subjects.
Xenophon's implied message is that the good manager, such as his
idealized Ischomachus, must not confine his management skills to the
private sphere but should apply them also to the conduct of the state,
in accordance with the laws.

Hiero the Tyrant, a supposed dialogue on the nature of sole rule
between Simonides the praise-poet from Ceos and his then employer
Hiero, tyrant of Syracuse in Sicily in the early fifth century BC (478–
467), is thus in several ways the negative image of the *Estate-manager*.
Simonides plays on the fact that in Greek, unlike English, the *tyrannos*
was fundamentally an un- or extra-constitutional ruler, so that 'good
tyrant' was not by definition oxymoronic. The tyrant, Simonides
urges, may gain personal happiness only if he rules well, that is in the
interests of his subjects.

Dialogue was utterly natural to the Greeks, and crucial for their
definition of self by literary means. In poetry it was of course common
enough in epic and was the very stuff of tragic and comic drama,
but in prose the dialogue form was essayed first in sophistic circles,
for instance in Protagoras' *Antilogiai* or 'Contrary Arguments'. In
its manner as well as its matter the so-called 'Melian Dialogue' in

3

Thucydides (5.84–113) bears witness to the genre's sophistic origins. But the form was brought to perfection for broadly philosophical purposes by Plato during the first quarter of the fourth century. Nor was the confrontation of despotic ruler and expert layman (*sophistes* in its original, non-pejorative sense) a scenario original to Xenophon. The literary prototype was the encounter, with supplied invented dialogue, between Croesus and Solon in the first book of Herodotus, by whom Xenophon was greatly influenced. Croesus, however, king of Lydia in Asia Minor, was a non-Greek, which accorded with Herodotus' preoccupation with representations of 'the Other' and added to the piquancy of autocratic tyranny the stigma of oriental barbarism. Hiero of Sicilian Syracuse, on the other hand, was a home-grown Greek tyrant, with high cultural pretensions – patron of Pindar, Bacchylides and Aeschylus, besides Simonides, and founder even of a new Greek city. That helped Xenophon firmly to focus his debate on the nature and meaning of autocracy within the context of Greek politics.

Another reason for Xenophon's selecting Hiero as his 'historical' example was his contemporary resonance. Possibly the most powerful and certainly one of the most colourful of the Greeks of Xenophon's own day was also precisely a tyrant of Syracuse: namely Dionysius I, who ruled much of Sicily and wielded considerable influence in Greece and the Adriatic between 405 and 367. Other 'Socratics' beside Xenophon are known to have taken a special philosophical interest in him. Plato indeed is even said to have tried to convert Dionysius into a prototype philosopher-king, and, predictably failing in that, to have borrowed from him many essential traits for his deadly portrait of the arch-tyrant in Book 9 of the *Republic*. Aristotle, who no doubt had read *Hiero* as well as the *Republic*, includes references to both Hiero and Dionysius in his no less unflattering discussion of tyranny as a mode of rule (*Politics* 1313). 'The typical tyrant', Aristotle declared, 'dislikes free-spirited people' – people, that is, such as Xenophon's Simonides, who had the reputation of being a sage and attracted numerous anecdotes.

Yet it is important to be clear that Xenophon was not against one-man rule as such – far from it: he shared to the full in the movement of reaction among Greek intellectuals away from what they saw as the almost unnatural defects of democracy or mob-rule and towards enlightened monarchy. One means of stigmatizing democracy, as in the clever piece of oligarchic pamphleteering represented by Xenophon's fictional dialogue between Pericles and his maverick ward Alcibiades in *Memoirs of Socrates* (1.2.40–46), was to characterize it as a form of collective tyranny, whereby the ignorant and ill-educated masses ruled despotically over the unwilling and unconsenting elite few. It was vital, therefore, for Xenophon here to draw the distinction as sharply as possible between the illegitimate and intolerable sole ruler, the tyrant, and, on the other hand, the wise and beneficent sole ruler, the legitimate and positively desirable king, who – regardless of ethnicity – might become the living embodiment of the conservatives' ideal of lawfulness, a 'seeing law', as Xenophon describes his idealized Persian Great King Cyrus in the *Education of Cyrus* (*Cyropaedia* 8.1.22). What 'Simonides' in effect sets out to teach 'Hiero' is how, though objectively a tyrant ruler, he can avoid ruling tyrannically.

It is one thing, however, to detect a general contemporary resonance in the dialogue, but it is quite another to argue for any one specific contemporary event having been the occasion for Xenophon's composing it. An old suggestion of George Grote (author of a pioneering history of ancient Greece, first published between 1846 and 1856) that Xenophon was provoked by Dionysius' arrogant behaviour at the Olympics of either 388 or 384 has been recently revived. Another suggestion, almost as old, has linked the composition rather with events occurring within the Thessalian tyrant house at Pherae in 358, described by Xenophon himself in *A History of My Times* (6.4.33–7). Neither suggested connection seems overwhelmingly compelling.

The literary confrontation of dictator and free-thinking subject has a long and continuing history. It has been exemplified in the Romanian writer Norman Manea's *On Clowns. The Dictator and the Artist* (1994), where his grim description of the tyrant as 'someone who manipulates, gives orders, enforces discipline, punishes and rewards according to the sovereign and sadistic laws of evil, ugliness, and mendacity' and his reference to 'our sadistic national clown' are easily seen as applying specifically to the late and unlamented Nicolae Ceausescu. However, entirely worthy of the universalizing philosophical tradition within which Xenophon the Socratic positioned his discussion is Manea's disturbing question: 'Is the dictator only the enemy or also the creation of the masses?'

HIERO THE TYRANT

CHAPTER I

Once upon a time the poet Simonides paid a visit to the tyrant Hiero. 1
When they had some time free from interruption, Simonides said,
'There's something I should like you to explain to me, Hiero, if you
would – something on which you're sure to be more knowledgeable
than I.'

'But you are such a learned person,' Hiero replied. 'What is this
subject on which I am supposedly more knowledgeable than you?'

'I'm aware that you were born an ordinary citizen,' he said, 'and 2
now you're a tyrant. Since you have experience of both walks of life,
you're sure to know better than I how the life of a tyrant differs from
that of an ordinary citizen with respect to the pleasures and pains of
human life.'

'Well,' said Hiero, 'you're still an ordinary citizen, so why don't 3
you remind me what it's like? That will make it much easier for me
to explain the differences between the two, I should think.'

So Simonides said: 'All right, Hiero. I think I can safely say, as a 4
result of my observations, that pleasure and pain come to ordinary
citizens through the agency of certain organs: the eyes in the case of
things they see, the ears for things they hear, the nostrils for scents,
their mouths for food and drink, and I don't need to mention the
organs used for sex. However, we use the whole body, I think, to 5
assess and find pleasure or distress in cold and heat, hardness and
softness, and lightness and heaviness. And it seems to me that we
sometimes use just the mind to feel pleasure or distress, as the case
may be, in things that are good and bad, but sometimes the mind in
combination with the body. I feel confident in my impression that 6
sleep gives us pleasure, but I'm somehow even more sure that I don't

understand how it does so, and what organ might be involved, and when the pleasure arises. But this is perhaps hardly surprising: after all, what happens to us when we're awake is bound to afford us clearer impressions than what happens during sleep.'

7 'For my part, Simonides,' Hiero replied, 'I don't see how a tyrant could possibly be conscious of any pleasures and pains apart from the ones you've mentioned, and so thus far I don't know if there's *any* difference between the life of a tyrant and that of an ordinary citizen.'

8 'Well, here's a difference,' Simonides went on. 'A tyrant gets far more pleasure and far less pain from each of these areas of life.'

'No, you're wrong, Simonides,' Hiero said. 'I can assure you that an ordinary citizen of adequate means experiences far more pleasure and suffers far less and far less intensely than a tyrant.'

9 'That's incredible,' said Simonides. 'I mean, if you're right, why is it that so many people – men of considerably more than adequate means, apparently – want to become tyrants? Why is it that tyrants are a universal object of envy?'

10 'Because, by Zeus, people don't have experience of both stations in life,' Hiero answered, 'and that influences their thinking about the matter. I'll try to show you that I'm right. Let's start with the sense of sight, which was the first item on your list, I seem to remember.

11 My reflections lead me to conclude that tyrants are worse off in this visual domain. There are things worth seeing everywhere in the world, and ordinary citizens travel around in search of these sights. They visit any state they want to as sightseers, and attend the international festivals where everything generally agreed to be especially

12 eye-catching comes together all at once.[1] A tyrant, however, is hardly concerned with going to festivals. It isn't safe for him to go to places where he would be no stronger than anyone else, and his status at home is not so secure that he can leave things in others' hands while he travels abroad. On top of his fear of losing his power, he would be worried about not being in a position to punish the wrongdoers.

13 "Ah, yes," you might argue, "but eye-catching spectacles come to him, without his having to leave home." That is certainly true, Simonides, but only of a small proportion of all the sights and spectacles there are in the world, and even then they are offered to a tyrant at

such a price that however unimpressive the show the exhibitors expect to leave the tyrant's presence having gained in a few hours many times more than they would earn in a lifetime from everyone else in the world.'

'All right,' Simonides said, 'you may be worse off in the visual 14 sphere, but you're better off where hearing is concerned. After all, you have a plentiful supply of the most pleasing sound there is – praise – since your courtiers never stop applauding every word you speak and every action you perform. And criticism,[2] the harshest sound in the world, never reaches your ears, because no one is prepared to condemn a tyrant in his presence.'

'Do you really think,' Hiero replied, 'that the fact that people 15 refrain from speaking ill of a tyrant can give him the slightest pleasure, when he knows for sure that for all their silence every single one of them is *thinking* ill of him? Do you really think this praise gives pleasure, when it looks very much as though its purpose is flattery?'[3]

'Well,' Simonides said, 'I do of course agree wholeheartedly with 16 you, Hiero, that the more independent a person is, the more pleasing it is to be praised by him. However, I'm sure you can see that nothing you have yet said would convince anyone that you tyrants do not get far more pleasure than the rest of us from the food and drink which sustain human life.'

'Yes, Simonides,' he said, 'I know that the food and drink we 17 tyrants have is generally supposed to be more pleasant than what ordinary citizens get. This view is based on the idea people have that *they* would enjoy the meals which are served up to us more than they do their own food, since anything that is a cut above what one is used to gives one pleasure. This explains why everyone looks forward to 18 the day of a festival – everyone except a tyrant, that is. Why not? Because his table has always been laden with food and drink in abundance, so there's nothing special about festival days for him. The first conclusion to be drawn, then, is that tyrants are in a worse situation than ordinary citizens in respect of this kind of anticipatory pleasure. Besides, as I'm sure you know perfectly well from your own 19 experience, the more superfluous food a person is served, the more quickly he gets sated, and this leads to a second conclusion, that being served a lot of food makes one less well off than a moderate life-style does in respect of the duration of the feeling of pleasure.'

20 'But surely as long as one has an appetite for the food,' Simonides argued, 'a luxurious meal is nicer than plain fare.'

21 'Now, Simonides,' Hiero said, 'don't you think that a person who finds something particularly enjoyable is also particularly desirous of this occupation?'

'Certainly,' he said.

'Well, in your experience do tyrants approach their meals with a higher degree of pleasure than ordinary citizens do theirs?'

'No, they certainly don't,' he said. 'In fact, their attitude is commonly supposed to border on distaste.'

22 'Of course,' said Hiero, 'and have you noticed all the artificial confections that are served up to tyrants, flavoured so as to taste sharp, bitter, sour and so on?'

'Yes, I have,' Simonides said, 'and they strike me as highly unnatural things for people to eat.'

23 'Surely,' Hiero continued, 'for an appetite to crave that kind of food it would have to be effete and debilitated, don't you think? I mean, you know as well as I that people who enjoy their food have no need of such contrivances.'

24 'Well,' said Simonides, 'I do think that the expensive perfumes with which you tyrants anoint your bodies are appreciated more by the people around you than by you yourselves, just as it isn't the actual person who has eaten strong-smelling food who notices any unpleasant smells on his breath, but rather his neighbours.'

25 'Yes, and the same goes for enjoyment of food too,' Hiero said. 'If there's no novelty for a person in having a sumptuous and varied diet, he doesn't fancy anything he is offered; it is the person for whom something is a rare treat who eats his fill with delight when it is served up to him.'

26 'It's beginning to look as though the only thing that makes people want to be tyrants is the satisfaction of sexual appetite,' Simonides said. 'I mean, in the sexual domain you are free to sleep with anyone you find particularly attractive.'[4]

27 'In actual fact,' Hiero replied, 'this is a sphere in which, I can assure

you, we are worse off than ordinary folk. Let's start with marriage. The best kind of marriage, as you know, is taken to be marriage into a family which has more property and influence than one's own; a man who makes this kind of marriage, it's said, may feel both pride and pleasure. The second-best kind is marriage between peers, while marrying beneath one is considered demeaning and worthless. But a tyrant is bound to marry a social inferior (unless he marries a foreign woman), and so the most satisfactory kind of marriage is denied him. 28

'Moreover, the higher the self-esteem of a woman, the more pleasant it is to be granted her favours; there is nothing at all satisfying, however, in obtaining a slave girl's favours, and any shortcomings in her services put one into a terrible temper and bad mood.

'Next, what about sex with boys? Here a tyrant finds even less pleasure than he does in his heterosexual relationships. The point is that, as everyone knows, desire is the element that makes sex far more enjoyable. Desire, however, is an extremely rare feature of a tyrant's life, because the pleasures of desire are not stimulated by things that are readily available, but by things that are hoped for in the future. Someone who has never experienced thirst cannot enjoy a drink, and by the same token a person who hasn't experienced desire has not experienced the true delights of sex.' 29 30

Simonides laughed at Hiero's words and said, 'What do you mean, Hiero? Are you really saying that a tyrant doesn't fancy young boys? What about your love for Daïlochus – the gorgeous Daïlochus, as people call him?' 31

'To be honest, Simonides,' he said, 'the reason is that what I most want to get from him is not what is, it seems, readily available, but something which a tyrant, of all people, is hardly likely to obtain. It is true that I do desire from Daïlochus those favours which it is perhaps inevitable, given human nature, that one will want from people one finds attractive, but I specifically want to obtain the object of my desire from a willing and affectionate partner. I think I'd rather do myself an injury than get them from him against his will. I mean, in my opinion, there's nothing nicer than taking things from one's enemies against their will, but the sweetest favours from a boy are those given freely, to my mind. For instance, when your affection is 32 33 34 35

returned, the glances that pass between the two of you are a delight, conversation with its questions and answers is a joy, and there's nothing more pleasant and erotic than wrestling and wrangling with your
36 loved one. But to have your way with him against his will is more like robbery than sex, I'd say. Actually, though, it affords a brigand some pleasure to get away with his haul and to cause an enemy pain, but to enjoy the pain of the one you love, to be hated even as you kiss, to touch someone who loathes your touch – surely this is a vile
37 and pitiful affliction. What I'm getting at is that the very act of gratification is immediate proof for an ordinary citizen that it is affection that makes his beloved compliant, because he knows that his submission isn't forced, whereas a tyrant can never be sure that he
38 is actually liked. I mean, we all know that when people submit out of fear they simulate as accurately as possible compliance born out of genuine affection. In fact, plots against tyrants are hatched, as often as not, by those who claim the greatest friendship towards them.'

CHAPTER 2

1 'As a matter of fact, though,' Simonides replied, 'I for one wouldn't count these points of yours as particularly important. I don't know about you, but I've certainly seen plenty of well-respected men voluntarily deny themselves food, drink and savouries,[1] and even
2 abstain from sex. No, the difference between you tyrants and ordinary citizens is that you can make mighty plans and rapidly put them into effect, you have a vast amount of luxuries, you own horses of outstanding quality, arms and armour of unrivalled magnificence, wonderful jewellery for your womenfolk and the most magnificent residences on the accoutrements of which no expense has been spared. In terms of their quantity and their technical accomplishments there are no better slaves than yours, and there is no one in a better position than you to harm your enemies and reward your friends.'[2]
3 'I don't find it at all surprising,' Hiero replied, 'that the mass of mankind are taken in by tyranny, since the rabble tend to assess
4 happiness and unhappiness by external appearances. Tyranny flaunts

in public its speciously valuable possessions, but there's another, darker side to it, which is kept hidden away in the minds of tyrants – in the place where human happiness and misery are stored. Anyway, as I say, it doesn't surprise me at all that the masses should have failed to notice this, but that even people like yourself – people with a reputation for judging most things in the clearer light of intelligence rather than by external appearances – this does strike me as astonishing. 5

'Speaking from personal experience, Simonides, I can tell you that no one is a more complete stranger to life's greatest blessings than a tyrant, and that no one has a greater share of life's worst troubles either. To take the first example that comes to mind, peace is held to be of immense benefit for mankind. It may be so, but tyrants have hardly a moment of peace in their lives. War is considered a disaster, but no one sees more of it than a tyrant. The point is that, unless their state is actually at war, ordinary citizens can go anywhere they want without fear of being killed by anyone; wherever tyrants go, however, they always treat it as enemy territory. At any rate, they think they have no choice but to spend their lives in armour and to take an armed escort with them at all times.[3] 6 7 8

'Secondly, even if ordinary citizens do go out on a campaign into enemy territory, they consider themselves safe once they return home; but back home is where a tyrant knows there is the highest concentration of his enemies. Thirdly, if the city is attacked by a superior invading force, the weaker side thinks it dangerous to be outside the city walls, but once behind the fortifications, they all regard their situation as one of safety. A tyrant, however, is not out of danger even when he enters his residence; in fact, he thinks he has to protect himself there more than anywhere else.[4] Fourthly, a truce or a permanent peace puts an end to war for ordinary citizens, but there's no peace between a tyrant and his subjects, and he cannot ever confidently rely on truces. 9 10 11

'So there are hostilities between states, and hostilities between tyrants and their oppressed subjects. All the hardships that are involved in wars between states are also suffered in the other kind of war by tyrants, in the sense that tyrants as well as the ordinary citizens of states have to bear arms, tread warily and face danger, and also because both groups are liable to suffer from any adverse consequences of defeat. 12 13

14 So far, then, both kinds of war are equal. However, the pleasures the citizens of a state* gain in wars between states are not available to
15 tyrants; this is where the similarity stops. For, as you know, when states win a battle, the pleasure the citizens get from forcing the enemy into retreat, from pursuing fugitives and killing their foes, beggars description. It's impossible to capture in words how they glory in their achievement, how they bask in the brilliance of their fame, how they are cheered by the thought that they have enhanced the power
16 of their community. Every one of them claims that he was privy to the plan and killed more people than anyone else; in fact, it's hard to find a space free of lies and exaggeration; all you find is people claiming to have killed more of the enemy than actually fell in the battle! This just goes to show what a fine thing they regard outright victory to
17 be. As for a tyrant, however, when he suspects some people of plotting against him, and then finds out that his suspicions are true and puts the conspirators to death, he is well aware that he is not enhancing the power of the community and that in future he will have fewer subjects to rule over; so far from finding it possible to be happy about what he is doing and to pride himself on it, he plays it down as much as he can and defends the justice of what he has done even while he is in the middle of doing it. This just goes to show how disgusted
18 even he feels about his actions. Even the death of people he feared doesn't boost his morale at all; in fact, he takes even more precautions than he did before. So this is the kind of war a tyrant spends his life fighting, as I have explained.'[5]

CHAPTER 3

1 'Next, consider how tyrants are placed with regard to friendship and affection. Let's start by trying to see how important a part they play
2 in helping a person to live well. I mean, people who like someone enjoy his company, gladly do him favours, miss him when he isn't there, are delighted when he returns, share his pleasure at his successes
3 and support him through any setbacks.[1] States too are well aware of the importance of the part friendship plays in helping people to live

well and pleasantly. At any rate, it is not uncommon for the legal code of states to allow people to kill adulterers, and only adulterers, with impunity, and the thinking behind this law is obviously that adultery impairs the affection a wife feels for her husband. After all, if sex takes place without the woman's consent, this does not make the slightest difference to the regard her husband feels for her, as long as the affection she feels for him clearly remains inviolate.[2] My own assessment of the importance of friendship and affection to the good life leads me to believe that when a person is liked he really doesn't have to seek for good things: they just come his way of their own accord, from both gods and men.

'That is how important a possession friendship is – but friendship is something else which a tyrant above all is denied. If you doubt the truth of what I'm saying, Simonides, why don't you look at it this way? The strongest bonds of affection, as you know, are held to be those felt by parents for their children, by children for their parents, by brothers for their brothers, by wives for their husbands and by comrades for their comrades. A little reflection will show you that this is far more true for ordinary citizens than for tyrants. Tyrants have often killed their own children or been killed themselves by their children; when brothers have been involved in tyranny together, it is not uncommon for them to have become one another's assassins; plenty of tyrants have even been killed by their own wives – yes, and also by comrades who were apparently their closest friends. In short, when the people who might naturally feel the most affection for them – or who at least might have been particularly impelled by convention to do so – hate them so much, how are we to suppose that anyone else feels affection for them?'

CHAPTER 4

'What about trust? Surely the less a person knows of trust, the more he is deprived of something of value. I mean, without trust what delight could we find in others' company? Without trust, what joy would there be in the relationship between man and wife? Without

2   trust, what pleasure would there be in owning a slave? Yet here again, in the matter of trusting people, a tyrant is worse off than anyone else. He lives in constant mistrust even of what he eats and drinks; before consecrating any food and drink to the gods he tells a servant to taste them, because he can't be sure that they won't have been poisoned.

3   'One of the most important things in the lives of ordinary citizens is the country they live in. The citizens of a country serve for free as one another's bodyguards against slaves and criminals, to make sure
4   that none of their fellow citizens meets a violent death.[1] They take this job of protecting one another so seriously that it is not uncommon for them to have a law that even the associates of a murderer are polluted.[2] And the upshot is that a country enables each of its citizens
5   to live in security. A tyrant's life, however, is the opposite of everyone else's in this respect too. So far from being punished, the murderer of a tyrant is greatly honoured by his fellow citizens; instead of being banned from the shrines, as the killers of ordinary citizens are, states erect statues of tyrannicides in their sanctuaries.[3]

6   'You might imagine that a tyrant's extra possessions afford him extra pleasure as well, but that would be wrong too, Simonides. Consider the analogy of a professional athlete, who doesn't get any pleasure from beating amateurs, but hates losing to his rivals.[4] The same goes for a tyrant: there's no pleasure for him in having conspicuously more than ordinary citizens, but it hurts him to have less than other tyrants, whom he regards as his competitors in wealth.

7   'Nor is it the case that a tyrant's wishes are more quickly realized than those of ordinary citizens. An ordinary citizen might want a house or a farm or a house-slave, but a tyrant wants whole cities, vast tracts of land, safe harbours and impregnable strongholds, which are far harder and riskier to come by than the things an ordinary citizen aims for.

8   'In actual fact, though, it is as common to find an impoverished tyrant as it is rare to meet poverty among ordinary citizens. The criterion of wealth and poverty is not quantity but a person's perceived needs,[5] which is why "plenty" means "more than enough" and "little"
9   means "less than enough". A tyrant is less capable of meeting his essential expenses with all his vast wealth than an ordinary citizen is

with his money, because an ordinary citizen can cut down what he spends on his daily needs in any way he chooses, whereas this is out of the question for a tyrant. After all, the most expensive and essential item for a tyrant is protecting his life, and cutting down what he spends on this would seem to be lethal.

'Then again, why should we pity people as poor when they can 10 honestly come by everything they need? Wouldn't it be fairer to count people wretched and poor when they are so badly off that they have no choice but to find criminal and degrading means of staying alive? Well, no one turns to crime more than a tyrant: he frequently 11 steals from temples[6] as well as from people, because he is in constant need of money to cover his necessary expenditure. You see, he has two options: either maintain an army all the time, as if there were a war on, or be killed.'

CHAPTER 5

'Here's another hardship a tyrant experiences, Simonides. He is just 1 as capable as any citizen of recognizing bravery, cleverness and moral rectitude in people, but instead of admiring such qualities, he is afraid of them. He worries about brave people using their courage in the service of freedom, about clever people intriguing against him and about morally good people being chosen by the general populace as their champions. So his fear makes him do away with such people, 2 but then whom is he left with? Only people who are without morality, lack self-discipline and are servile. He puts his trust in immoral people because they share his fear about the state some day winning its freedom and getting them in its power, in weak-willed people because of their laissez-faire attitude towards whatever is going on, and in servile people because they don't even value freedom. So to my mind this is another hardship, to have to be intimately involved with people other than those one thinks good.

'Moreover, although even a tyrant is bound to be patriotic (because 3 he relies on the state for his life and happiness), nevertheless his situation as tyrant forces him to have a deleterious effect on the state.

The point is that he doesn't like to develop combativeness and military skills in the citizens of his state; it gives him greater pleasure to make his foreign militia a more formidable fighting force than his fellow
4 countrymen and to use them as his personal guards. Also, even in years of plenty, when the state is overflowing with good things, a tyrant does not share in the celebrations, because he thinks he will find his subjects more submissive the needier they are.'

CHAPTER 6

1 'Simonides,' Hiero went on, 'I would also like to tell you about all the pleasures *I* enjoyed as an ordinary citizen, but which I am aware
2 of lacking now that I have become a tyrant. I used to enjoy the company of friends and acquaintances of my own age, as they enjoyed mine too; I used to spend time with myself when I wanted a bit of peace and quiet; I used to while away the hours at symposia, often until I forgot all the hardships of human life, often until my mind was fully taken up with the singing and dancing and fun, and often until
3 sleep was all I and my companions wanted.[1] But now I have no one to enjoy my company because my comrades are slaves instead of friends, and there's no pleasure in my association with them because I can see in them no flicker of warmth towards me. I am as wary of drunkenness and sleep as I would be of a trap.[2]

4 'To be frightened of a crowd and also of solitude, to be frightened of being unguarded and also of your very guards, to be reluctant to have unarmed people around you and yet to find the sight of armed
5 men alarming – isn't this a horrible situation? And then to trust strangers rather than your fellow citizens and non-Greeks rather than Greeks, to want to turn free men into slaves and yet to be forced to make slaves free[3] – doesn't all this strike you as evidence of a mind
6 cowed by fears?[4] And* fear, you know, not only is painful in itself, by its mere presence in the mind, but also haunts all our pleasures and spoils them.

7 'If you have experience of warfare, Simonides, as I do, and were ever stationed with enemy lines close at hand confronting you, call

to mind how you approached your food at the time and what the quality of your sleep was. Tyrants are prey to all the fears that troubled you then, and to more terrifying ones as well, since the enemies they seem to see are all around them, not just in front of them.' 8

'I absolutely agree with some of what you're saying,' Simonides replied. 'War *is* a frightening thing. All the same, Hiero, we reduce the fears that trouble our meals and sleep on campaign by stationing guards out in front of our position.' 9

'Of course you do, Simonides,' Hiero said. 'And these guards in their turn are watched over by the laws of the state, which guarantee that they fear to neglect their duty as well as taking on your fears. But tyrants hire guards for pay, as if they were labourers at harvest-time.[5] Now, the most important requirement for guards, I imagine, is trust-worthiness, but it's far easier to find scores of labourers for agricultural or any other kind of work than it is to find a single trustworthy guard, especially when money is what induces them to become guards in the first place and they can earn far more in a few moments by killing the tyrant than they would receive from him in pay for a lengthy stint of protecting him. 10 11

'You said you envied our ability to help our friends immensely and do the utmost harm to our enemies, but again you're wrong. I mean, could you really tell yourself that you're helping friends when you know perfectly well that the more people receive from you the more quickly they want to get out of your sight? For a tyrant's gifts are never regarded as a person's property until he is beyond his reach. Or again, how does your claim that a tyrant can do particular harm to his enemies fare in the light of the fact that he knows perfectly well that every single one of his subjects is his enemy and that he can't have them all put to death or thrown into prison – whom would he rule if he did that? – but has to protect them and be involved with them, even while knowing their hatred for him? 12 13 14

'Another point, Simonides. I can assure you that when a tyrant is afraid of any of his subjects, it is hard for him to see them alive, but also hard for him to kill them. As an analogy, imagine someone with a good horse who is nevertheless worried that it might fatally let him down: the horse's good points make it hard for him to kill it, yet it 15

16 is also hard for him to keep it alive and make use of it, when he is worried that in a dangerous situation it might prove fatal for him. The same goes, in fact, for any possession that is irritating but useful: it is as much of a nuisance to have it as it is to do without it.'

CHAPTER 7

1 Simonides' response to this was to say, 'What an important thing prestige seems to be, Hiero! People long for it so much that they're prepared to do anything, no matter how exhausting and dangerous it 2 may be, to get it. Look at all the trials and tribulations tyranny apparently involves, according to you – but you tyrants still hurtle headlong towards it, drawn by the prestige it carries and by the desire to have everyone unswervingly and subserviently carry out all your commands. You want everyone around you, wherever you are, to look up to you in admiration, yield their seats to you and get out of the way in the streets for you, and make you the revered object of everything they say and do in your presence. After all, these are the typical behaviour patterns displayed by people towards a tyrant they are subject to and towards anyone else they respect.

3 'In my opinion, you see, Hiero, our craving for prestige is a point of difference between us humans and the other animals. I mean, it looks as though the pleasures of eating, drinking, sleep and sex are available to all creatures equally, but love of honour isn't a natural feature of the irrational animals, or even of all humans. People with this innate love of honour and praise are the ones who are furthest removed from the animal realm; they are regarded as men and not 4 just as human beings.[1] I don't find it surprising, then, that you tyrants put up with all the hardship tyranny involves, given the extraordinary amount of honour you receive. For it seems to me that our delight in status and prestige is the closest we humans can get to the kind of pleasure the gods experience.'

5 'No, Simonides,' Hiero replied. 'I think even a tyrant's prestige has 6 much in common with his sex-life, as I described it to you. We agreed that favours granted by people who don't reciprocate one's affection

are not acts of kindness, and also that sex with an unwilling partner is not enjoyable. By the same token, services rendered by men out of fear are not acts of respect. I mean, surely we wouldn't describe it as 7 a sign of respect for the offender in either case, when people yield their seats against their will or when they make way under duress for someone who is their social superior? And it's very common for 8 people to give gifts to those they hate, especially when they are particularly afraid of something bad happening to them at their hands.

'It would be reasonable, I think, to regard this behaviour as prompted by servility, but acts of respect seem to me to stem from the opposite condition. When people think that someone is in a position to do 9 them good and that it is thanks to him that their situation is improving, and so his name is always on their lips and they are constantly singing his praises; when each one of them looks on him as his own personal benefactor, and of their own free will they make way for him and yield their seats to him, out of affection, not fear; when they present him with garlands for his good services, from which they all benefit, and freely offer him gifts; *that* – the kind of service I've described – seems to me to be true respect, and when a man is taken to deserve this kind of treatment, I would say that he is the recipient of genuine honour. And I, for my part, would count someone who is honoured 10 like this a happy man, because as far as I can see he is not the target of conspiracies, but the object of concern for his well-being, and he lives a life untroubled by fear and the malice of others, free from danger and misery. A tyrant, however, I can assure you, Simonides, spends all his time, day and night, as if he had been condemned to death by the whole human race for his iniquity.'

After listening to this speech of Hiero's, Simonides said, 'If it's so 11 awful to be a tyrant, Hiero, and you've come to this conclusion about it, why haven't you shed this terrible burden? Why is it that no one – neither you nor anyone else – ever willingly gives up his position as a tyrant, once he has gained it?'

'Yes, Simonides,' he said, 'this is exactly the most pitiful aspect of 12 tyranny. It is impossible to let go of it. How could a tyrant ever raise enough money to pay back in full the people he stole from, or serve all the prison sentences to compensate those he imprisoned? How

could he recompense all the people he put to death by coming up
13 with an adequate number of deaths to die? Do you want to know
what I think, Simonides? I think that the only person who might
profit by hanging himself is a tyrant; I have come to the conclusion
that he is more likely than anyone to gain from this course of action,
because he is the only person in the world whose interest is as little
served by getting rid of his misfortunes as it is by keeping them.'

CHAPTER 8

1 'Well, Hiero,' Simonides replied, 'your current state of depression
about tyranny doesn't surprise me, since you think it stops you achieving
your goal of being liked by people. I think I can teach you, however,
that rulership does not prevent you being liked and that in fact you're
2 better off than ordinary citizens in this respect. In considering whether
or not I'm right, let's ignore for the time being the issue of whether the
greater power a ruler wields means that he can also confer a greater
number of favours; what I want us to do instead is imagine an ordinary
citizen and a tyrant performing the same service and then try to see
which of them would win more gratitude from their identical acts.

'I'll start with the most trivial examples and go on from there.
3 Imagine, first, a ruler and an ordinary citizen catching sight of someone
and greeting him in a friendly fashion. In this example, whose greeting,
do you think, would be more welcome? Now let's have both of them
complimenting the man. Whose compliments would afford more
pleasure, do you think? Suppose each of them honours the man with
an invitation to a sacrificial feast. Whose invitation would be more
4 gratefully received, in your opinion? Imagine both of them looking
after a sick man. Isn't it obvious that the more powerful the person,
the more his ministrations will delight the patient? Now let's have
them giving identical presents. Isn't the answer obvious in this case
too? The most powerful members of society could be half as generous
as an ordinary person, and their gifts would still count for more.
5 'In fact I'd go so far as to say that the gods cause a kind of aura of
dignity and grace to surround a ruler. Not only does authority make

a man more prepossessing, but despite the fact that it's still the same person, we also get more pleasure from seeing him when he is in a position of authority than we did when he was an ordinary citizen, and it's more of a thrill to talk to eminent members of society than it is to talk to our social equals.

'Now, you were particularly bitter about the tyrant's situation with regard to affairs with boys, but they're not put off in the slightest by old age in a ruler, nor do they take any account of ugliness in the person they've taken up with, because by itself high standing in society vitally enhances a person's appearance, so that blemishes disappear and attractive features shine out even more clearly. 6

'So identical acts of kindness are appreciated more when performed by tyrants than they are when performed by ordinary citizens. Under these circumstances, since you're actually capable of doing far greater favours and of giving far more generous gifts than ordinary citizens can, doesn't it follow that you're bound to be liked much more than ordinary people as well?' 7

Hiero wasted no time in replying. 'No, of course it doesn't, Simonides,' he said, 'because we're also forced to put into effect, far more commonly than ordinary citizens are, the kinds of measures which make people unpopular. We have to exact money to cover essential costs, compel people to protect all the things that need protection, punish criminals, curb potential violence; and when the time for rapid action comes and a land or naval expedition is called for, we have to see that the people in charge take their responsibilities seriously. Moreover, a tyrant needs mercenary troops, and this financial burden is particularly resented by his subjects because they think that the point of keeping these troops is self-interest rather than the promotion of social equality.'[1] 8 9 10

CHAPTER 9

'Well, Hiero,' Simonides replied, 'I'm not going to deny that you have to concern yourself with all these matters, but I do think that although some of your concerns certainly lead to unpopularity, others 1

2 are richly appreciated. For instance, instructing people in excellence – that is, showing how much you admire and value the best and most excellent achievements – is a concern which is appreciated. However, the task of censuring, disciplining and imposing penalties and punish-

3 ments on underachievers is bound to incur unpopularity. In my opinion, then, a ruler should delegate to others the task of punishing anyone who needs disciplinary action, but should retain for himself the job of awarding prizes. The soundness of this idea is confirmed by

4 experience. For instance, when we want to hold a choral competition, it is the ruler[1] who puts up the prizes, while the job of assembling the choirs is given to impresarios, and it is left to others to train them and to discipline those who fail to come up to scratch in some way. The immediate result in this case is that the agreeable aspect of the competition is due to the ruler, while the disagreeable aspects are left to others.

5 'Why shouldn't all other public business be carried out on the same principle? Every state is divided into tribes or regiments or companies,

6 with officers put in charge of each division.[2] If one were to treat these divisions like choirs and offer them prizes for excellence of equipment, drill, horsemanship, courage in battle and honesty in negotiations, it seems reasonable to assume that enough rivalry would develop for all

7 these qualities to be assiduously cultivated. There can be no doubt that, motivated by the passionate desire to win an award, troops would set out for their destination with greater alacrity, and that in a time of taxation people would pay up more promptly.

'Another beneficiary would be agriculture, a pursuit of the greatest utility, but which, as things stand, is singularly lacking in the spirit of rivalry. But agriculture would improve immensely if one were to offer prizes for the estate or village which farmed the land most admirably, and there would also be a great many beneficial consequences for those of your subjects who channelled their energies into

8 farming.[3] For example, their incomes would go up, self-discipline and industry generally go together, and when people have work to do they rarely turn to crime.

9 'Again, if trade is an activity which does a community some good, offering a reward for the person who brings in the most business would also serve to encourage more people to become traders. And

if it were known that anyone who discovers a way to make money which doesn't involve any inconvenience will be honoured by his state, then this is another area where research would flourish. In short, 10 if it were clear that good innovations in *any* area of life will not go unrewarded, this too would encourage large numbers of people to make it their business to try to discover something useful. And when benefit is occupying the minds of large numbers of people, more ways will inevitably be found to promote it and bring it about.[4]

'In case you're anxiously thinking that offering prizes for such a lot 11 of occupations will be very expensive, Hiero, you should bear in mind that there are no more cost-effective commodities than those which are paid for with prizes. Just look at the vast amounts of money, effort and attention people are willing to spend preparing for horse-races, athletic contests and choral competitions.'[5]

CHAPTER 10

'I suppose you may well be right on this, Simonides,' Hiero said, 'but 1 can you tell me how I can employ my mercenaries without being hated for it? Or do you think that once a ruler has become popular he has no further need of bodyguards?'

'No, of course he'll continue to need them,' Simonides answered. 2 'I am well aware that human beings are no different from horses in the sense that some of them become more ungovernable the more their needs are satisfied.[1] Fear of bodyguards is quite an effective way 3 to control that kind of person. At the same time I don't think you'd find anything that would be more helpful to the gentry than your guards. I'm sure you keep them as your own personal guards, but a 4 great many masters have in the past been murdered by their slaves, so the mercenaries should be instructed, right from the start, to act as the personal guards of every single citizen of the state and to go to their assistance if they find anything like that happening. I mean, we all know that states do have a criminal element, so if your guards had orders to protect the citizens too, their help would constitute another service your subjects would appreciate.

5   'Moreover, your mercenaries could probably be more successful
than anyone at calming the fears of country folk as they go about their
business and at providing security for them and their flocks, not only
on your own estates, but all over the countryside. By guarding the
crucial positions they can give your subjects time to look after their
own affairs.

6   'Then again, who would be better placed to gain advance intelligence of secret and unexpected enemy incursions, and to forestall
them, than a standing force of armed and organized troops? And in
times of war, what could be more useful to your subjects than a
mercenary force which will probably be perfectly ready to relieve
them of most of the hard work, danger and need for vigilance?

7 And wouldn't the presence of a standing force inevitably make any
neighbouring states clearly see the desirability of peace, since nothing
is better than an organized body of troops at keeping one's own side
safe and at upsetting the enemy's plans?

8   'Once your subjects realize that your mercenaries are no threat to
anyone unless he is a criminal, that they deter potential criminals and
help the victims of crime, watch out for the citizen body and face
danger in its defence, surely they're bound to be absolutely delighted
to bear the costs of maintaining such a force, aren't they? At any rate,
the guards they keep on their own property are used for more trivial
tasks than these.'[2]

CHAPTER II

1 'Another point to note, Hiero, is that you shouldn't hesitate to draw
on your own personal funds to pay for projects that enhance the
common good. It seems to me that money spent by a tyrant on public
projects comes closer to being essential expenditure than money he
spends on himself. But let's consider all the relevant points one by
one.

2   'In the first place, then, which do you think brings you more
credit,* a residence gorgeously furnished at extraordinary expense, or
the whole city equipped with defensive walls, temples, colonnades,

squares and harbours? Are you more likely to strike fear into the   3
enemy if you personally are decked out with astounding arms and
armour, or if the whole city is properly armed? Do you think more   4
income would be generated if you were to keep only your own estates
farmed or if you were to ensure that all the estates owned by your
subjects were farmed? As for the occupation which is generally   5
regarded as the noblest and grandest there is – that is, the breeding of
horses for chariot-racing – which approach do you think will bring
you the most credit, if you personally were to breed more teams than
anyone else in Greece and enter them at the great festivals, or if
your community were to produce more breeders and provide more
contestants than any other state in Greece? And would you prefer any
victory you won to be due to the excellence of your team or to the
flourishing of the community over which you preside?[1]

'In my opinion, you see, it's actually misguided for a tyrant to   6
compete against ordinary people. Rather than admiration, a victory
would stir up malicious talk about all the estates which contributed
towards his expenses, while a defeat would make him completely
ridiculous. No, I tell you, Hiero, your competition is against other   7
heads of state, and if you make the state you rule flourish more than
any others, *then* you will be* the victor in the noblest and grandest
contest in the world.

'The first and immediate result will be the attainment of your goal: 8
you will be liked by your subjects. Secondly, your victory will not
be proclaimed just by a single crier: the whole world will resound
with praise of your excellence. State after state, not just ordinary   9
citizens, will look up to you with warmth and admiration, and
throughout the world you will receive public tributes,[2] rather than
mere private acclaim.

'Moreover, on the issue of safety, you'll be able to travel wherever   10
you like to see the sights, or to stay where you are and do so. A
constant procession of people will pass before your eyes, all with
something clever or beautiful or good to show you, all desiring to
serve you. Everyone around you will wish you well, and everyone   11
away from you will long to see you.

'What people will feel for you, then, is passionate love rather than mere liking. You won't have to make advances to good-looking men, but to bear with their advances.[3] You won't be afraid, but you will make others afraid, for your well-being. Your subjects' state will be one of voluntary acquiescence, and their willing consideration for you will be obvious. In times of danger you'll find them not just fighting by your side, but shielding you – even eagerly shielding you – with their bodies. They will want to shower you with gifts, and you'll never be at a loss for a person of goodwill with whom to share them. You'll find them rejoicing with you at your successes and fighting for your interests as though they were their own. You'll be able to treat your friends' entire assets as your funds.

'So you can enrich your friends, Hiero, without worrying, because you'll be enriching yourself; you can enhance the power of your community, because you'll be conferring power on yourself; you can win allies for the state, <because you'll be gaining them for yourself.>* The whole country you can consider your estate, the citizens your comrades; you can regard your friends as your own children, and your sons as indistinguishable from your life.[4] Try to outdo all these people in benevolence, because if you beat your friends in benevolence, your enemies will never be able to stand up to you. If you do all this, there is no doubt that you will be endowed with the most wonderful and blessed possession in the world – you will be prosperous and happy and yet not be envied for it.'

AGESILAUS

INTRODUCTION

Agesilaus II, king (or strictly joint king) of Sparta, was one of the most interesting and important figures of his day (*c.* 445–360), a highly suitable case for biographical treatment. For the Greeks of the fourth century, biography was a novel art-form, being pioneered jointly by Xenophon and by Plato's great rival as pedagogue, the Athenian rhetoric teacher Isocrates (436–338), who wrote encomiastic biography of two rulers, really tyrants, of Greek Cyprus, Euagoras (awarded Athenian citizenship) and his son Nicocles of Salamis. But Xenophon was not interested in life-writing simply for its own sake. He owed Agesilaus an encomium of some sort, for great personal services rendered (see main Introduction), and he felt duty-bound to defend his deceased patron's good name against the large numbers of articulate enemies that the king's uncompromising policies had generated. He wished, above all, to treat Agesilaus as a paradigm case, an exemplum of a moral-political thesis about leadership and the other components of what he calls compendiously 'manly virtue' (*andragathia*, 10.2).

The main point of *Agesilaus* is thus to exhibit the talents that had enabled Agesilaus to be both a perfectly good man, morally speaking, and – therefore – a great leader and ruler. Since Xenophon also 'covered' the career of Agesilaus in some considerable detail in his general history of Greece, sometimes in almost the same words, it is possible for us – as for his original readers – to compare and contrast the content, arrangement and emphases of the two works. Hardly surprisingly, the *Agesilaus* version emerges as consistently the more positive – the work is, after all, explicitly an encomium, not an objective description and explanation of a man's career (in so far as that would have been within the scope of Xenophon's intellectual capacity or philosophical ambitions). One example will speak for many.

Referring to Agesilaus' campaign against the Peloponnesian city of Phleious, a recalcitrant ally of Sparta, Xenophon writes here that, although it 'may perhaps be criticized on other grounds', there can be no doubting that it was 'prompted by loyalty to his comrades' (2.21), which was a virtuous and entirely admirable motivation. What those 'other grounds' actually were, so delicately alluded to here, are made explicit in *A History of My Times*. Phleious put up an extremely resolute and politically astute resistance to Agesilaus – it took him almost two years to complete the siege successfully, and the Phleiasian democratic leadership rightly thought it worth appealing against Agesilaus to his co-king. For, quite exceptionally, Agesilaus's action engendered significant and vocal opposition even among his own habitually loyal people: 'There were a number of Spartans who complained that for the sake of a few individuals they were making themselves hated by a city of more than 5,000 men' (5.3.16; cf. Cartledge, *Agesilaos*, p. 265). Scholars today differ strongly over the political wisdom of Agesilaus' hardline, pro-oligarchic policy towards Sparta's disaffected Peloponnesian League allies, but supposing we had only the *Agesilaus* version, we could not even begin to argue the issue rationally.

That political calculus, however, is beside Xenophon's point in the biography. Once the outline sketch of Agesilaus' deeds has been got out of the way at breakneck speed in his first two chapters, Xenophon can lovingly enumerate and illustrate his hero's principal virtues, above all – and in this significant order – piety, justice, self-control, courage and wisdom. At the end of the *Memoirs of Socrates*, in respect of Socrates, and again towards the end of the *Cyropaedia* (8.1.23–33), we find the same first three of these virtues singled out, and in the same order. But *eusebeia* or duly reverential attitude and practice in relation to what Xenophon calls variously *ho theos* ('the god'), *hoi theoi* ('the gods'), *to theion/ta theia* ('the divine matter(s)') or *to daimonion* ('the supernatural') – that for him was always the cardinal virtue, the primary point of reference on his moral map.

AGESILAUS

CHAPTER I

I am well aware of the difficulty of writing a tribute to Agesilaus that 1
does justice to his virtue and reputation, but all the same the attempt
has to be made. It would be wrong for a man's perfect goodness to
condemn him to receiving no acclaim, however inadequate!

First, then, on the nobility of his lineage, could one find more 2
telling or excellent evidence than the fact that even today people
count the generations of illustrious ancestors – no ordinary citizens,
but kings and the sons of kings – who constitute his descent from
Heracles?[1] Nor could one find fault with them by claiming that, 3
although they were kings, the state they ruled over was an insignificant
one. No, the supreme regard in which their line is held in their
fatherland is matched by the pre-eminent position their state occupies
in Greece, and so they were not the first citizens of a second-rate
country, but leaders among leaders. Both the country and lineage of 4
Agesilaus also merit joint acclaim because the community never let
envy of his ancestors lead them to attempt to put an end to their rule
and the kings never lusted after more power than they originally
received at their accession. That is why, as is apparent, no other
government – whether it was a democracy, an oligarchy, a tyranny
or a kingship – has enjoyed unbroken continuity, while this one alone,
his ancestral kingship, has had a continuous existence.[2]

Moreover, it is clear that Agesilaus was considered worthy of the 5
throne even before his reign began, because after the death of King
Agis, when the throne was disputed between Leotychidas (on the
grounds that he was the son of Agis) and Agesilaus (on the grounds
that he was the son of Archidamus), the state judged Agesilaus to be
the more suitable candidate, thanks to his lineage and his virtue, and

they accordingly chose him as their king.[3] And what further evidence is needed of his virtue as far as the period before he ascended to the throne is concerned, than the fact that he was judged worthy of the highest office[4] in the most powerful state by the best of men?

6   I will next give an account of all the things he achieved during his reign, because in my opinion there is no better way to gain insight into his character than by considering his deeds.[5]

Agesilaus was no longer* a young man at the time of his accession to the throne. His reign was not far advanced when the news arrived that the Persian king was mustering a huge fleet and land army to 7 attack Greece. In the course of the ensuing debate, as the Spartans and their allies tried to decide what to do, Agesilaus said that if they gave him thirty Spartiates, 2,000 ex-Helots[6] and a contingent of 6,000 allied troops, he would cross over to Asia and try to negotiate a peace – or, if the Persian's mind was set on war, he guaranteed to keep him 8 too busy to attack the Greeks.[7] This immediately earned him a great deal of admiration from all quarters. In the first place, there was his desire to pay the Persian back for his earlier invasion of Greece by crossing over to Asia;[8] then there were his preference for taking the war to the enemy rather than waiting for him to attack and his intention that the cost of the war should fall on the Persians, not the Greeks;[9] but the best aspect of his plan, to people's minds,[10] was the possibility of making Asia rather than Greece the prize of the war.

9   No clearer demonstration could be given of the kind of commander he proved to be, once he had been assigned the army and had sailed 10 off to Asia, than a narrative of his achievements.[11] His first action on arriving in Asia was as follows. Tissaphernes swore an oath to Agesilaus to the effect that, if Agesilaus would honour a truce until the return of the couriers whom he, Tissaphernes, had dispatched to the Persian king, he would see that the Greek cities in Asia regained their independence and were handed over to him.[12] Agesilaus, in his turn, swore to keep the truce without treachery and set a term of three months for the completion of Tissaphernes' side of the bargain.[13]
11   Tissaphernes, however, immediately broke his oath; instead of arranging for an end to hostilities, he asked the Persian king to send him a sizeable army, over and above the one he already had. Although

Agesilaus found out what was going on, he continued to abide by the truce. This, then, seems to me to constitute his first fine achievement: 12 he exposed Tissaphernes as a perjurer, so making him universally distrusted, and revealed himself by contrast to be the kind of man who not only approves and sanctions oaths, but also honours his agreements, thereby making everyone, both Greeks and non-Greeks, enter confidently into agreements with him whenever he wanted.

With the arrival of the fresh army, Tissaphernes arrogantly threat- 13 ened Agesilaus with war, unless he left Asia. All Agesilaus' staff, including the Spartans who were there, openly expressed the dismay they felt at the thought that the forces available to Agesilaus were weaker than the Persian king's resources – but Agesilaus looked positively radiant as he told the delegation to convey his profound thanks to Tissaphernes for having failed to keep his word, because the upshot was that he had earned the gods' hostility and made them allies of the Greeks. Next, Agesilaus lost no time in ordering his troops 14 to pack up their gear in preparation for going to war, and in warning the communities on his route to Caria to have supplies ready for him. He also told the Ionian, Aeolian and Hellespontine Greeks by dispatch to send reinforcements to him at Ephesus.

Tissaphernes' strategy was based on considering that Agesilaus had 15 no cavalry and that the terrain of Caria was not suitable for cavalry manoeuvres, and on the supposition that Agesilaus was angry with him personally for his deception. Having come to the conclusion that Agesilaus' real target in Caria was his domain, he sent the whole of his infantry over there, while bringing his cavalry round to the plain of the River Meander. He thought that he had the capacity to crush the Greeks with his mounted troops before they reached bad cavalry country. Agesilaus, however, immediately went in the opposite direc- 16 tion and marched on Phrygia instead of Caria. He proceeded to conscript into his army any forces he encountered during his march and to reduce the cities, and his surprise attacks gained him huge quantities of booty.

Further evidence of Agesilaus' accomplishment as a military com- 17 mander was found in the fact that, once war had been declared and deception therefore became just and fair, he showed Tissaphernes to be a mere child at deception. His friends also apparently benefited

18 financially from his sound advice at this point. He had captured so much property that goods were selling for next to nothing, so he told his friends to buy things up, explaining that he would soon be taking his army down to the coast. He told the quartermasters responsible for selling the booty to give the goods away, while keeping a record of their current market value; this enabled all his friends to gain huge quantities of valuable property without putting any money down in

19 advance and without causing any loss to the army funds. Moreover, whenever deserters came* to the king, as one might expect they would, and offered to show him where there was some property to be taken, he made sure that it was his friends who were responsible for taking possession of these goods too, so that at one and the same time they could increase both their profits and their reputations. The immediate result of this was that his friendship was ardently wooed by large numbers of people.[14]

20   Agesilaus appreciated that a devastated and depopulated land would be unable to support an army for long, whereas an inhabited and cultivated land would be a permanent source of nourishment, so he took care to win some of his enemies over with leniency, as well as

21 defeating others by force of arms. It was a frequent injunction of his to his men not to treat prisoners-of-war as criminals to be punished,[15] but as human beings to be guarded; and if he ever noticed, when shifting camps, that any small children had been abandoned by the dealers (who would commonly try to sell the children because they doubted that they would be able to support them and feed them), he

22 took care that they were rounded up and taken off somewhere.[16] He also gave orders that any prisoners who were abandoned because of their old age were to be provided for, to prevent their being killed by dogs or wolves. Consequently, he came to be regarded with goodwill not just by those who heard about this behaviour of his, but even by his prisoners-of-war. Whenever he brought a community over to his side, he refused to let the inhabitants serve him as slaves serve their masters and required from them only the obedience due to a ruler from free subjects; and his kindness gained him control even of strongholds which were impervious to brute force.

Now, since Pharnabazus and his cavalry were making it impossible 23
for him to fight on the plains, even in Phrygia,[17] he decided that he
had to equip himself with a troop of cavalry or else be condemned
to wage a fugitive's war. He therefore drew up a list of the richest
men from all the communities there who could maintain a horse, and 24
announced that if any of them supplied a horse, arms and armour,
and a reliable man, he would be exempt from military service. In
this way he gained their commitment to the project – the kind of
wholehearted commitment that comes with looking for someone to
die in one's place![18] He also charged certain communities with providing cavalry units, the idea being that horse-breeding communities
would in all probability find it simple to come up with self-assured
horsemen. This too was considered a *tour de force*, in the sense that no
sooner had he gained a troop of cavalry than it was a potent and
effective unit.[19]

Early the following spring,[20] he assembled his entire army at Ephesus. 25
In order to motivate their training, he offered the cavalry contingents
a prize for expertise on horseback and the heavy infantry contingents
a prize for physical fitness. He also offered the light infantry units[21]
and the bowmen prizes for displaying excellence at their particular
jobs. And so you could have seen the gymnasia crammed with men
at their exercises, the horse-track filled with cavalrymen on horseback,
and the javelineers and bowmen shooting at the target pillar.[22] In fact, 26
he made the whole city where he was a remarkable sight. The city
square was so filled with all kinds of armour and horses for sale, and
every single bronze-smith, carpenter, ironsmith, leather-worker and
engraver was so busy working on weapons of war, that you would
literally have thought the city a workshop of war.[23] And the sight of 27
Agesilaus at the head of his men as they came garlanded from the
gymnasia and dedicated their chaplets to Artemis[24] would have put
heart into anyone, since every aspect of a situation where men are
showing reverence to the gods, practising the arts of war and cultivating
obedience to authority is naturally bound to raise good hopes.[25]

Another thing he did was tell the auctioneers to offer any barbarians 28
captured by his raiders for sale naked, the idea being that contempt
for the enemy fuels strength for battle. So the sight of their pale,

37

overweight and unfit bodies (because barbarians never used to strip and always relied on some kind of transport) made his men think that the forthcoming war would be just like having to fight women.

He also told his men that he would very soon be taking them by the shortest route to the best parts of the region, where he could have them directly prepare their bodies and minds for the coming conflict.

29 Now, Tissaphernes judged this announcement to be another deliberate decoy, and thought that this time Agesilaus really was going to invade Caria. So he sent his infantry over there, just as he had before, and stationed his cavalry on the plain of the Meander. Agesilaus meant no deceit, however; he kept to the terms of his announcement and went straight to the district of Sardis. For three days he made his way through territory devoid of enemy troops, which enabled his men to stock up with plenty of supplies.

30 On the fourth day, however, the enemy cavalry arrived. While the officer in charge of the baggage train crossed the River Pactolus and made camp, as instructed by his commander, the actual cavalry caught sight of the Greek camp-followers, who were spread out in search of plunder, and killed a fair number of them. Once Agesilaus realized what was happening, he ordered his horsemen to mount a rescue operation. When the Persians saw these reinforcements coming, they regrouped and took up a position confronting the Greeks. All their

31 cavalry units – huge numbers of men – were involved in this. This was the point at which Agesilaus realized that he was at full strength, while the enemy was still without their infantry; it seemed the right time to join battle, if possible.[26] As soon as he had offered up a sacrifice,[27] he led his men in battle array against the cavalry formation. The heavy-armed troops from the ten youngest year-groups had orders to rush in and close with the enemy, while the light infantry were to lead the charge. He also ordered his cavalrymen to attack with the knowledge that he was backing them up with all the rest of

32 the army. It was the crack Persian troops who received the Greek cavalry attack, but they fell back in the face of the all-out shock of the assault. Some of them were cut down there and then in the river, while the rest fled. The Greeks set out in pursuit and captured the Persian camp as well. The light infantry began to turn to pillage, as

one might have expected, but Agesilaus had his men form a circular camp, enclosing both their own and the enemy's property.[28]

News reached him that mutual recriminations over what had happened were keeping the enemy in disarray, so he immediately set out against Sardis. On arriving there, he proceeded to burn and ransack the outskirts of the city, and at the same time he also issued a proclamation to the effect that those who wanted freedom would find him their ally, while those who claimed Asia as their own would find her liberators ready to decide the issue by trial of arms.[29] However, since no one came out to confront him, he set about his campaign from then on with confidence. He began to see Greeks who had previously been forced to abase themselves being regarded with respect by their former oppressors; he made those who had actually expected to enjoy the honours due to the gods incapable of even looking a Greek in the eye;[30] he made his friends' land safe from incursions, while picking his enemies' land so clean that in two years he consecrated more than 100 talents to the god at Delphi as a tithe of his booty.[31]

The Persian king, however, had Tissaphernes beheaded, because he blamed him for these setbacks to his power, and sent Tithraustes down to the coast instead. But subsequently the Persians' affairs began to look even more bleak, while Agesilaus' went from strength to strength. Every tribe and nation sent envoys to seek his friendship, and a number of places longed for freedom so much that they went so far as to rebel against Persia and seek his protection instead, with the result that Agesilaus found himself becoming the leader not only of Greeks but even of large numbers of non-Greeks.

He behaved in these circumstances in a way that deserves an extraordinary degree of admiration. He was now the ruler of a great many communities on the mainland, and a great many of the Aegean islands too, since the state had attached the fleet to his command as well; his fame and power were on the increase, there was nothing to stop him doing as he wanted with all the advantages available to him, and on top of everything he was intending and hoping to overthrow the empire which had in the past invaded Greece.[32] Nevertheless, he did not succumb to any of these temptations, and when he was summoned by the authorities at home to return to help his fatherland, he obeyed the state's command as readily as if he had in fact been standing in the Ephors' office all alone before the five of them.[33] So he made it perfectly clear that he preferred his fatherland to the whole world, old loyalties to newly acquired friends, risky but honourable and just gains to risk-free but shameful ones.

37   How else could one describe another achievement of his during the period of his command except as the mark of a king who deserves our admiration? He found the communities he left Sparta to rule over torn by feuds because of the political turmoil engendered by the collapse of the Athenian empire, but as long as he was personally present he managed to get them to reach political unanimity and live in prosperity without the inhabitants having to resort to banishing
38 and executing one another.[34] That is why the Asian Greeks were saddened by his departure; they felt they were losing not just a ruler, but a father and a comrade. And at the finish they showed that the friendship they were offering was no sham, because they volunteered to help him protect Sparta, and did so even though they knew that they would be up against an enemy who was at least their equal. Anyway, this brought his exploits in Asia to an end.

CHAPTER 2

1 His route once he had crossed the Hellespont was identical to the one taken by the Persian king with his vast army, through the territory of the same peoples, and yet Agesilaus covered in less than a month the distance which took the Persians a year, because he had no intention
2 of being too late to help his fatherland. In Thessaly (that is, after he had passed through Macedon), the people of Larissa, Crannon, Scotousa and Pharsalus, who were allies of the Boeotians – in fact the whole Thessalian population apart from those who happened to be in exile at the time – kept tailing him and harassing him. For a while he had his men adopt a hollow-square formation while on the move, with half the cavalry up in front and the other half in the rear, but the Thessalians' attacks on the rearguard hindered his progress, so he

sent all the horsemen except his personal entourage round from the van to support the rear.

When the two armies were at battle stations facing each other, the Thessalians thought better of engaging heavy infantry with their cavalry, so they turned and began gradually to withdraw.[1] Agesilaus' army followed them, but very circumspectly. Agesilaus realized that both sides were making mistakes, so he sent his own personal unit of hardy horsemen up to the front with instructions to tell the others to join them in a full-blooded pursuit and not to let the Thessalians turn and make a stand. Those of the Thessalians who tried to wheel round to face the unexpected charge – as not all of them did – were caught with their horses side on to the attack and were captured. Only the Pharsalian cavalry commander, Polycharmus, succeeded in rallying his unit. He and his entourage died fighting, and at this the Thessalian army fled in complete disarray. Those who avoided death or capture did not stop running until they reached Mount Narthacium. That day Agesilaus commemorated the victory by setting up a trophy between Pras and Narthacium, and stayed on the battlefield, relishing having defeated people who particularly prided themselves on their horsemanship with a cavalry force of his own devising.

The next day he crossed the Achaean mountain range in Phthia and headed for the Boeotian border, passing through nothing but friendly territory. At the border with Boeotia he found an army drawn up ready to do battle with him, consisting of contingents from Thebes, Athens, Argos, Corinth, the Aenianians, Euboea and both the Locrian peoples.[2] With no hesitation, and in full view of the enemy, he had his men take up their battle stations. He had a regiment and a half of Spartans and some men from Phocis and Orchomenus (which were the only local places to offer support), as well as the army he had brought with him from Asia. Now, I am not going to claim that he took on the enemy despite being vastly outnumbered and outclassed, because that would make Agesilaus seem mad, in my opinion, as well as showing up my own foolishness for praising someone who casually put the most vital concerns at risk. No, what I do admire in the man is that he took to the field with a force of at least the same size as the enemy's, armed his men so as to present a solid mass of bronze and

8 red, took pains to ensure that his men were capable of strenuous efforts and filled their minds with the proud certainty that they were a match for anyone they had to fight; he also made them want to compete with their comrades to see who would demonstrate the most valour, and led them all to expect that their common good would be well served if they proved themselves to be brave and true men. For it was his view that this is the way to get men to commit themselves wholeheartedly to fighting the enemy.[3]

9 As a matter of fact, he was not proved wrong – but I will describe the course of the battle, because it was the most remarkable battle of modern times.[4] The two sides converged on the plain near Coroneia, with Agesilaus and his men coming from the direction of the Cephisus, and the Thebans and their allies from the direction of Mount Helicon. It was obvious to both sides that their infantry lines were evenly matched, and their cavalry units were much the same size as well. Agesilaus held the right wing of his army, with the Orchomenians[5] at the other end on the left, while on the Theban side the Thebans themselves were on the right, with the Argives holding the left wing.

10 As they converged a deep silence fell on both sides for a while, but when about a stade[6] separated them the Thebans raised the war cry and charged into the attack.

When the gap was down to three plethra[7] a countercharge was launched from Agesilaus' lines by Herippidas and his mercenary unit,

11 consisting of men who had marched with Agesilaus ever since he left home, along with some Cyreians;[8] the Ionians, Aeolians and Hellespontine Greeks were close behind and all joined in the charge. They were just a spear's thrust from the enemy when the lines facing them gave way. And the Argives did not even wait for Agesilaus and his men, but turned and ran for Helicon. At this point some of the mercenary troops[9] were already crowning Agesilaus with a victory garland, but then he received a report that the Thebans had cut through the Orchomenian lines and were among the baggage train. He immediately wheeled his phalanx round and led it against the Thebans. However, the Thebans had seen their allies make good their escape to near Mount Helicon, and they wanted to break out and regroup with their own side, so they pushed forward resolutely.

Agesilaus' next actions can unequivocally be described as cour- 12
ageous, but it must be said that he did not choose the safest course.
He could have let them pass through, come up behind them and
defeated their rearguard, but that is not what he did. Instead he
smashed head on into the Thebans. So with shield thrust against shield
they pushed,[10] fought, killed, died. The air was not filled with cries,
but it was not silent either: there were the typical sounds made by
men in the heat of battle fury. In the end some of the Thebans did
break through to Helicon, but many of them retreated and were
killed.

Now that victory was his, Agesilaus had himself carried – he had 13
been wounded – up to his men in their battle lines. Just then some
of his horsemen rode up with the news that eighty of the enemy,
fully armed, had taken cover up against the temple, and they asked
him what they should do. Even the many wounds he had received
all over his body from all kinds of weapons did not make him forget
the gods;[11] his instructions were that the men should be allowed to
go wherever they wanted without coming to any harm, and he
ordered his personal mounted guard to escort them to a place of safety.

With the fighting over, the battlefield presented a vision of blood- 14
stained earth, corpses of friends and foes lying intermingled, shattered
shields, splintered spears and daggers bare of their sheaths – some on
the ground, some sticking out of bodies, some still clasped in hands.
By now it was late in the afternoon, so once they had dragged the 15
bodies of the enemy dead inside their lines, they ate and bedded down
for the night. Early the next day Agesilaus gave Gylis the polemarch[12]
his orders: he was to deploy the men at battle stations and set up a
trophy, all the men were to wear garlands in honour of the god, and
all the pipe-players were to play their pipes.[13] While they were busy 16
carrying out these orders, the Thebans sent a herald to ask for a truce
to bury their dead. This led to a truce, of course, and then Agesilaus
set off for home. And so he rejected supreme power in Asia in favour
of the traditional norms of ruling and being ruled at home in Sparta.[14]

Subsequently[15] he noticed that although the Argives could comfort- 17
ably live off their own land, they had also appropriated Corinth and
were enjoying success in the war.[16] So he mounted an expedition

against them. He laid waste to all their territory and then immediately took the pass at Tenea* and went to Corinth, where he captured the wall connecting Corinth to the port of Lechaeum.[17] Having re-opened the gates to the Peloponnese, he returned home to play his part as directed by the choirmaster in singing the hymn of praise to the god at the Hyacinthia.[18]

18   Later, however, it came to his attention that the Corinthians were using Peiraeum as a place to safeguard all their herds and flocks, and were cultivating and harvesting the whole promontory there; moreover – and most importantly, to his mind – that the Boeotians were finding it easy to get through to the Corinthians via Peiraeum from Creusis. He therefore marched on Peiraeum, but found it heavily defended. What he did, then, was move camp (after his men had eaten their morning meal) close to Corinth, to give the impression

19   that the city was about to surrender. Reinforcements were hastily sent from Peiraeum to the city under cover of darkness – but not without Agesilaus becoming aware of it. At dawn the next day he turned back and captured Peiraeum, which he found undefended. He took possession of everything in the area, including the defensive walls which had been built. Then he returned home to Sparta.

20   Some time later, the Achaeans desperately wanted to enter into an alliance with the Spartans and were asking for support in their campaign against Acarnania. <. . .>* When the Acarnanians attacked him in a pass, he occupied the heights above them with his light infantry,** joined battle and inflicted heavy losses on them. He set up a trophy commemorating the victory, but he did not leave matters there: he improved relations between the Achaeans and the Acarnanians, Aetolians and Argives, and entered into an alliance with these four nations too.[19]

21   When the enemy[20] sent a delegation to sue for peace, Agesilaus spoke out against it, until he forced Corinth and Argos to allow the banished members of the pro-Spartan party to return home. And on another occasion, later than this,[21] he personally undertook a campaign against Phleious and restored those who had been banished from there for their Spartan sympathies. These campaigns may perhaps be criticized on other grounds,[22] but there can be no doubt that they

were prompted by loyalty to his comrades. After all, he also marched 22
on Thebes to help the pro-Spartans* there when they were being
massacred by their opponents.[23] He found all the approaches to the
city thoroughly protected by trenches and stockades, but he crossed
over by the pass at Cynoscephalae and laid waste to Theban territory
right up to the city itself, challenging the Thebans to choose their
own ground and meet him in battle either on the plain or in the hills.
A year later he launched another campaign against Thebes; this time
he passed through the stockades and trenches at Scolus and laid waste
to the rest of Boeotia.

So far both he and the state had jointly enjoyed success, and although 23
there were setbacks in the years that followed, no one could claim
that any of them happened under Agesilaus' leadership.[24] However,
after the disaster at Leuctra, when the prevalent view was that the
Spartans would not dare to stir from their country for a long time,
Agesilaus marched out against the Tegeans at the head of an army
consisting only of Spartans, despite the fact that all the Boeotians,
Arcadians and Eleans had formed an alliance, because his political
opponents in Tegea, supported by the Mantineans, were murdering
his supporters and guest-friends. He devastated the lands of those who
were doing the killing and then returned to Sparta.

As a result of this expedition of his, Sparta was attacked by an army 24
consisting of contingents from every community in Arcadia, along
with the Argives, Eleans and Boeotians, and supported by men from
Phocis, both Locrian peoples, Thessaly, the Aenianians, Acarnania
and Euboea.[25] As if that was not enough, there was an on-going revolt
involving their slaves and a number of their dependent towns as well,
and the Spartiate population had been at least halved by their losses
at Leuctra.[26] Despite all this, and despite the city's lack of a defensive
wall, he kept it safe. He never ventured out when the terrain would
unequivocally favour the enemy, but wherever the terrain would give
the advantage to his fellow citizens, he had them deploy and give
battle with all their might; his thinking was that if he ventured out
on to the plain he would be surrounded on all sides, whereas if he
kept to the passes and the heights he could get the better of anyone.[27]

The way in which he acted subsequently, after the enemy had 25 retreated, showed undeniable good sense. He was now too old for campaigning on foot or horseback, but he realized that in order to win military support, the state needed money. He therefore made it his business to raise money.[28] He not only did everything that could be done from Sparta, but he did not hesitate to make the most of any opportunity that presented itself, and even though he could not act as a military commander, he did not think it beneath his dignity to serve as an ambassador, if this meant that he could do the state some

26 good. Nevertheless, even as an ambassador he achieved feats of which any military commander might have been proud. For instance, Autophradates was so afraid of him that he fled from Assus, where he had been besieging Ariobarzanes, who was an ally of Sparta; and Cotys also abandoned his siege of Sestus (which was at that time still in the hands of Ariobarzanes) and withdrew.[29] In other words, it would* not have been unreasonable for him to have set up a trophy commemorating victories over his enemies even as a result of his ambassadorial work. Moreover, Mausolus was blockading both Sestus and Assus by sea with 100 ships, but he too left, although it was not fear that induced

27 him to do so, but Agesilaus' powers of persuasion.[30] <In this business>* he was remarkably successful, in the sense that he received money from both parties – the people he drove away, as well as those who considered themselves in his debt. Tachos and Mausolus (the latter being one of those who contributed money to Sparta, in his case because of his long-standing ties of guest-friendship with Agesilaus) also gave him a magnificent escort for his homeward journey.[31]

28 Later, when he was about eighty years old, it came to his attention that the king of Egypt wanted to go to war with Persia, and that he had foot-soldiers, horsemen and money in abundance. When a message arrived appealing for his assistance, and even promising him command

29 of the expedition, he was pleased, since he thought that at a stroke he could repay the Egyptian king for the favours he had done Sparta, restore the Asian Greeks' independence and punish the Persian king not only for past wrongs, but also because, while claiming to be an ally of the Spartans, he was demanding that they relinquish Messene.[32]

30 However, the Egyptian who was asking for his help withdrew his offer of command of the expedition, and this made Agesilaus uncertain

what he should do, since he had been so emphatically misled. Next, a division of the Egyptian army which was on a separate campaign rose up against the king, and then all the rest of his troops abandoned him too. The king fled the country in fear and took refuge in Sidon in Phoenicia, while civil war broke out in Egypt and *two* kings were chosen. Agesilaus realized at this point that if he supported neither of the two kings, not only would the Greeks not be paid or provisioned by either of them, but also the eventual victor would bear them a grudge, whereas if he helped one or the other of them, whichever one he helped would probably repay the favour with goodwill. So he decided which of the two kings was apparently more pro-Greek, joined forces with him, defeated the anti-Greek one in battle and helped to settle the other one on the throne. So he established friendly relations between Egypt and Sparta, and gained a great deal of money.[33] It was now the middle of winter, but even so he sailed back home, because he was in a hurry to ensure that the state would be able to mount an effective campaign against its enemies in the following summer.

CHAPTER 3

So much, then, for Agesilaus' public exploits, accomplished in front of a host of witnesses. Achievements of this kind do not need supporting evidence: the mere mention of them is enough to win instant belief. However, I shall now try to present a picture of the virtue which resided in his soul, because it was this that motivated all these achievements and prompted him to feel such a passionate desire for morality and abhorrence for immorality.

Agesilaus was so religious that even his enemies trusted his oaths and treaties more than they did their own ties of friendship. Although they were reluctant to meet <, for instance, when dealing with one another>,* they would put themselves into Agesilaus' hands. To allay any disbelief, I wish actually to mention some specific cases involving particularly eminent people. First, then, when Spithridates the Persian was faced with what he regarded as the monstrous behaviour of Pharnabazus, who was arranging to marry the Persian king's daughter, but still intended to have Spithridates' daughter as an unmarried concubine, he entrusted himself, his wife, his children and his assets

4   to Agesilaus. Then again, when Cotys,[1] the ruler of Paphlagonia, refused to comply with the Persian king's wishes, even though the demand was accompanied by the king's personal assurances,[2] he became afraid of being taken into custody and either fined a great deal of money or even put to death, but he too trusted the truce he made with Agesilaus and paid him a visit in his camp, which resulted in his entering into an alliance with Agesilaus and choosing to have his 2,000 horsemen and 4,000* light foot-soldiers fight alongside

5   Agesilaus and his men. Even Pharnabazus came and met with Agesilaus, and arranged to rebel against the Persian king if he were not given supreme command of the army. 'However,' he added, 'if I *do* become commander-in-chief, I will do my utmost to win the war against you, Agesilaus.' He could not have made this threat unless he had complete confidence that Agesilaus would honour the terms of their truce in his dealings with him.[3] All this just goes to show how vital and admirable it is for anyone, but especially a military commander, to have and be known to have piety and trustworthiness. Anyway, so much for his religious sensibility.

CHAPTER 4

1   As for his honesty in financial dealings, surely there could be no more telling proof than to point out that while no one ever claimed that he had been defrauded of anything by Agesilaus, many people used to acknowledge that they had benefited from his kindness. When it affords a person pleasure to give his own money away to help others, how could he think of stealing someone else's money and so tarnishing his honour? After all, if he wanted money, it would be far simpler for him to keep his own instead of taking what does not belong to him.

2   A person cannot be taken to court for failing to pay a debt of gratitude, so it is surely unthinkable that someone who would not deprive others of thanks might be prepared to deprive them of money, when this would actually be a crime under the law. And Agesilaus

not only judged it wrong to fail to pay a debt of gratitude, but also for someone with greater resources not to pay considerable interest on the debt. How could anyone plausibly accuse him of stealing from 3 the state when he handed over to his country, for the public benefit, the tokens of gratitude due to him? And what about the fact that, whenever he wanted to offer a state or some friends financial assistance, he was able to help by getting the money from others? Does this not clearly imply that he was not corruptible by money, because if he had 4 been in the habit of selling his favours or accepting bribes for his services, no one would have felt at all in his debt? On the contrary, it is when favours are freely given that people are glad to do something for their benefactor, not just to repay the favour, but also in gratitude for being judged trustworthy enough to safeguard the advance loan of a favour.[1]

Also, when a person invariably chooses honesty and relative poverty 5 rather than dishonesty and excess, it is surely easy to acquit him of the charge of avarice. Well, when the state decreed that Agesilaus should receive Agis' property in its entirety, he gave half of it to his relatives on his mother's side, because he saw that they were not well off. The whole state, everyone in Sparta, can bear witness to the truth of this.[2] When Tithraustes offered to shower him with gifts if he 6 would only leave the country, Agesilaus replied: 'Where I come from, Tithraustes, it is considered better for a ruler to enrich his army rather than himself – that is, to try to take booty rather than gifts from the enemy.'

CHAPTER 5

What about all the pleasures to which people commonly succumb? 1 Does anyone know of Agesilaus having been conquered by them? This was a man who would no more choose drunkenness than madness, or overeating than idleness.* He never used to eat the two portions he was served at feasts, but gave them away, leaving neither for himself, because in his opinion the reason why the king was served double the amount was not so that he could overeat, but so that he

could use it as another way of conferring honour on anyone he wanted
2 to.[1] He treated sleep as the subject rather than the master of his
activities, and was visibly embarrassed if his bed was not the most
modest one around, because he thought that a ruler should be tougher,
3 not softer, than ordinary citizens.[2] There were, however, some things
of which he was not ashamed to have more than his share – such as
direct sunlight in summer and cold in winter – and he made himself
work harder than anyone else whenever hard work was called for out
on campaign. He thought that this sort of thing would raise morale
among his men. In short, then, Agesilaus revelled in hard work and
totally avoided idleness.

4 Where sex was concerned, his self-control was amazing, and is
surely worth mentioning for this reason alone. If his abstinence had
been due to lack of desire, it would be true to say that anyone else
would have done the same; but in fact the desire he felt for Megabates
the son of Spithridates was as strong as such a passionate man might
be expected to feel for such a good-looking boy. Even so, when
Megabates tried to kiss Agesilaus – it is the native Persian way to greet
people they respect with a kiss[3] – Agesilaus resisted with all his might
and refused to let him kiss him. Does this not already indicate a
5 superhuman degree of self-restraint? After that Megabates never tried
to kiss him, because he felt insulted, so Agesilaus asked one of his
comrades to persuade Megabates to pay his respects to him again. The
comrade asked whether Agesilaus would kiss Megabates if his suit was
successful. Agesilaus was silent for a while, and then said, 'By the two
gods,[4] no – not even if I were suddenly to become the best-looking
man in the world, and the strongest, and the fastest runner! I swear
by all the gods that I would rather fight that battle all over again than
6 have everything I see turn to gold!'[5] Opinions differ on this, I know,
but I would maintain with some confidence that for most people
these temptations prove more difficult to resist than their enemies
do.[6] Disbelief may be the general reaction to *this* statement, since only
a few people recognize its truth, but we all know that the more a
person is in the public eye, the less he can hide anything he does.[7]
And yet no one ever reported seeing Agesilaus get up to this kind of
activity, and idle conjectures on this score would just have seemed

implausible, because when he was abroad he was not in the habit of 7
taking a private house to stay in, but could always be found either in
a shrine, where it is impossible to do anything of the kind, or in the
open, with the result that everyone could vouch for his self-control,
having seen evidence of it with their very own eyes. The whole of
Greece knows the facts of this matter, so for me to lie about it
would be to fail in my aim of praising Agesilaus and succeed only in
incriminating myself.

CHAPTER 6

As for courage, two features of his behaviour seem to me to provide 1
clear evidence of this virtue: first, the enemies he undertook to fight
were always the ones who constituted the worst threat to his state
and to Greece as a whole; second, in engaging these enemies, he
always posted himself in the front line. When his opponents were 2
prepared to join battle, it was not panic-stricken flight on their part
that enabled him to defeat them: no, if he set up a victory trophy it
was after overcoming his enemies in a close-fought battle. He not
only bequeathed to future generations undying memorials of his
bravery, but also bore off the field visible signs of the heat of the
fighting,[1] so that people could use their eyes to assess his character,
rather than having to rely on listening to tales.

In actual fact one should really count all the campaigns he launched 3
rather than the victory trophies he set up, because even when his
adversaries refused to fight he still overcame them, and did so with
less risk and more benefit to the state and his allies. It is the same in
athletic competitions too: those who go through uncontested[2] win
the garland just as much as those who have to fight for their victory.

Turning to his skill, it is impossible to find any of his achievements 4
which do not display it. His attitude towards his fatherland was such
that as a result of his exemplary obedience <. . .>* and because he
was so devoted to his friends he earned the unswerving[3] loyalty of
his friends. He also made his troops both obedient and loyal – and
are there any factors more important for the effectiveness of a phalanx

of men than good discipline and reliability, the first of which is engendered by obedience and the second by loyalty towards the commander?

5   He made it impossible for his enemies to find fault with him – though they could not help resenting him, since he always found a scheme which enabled his side to get the better of them. He would trick them when the opportunity presented itself, beat them to some objective when speed was called for, hide when appropriate, and generally treat them in quite the opposite way from the way he treated

6 his friends. For instance, he treated night exactly like day and, by disguising his location, destination and intentions, treated day like night as well. He negated the strength of his opponents' strongholds

7 by circumventing, overrunning or stealing into them. Whenever he was on the march and knew that the enemy might choose to engage him in battle, he led his men in a tight formation to enable his efforts to be as concerted as possible, and had their progress resemble that of the most modest of maidens in its orderliness,[4] the idea being that this would reduce his men's liability to fear, dismay, confusion, error and

8 ambush. These tactics of his explain why he was so formidable to his enemies and such a source of encouragement and energy for his friends. And so he lived his life without his enemies ever treating him lightly, without his fellow citizens punishing him, without his friends ever finding fault with him; he was everyone's favourite and the most idolized person in the world.

CHAPTER 7

1   As for his patriotism, it would take too long to go through the evidence of this in detail; I think that every single one of his accomplishments is relevant in this context. In brief, then, we all know that if Agesilaus ever thought he could do his fatherland some good, he would not spare any effort, shrink from any danger, hold back any money, or use his physical state or his old age as an excuse.[1] No, it was his view that it is in fact the job of a good king to do his subjects as much good as possible.

2   An aspect of his behaviour that I would count as one of the most

important benefits he conferred on his state was that despite his unrivalled political power he was obviously the most assiduous servant of the laws. After all, how could anyone have been prepared to break the law when he saw how law-abiding the king was? How could anyone have attempted a coup out of dissatisfaction with his lot when he knew that the king put up even with restrictions to his power without turning against the laws?[2] His attitude towards his political 3 opponents was that of a father towards his sons. He would tell them off for their mistakes, but congratulate them on their creditable achievements and support them in times of trouble. He refused to regard any of his fellow citizens as an enemy and found something to approve of in all of them; he counted the preservation of each and every one of them as a profit and the death of even a worthless one as a loss. He obviously thought that his fatherland's prosperity depended on his fellow citizens continuing to live in peaceful observance of the laws, and that it would remain strong as long as the Greeks behaved sensibly.

Then again, if it is true that a good Greek is a supporter of Greece, 4 I challenge anyone to name another military commander who would refuse to take a city if he thought that would involve destroying it, and who considered victory in a war against Greeks a catastrophe.[3] Once, when he received a report that in the battle at Corinth only 5 eight Spartans had been killed, compared with almost 10,000 of the enemy, it was plain to see that the news distressed him. In fact he said: 'Alas, poor Greece! Enough men have just died to have defeated in battle, were they alive, the whole Persian army.'[4] And when the 6 Corinthian exiles informed him of the city's imminent surrender and pointed to the siege-engines with which they confidently expected to take the walls, he refused to attack, and argued that the proper course of action in the case of Greek cities was to discipline them rather than enslave them. 'If we annihilate those of our own people who make mistakes,' he added, 'the chances are that we will fail to have the means to overcome the Persians.'[5]

Moreover, if hatred of Persia is also a valid stance, not just because 7 of their earlier invasion, the purpose of which was to reduce Greece to slavery, but also because of their current policy of allying themselves with whichever side in a conflict will enable them to do Greece the most harm, because they bribe those individuals who they think will then be particularly bad for Greece, and because they negotiate a peace which will, in their opinion, be extremely successful at getting us to fight one another – well, it is obvious to everyone what Persia is up to, but who else, apart from Agesilaus, ever got a tribe to revolt against Persia, or made the security of a rebel tribe his responsibility, or, in general, ensured that the Persian king had enough problems to stop him making trouble for Greece? Even when his fatherland was involved in a war against other Greeks, he still bore the common good of Greece in mind and set out by sea with the intention of harassing the Persians in any way that he could.[6]

CHAPTER 8

1   Another quality of his that deserves mention is his charm. He had prestige and power and, as if that were not enough, a kingship that was not plotted against, but welcomed, yet no one ever found a trace of arrogance in him; instead, the traits even a casual observer would have noticed were affection and a desire to serve his friends.

2   While he enjoyed taking part in playful conversations, he also took helping his friends seriously, whenever necessary. His optimism, good humour and constant geniality made people seek his company in large numbers, not just because they hoped to accomplish some business, but also because it was pleasant to spend time with him. Although he was the last person to boast, he was still tolerant of others praising themselves in his hearing, because he did not think they were doing themselves any harm and at the same time were setting themselves good goals to live up to.

3   However, he could, if the occasion called for it, express himself with haughtiness as well, and this should also not go unrecorded. For instance, he once received from the Persian king a letter on the subject of forging links of hospitality and friendship between them. The letter was brought to him by the Persian who accompanied Callias of Sparta. Agesilaus, however, refused to accept it. He asked the Persian to tell

the king that there was no need for him to send him private letters, but that if he showed himself to be a true friend to Sparta and Greece, he would find no more wholehearted friend than Agesilaus. 'However,' he went on, 'if we find out that he is plotting against us, he can send me all the letters he likes, but he should not imagine that he will have my friendship.'[1] As far as I am concerned, it is another point to Agesilaus' credit that he snubbed the king's offer of guest-friendship and preferred to win the approval of the Greeks.

Something else I applaud in Agesilaus is that he did not think rulers should pride themselves on their relative wealth or on having a greater number of subjects than the next ruler, but on being better people and on having better people under them.

Here is an example of his foresight which I find admirable. Bearing in mind that the more satraps rebelled against the Persian king, the better it would be for Greece, he was not overcome either by the king's bribes or his power, and refused to enter into formal ties of guest-friendship with him, to make sure that any satraps who wanted to rebel would trust him.

Who could fail to admire the fact that in contrast to the Persian king (who believed that by acquiring a huge fortune he would gain control over the whole world, and so tried to amass all the gold, silver and precious objects in the world), the trappings of Agesilaus' residence were such that he did not need any of these things. Anyone who finds this hard to believe should look at the kind of house that was sufficient for Agesilaus, and in particular at the front doors. It would not be implausible to think that these were the very doors that Heracles' descendant, Aristodemus, acquired and set up on his return home.[2] He should also look at the furnishings inside the house, if he can, reflect on the kind of feasts Agesilaus used to provide during sacrificial festivals and listen to the story of how his daughter used to travel down to Amyclae by public cart.[3] And so, because he fitted his expenditure to his income in this way, he never had to do wrong for the sake of money. For all that it is held to be a fine thing to acquire strongholds which are invulnerable to enemy attacks, it is in my opinion far better to equip oneself with a mind that is invulnerable to money, pleasure and fear.[4]

CHAPTER 9

1   I shall now go on to explain the difference between his way of life and the boastful pretensions of the Persian king. First, while the Persian made himself seem special by rarely letting himself be seen, Agesilaus enjoyed being constantly in the public eye, because he thought that only offensive practices need be concealed, whereas a life dedicated
2   to noble pursuits gains in lustre from being out in the open. Second, while the Persian prided himself on being hard to approach, Agesilaus was happy to be approachable by anyone. Third, one of the Persian's affectations was to be slow at conducting business, whereas it gave Agesilaus particular pleasure to grant petitioners' requests as quickly as possible and send them on their way.[1]

3   In the matter of personal comfort too it is worth observing how much more easy and simple it was to satisfy Agesilaus. People travelled the world hunting down drinks the Persian king would enjoy, while countless cooks contrived delicacies for him to eat, and the business of getting him to sleep was indescribably complicated. Agesilaus, however, was so hard-working that he was content to eat and drink whatever was accessible and available, and anywhere was good enough
4   for him to take his rest. Apart from the enjoyment he derived from these actual practices, it also made him happy to reflect that while he found his treats all around him, the Persian king patently had to draw his pleasures from the ends of the earth, just to live without distress.
5   It also gave him pleasure to observe that while he knew he could cope without suffering with the structure of things as devised by the gods, the Persian king had too feeble a temperament to endure heat and cold, and had to live like the most helpless of wild creatures, not like a true man.

6   Here is another exploit of his which is, of course, admirable and impressive. He enhanced his own estate with the kinds of artefacts and possessions you might expect a man to own – that is, he kept a large number of hunting dogs and war-horses – but at the same time he also persuaded his sister Cynisca to breed a team of horses for chariot-racing and so, when she won a victory at the games, he proved

that to keep such a team is not a mark of manly virtue but merely of wealth.[2] And what about the nobility of the following view of his? It 7 was his opinion that his renown would not be increased in the slightest by a victory over ordinary citizens in a chariot-race; but if he won more loyalty from the community than anyone else, gained large numbers of friends of high quality throughout the world, outdid everyone in serving his fatherland and his comrades, and punished his adversaries, this, in his opinion, would make him a champion in the noblest and grandest contest there is,[3] and would earn him the best of reputations not only during his lifetime, but after his death as well.

CHAPTER 10

So much for my tribute to Agesilaus. There is an essential difference 1 between these qualities of his and those of someone who, say, discovers a treasure trove and so increases his wealth, but not his capacity to manage an estate, or of someone who wins a victory thanks to an epidemic in the enemy camp, and so increases his success, but not his military expertise. Anyone who excels in endurance when the time for effort arrives, in bravery when courage is to be tested and in wisdom when there is a need for deliberation, may, it seems to me, fairly be regarded as a man of all-round virtue. The value of the 2 invention of the chalk line and ruler is that without them people could not give their productions straight edges; by analogy, Agesilaus' virtue seems to me to set an excellent example for anyone who intends to try to acquire manly virtue. I mean, how could anyone become irreligious if he modelled himself on a god-fearing person? How could he become dishonest, violently lawless or weak-willed if he modelled himself on someone who was honest, restrained and his own master? For what was a source of pride for Agesilaus was the fact that he ruled himself rather than the fact that he ruled others; it was not guiding his subjects towards the enemy that made him feel proud, but guiding them towards virtue in all its forms.

It is true that my tribute to Agesilaus follows his death, but I would 3 not have this treatise regarded for that reason as a lament.[1] It is in fact a celebration of his life. After all, what I am saying about him now is no more than others used to say about him during his lifetime. Moreover, a life that brought fame and a death that arrived when it was due are hardly the proper subjects for lamentation. On the other hand, what could constitute more fitting themes for celebration than utterly glorious victories and outstandingly valuable achievements?

4 And it can scarcely be right to mourn a person who from childhood onwards longed passionately for fame and won more of it than any of his contemporaries, who was firmly resolved to gain high office and remained undefeated after becoming king, and who after living as long as any human being can expect died with an unblemished record as regards both those he led and those he fought.

CHAPTER II

1 I want briefly to recapitulate the various aspects of his virtue, to make my tribute easier to remember.

Agesilaus was a scrupulous observer of sacred places even when they lay in enemy territory, because he thought it just as important to win the gods over to his side on enemy ground as it was in friendly territory.

He never did violence to anyone, even an enemy, who had taken refuge in the sanctuary of a god, because he considered it irrational to describe people who steal from temples as sacrilegious, and then to think that there is nothing irreligious about pulling a suppliant away from the altar where he has taken refuge.[1]

2 He could constantly be heard to voice his opinion that the gods gain just as much pleasure from pious actions as they do from sanctified shrines.

Success did not make him disdain other people, but give thanks to the gods. He offered up more sacrifices when confident than prayers when hesitant.

He trained himself to respond to fear with a cheerful countenance and to be calm when successful.

3 The friends he particularly welcomed were not the ones with the

most power, but the ones who were most wholehearted in their friendship.

He never thought the worse of a person for defending himself against injustice, but he did of failure to express gratitude for a favour.[2]

He rejoiced to see those who sought base gain living in poverty, and he enjoyed enriching upright people, because he wanted to make it possible for honesty to be more rewarding than dishonesty.

It was his practice to be acquainted with all kinds of people, but to be intimate only with the good. 4

He thought that praise or criticism gave him as much insight into the character of the speakers as it did into the people they were speaking about.

He did not blame people for being taken in by their friends, but he was very severely critical when they were tricked by their enemies; and he thought it clever to practise deception on a mistrustful person, but immoral to do so on a gullible person.

He appreciated being praised by people who were also prepared to find fault with things they found displeasing, and he did not find honest bluntness offensive, but he was as wary of insincerity as of a trap. 5

He loathed malicious gossip even more than he hated theft, on the grounds that loss of friends is worse than loss of property.

He was tolerant of the mistakes of ordinary citizens, with their limited consequences, but took the mistakes of rulers seriously, on the grounds that they could do far more damage. 6

In his opinion, manly virtue rather than idleness was appropriate for a king.

Although he received plenty of offers from people who would have done the work for free, he refused to have a physical likeness of himself set up; however, he never stopped working on memorials of his character. He thought that physical likenesses were the province of sculptors, whereas memorials of his character were up to him alone, and added that whereas wealthy people might want to leave the first kind of memorial, virtuous people would want to leave the second kind.[3] 7

His attitude towards money was generous as well as honest. The difference, as he saw it, was that while an honest person was content 8 to leave other people's money alone, a generous person also had to spend his own money to help others.

He was always in awe of the supernatural, since he believed that a good life is no guarantee of happiness, and that only those who have died a glorious death are happy.

9 Unwitting neglect of virtue was bad enough, but in his opinion deliberate neglect of virtue was a worse calamity.

He had no desire to be famous for anything unless he had put in the relevant work.

He struck me as one of the few people who regard virtue not as something to be endured but as a comfort to be enjoyed. At any rate, praise gave him more pleasure than money.

The courage he displayed was invariably accompanied by good sense rather than foolish risks,[4] and he made a habit of putting his intelligence into practice rather than into theory.

10 There was no one who was more easy-going with his friends, and no one who was more terrifying to his enemies either. While he could stand any amount of hard work, he was always delighted to give in to a comrade, though he preferred good deeds to physical good looks.

He combined the ability to control himself when things were going well with the ability to be resolute in times of danger.

11 His cultivation of charm was implemented by his whole way of life rather than by flippancy, and his occasional haughtiness was supported by intelligence rather than insolence. At any rate, he despised arrogance and outdid unassuming people in humility. For instance, he took pride in the plainness of his own dress and the splendid equipment of his troops, in the modesty of his own needs and his generosity towards his friends.

12 In addition, he was the most implacable of adversaries, but the most lenient of victors.

He was particularly mistrustful of his enemies' ploys, but particularly amenable to his friends' requests.

He combined constantly seeing to the safety of his own side with constantly making it his business to nullify the enemy's plans.

13 His relatives labelled him 'a devoted family man', his intimates 'unswerving', his clients 'ever-mindful'; the oppressed called him their

'champion', and those who followed him into danger their 'saviour, second only to the gods'.

He was the only person, as far as I know, ever to have proved that 14 while physical vigour may deteriorate with age, in good people mental strength is not subject to the ageing process.[5] At any rate, he never stopped aspiring to a high and noble reputation, as long as* his body was capable of acting as a vehicle for his mental strength. And so was 15 there anyone who did not prove to be outshone in his youth by the elderly Agesilaus? Was there anyone who in his prime was as terrifying to his enemies as Agesilaus was when he was at the extremity of old age? Whose departure was a greater cause for rejoicing among the enemy than that of Agesilaus, despite the fact that he was an old man when he died? Who could compare with Agesilaus, even when he was on the verge of death, in raising the morale of the troops fighting alongside him? Was there any young man who was missed after his death more than Agesilaus, for all his age? His service to his fatherland 16 during his lifetime was so perfect that even after his death he was still a major benefactor of the state. And so he was brought back to his eternal dwelling-place, with memorials to his courage scattered throughout the world, and a royal tomb in his fatherland.[6]

HOW TO BE A GOOD
CAVALRY COMMANDER
(Hipparchicus)

INTRODUCTION

Within two decades of Xenophon's death, Alexander the Great's leadership of the elite Macedonian Companion Cavalry at Chaeroneia in Boeotia in 338 was a crucial factor in his father Philip's devastating defeat of the Athenians and Thebans that led to Greece's subjection to Macedon. But Macedon was exceptional among states of the Greek mainland for giving a decisive role to cavalry; another great exception was Thessaly, and a significant though lesser one Boeotia. Elsewhere in Greece the front-line force was the phalanx of heavy-armed hoplite infantrymen, or at Athens, exceptional in another way, its fleet of triremes. Even the Peloponnesian War, which brought about so many military innovations, did not result in a significant promotion of Greek cavalry warfare. For a start, the terrain was usually against it; so too were the Greeks' generally low level of technology and relatively egalitarian social organization. Here therefore, as often, Xenophon was arguing something of a rearguard case, although the Athenian cavalry seems to have shed most of the odium in which it had been clothed some three to four decades earlier.

The treatise is based on Xenophon's own extensive personal experience and expertise both at home in Greece and in Asia Minor. The command of technical detail is formidable. Xenophon was, in the words of the Loeb editor, E. C. Marchant, 'both an excellent judge of a horse and a highly accomplished horseman' and had a 'profound interest in cavalry and knowledge of its use' (Marchant, pp. xxxiii, xxviii). Specifically, the work is addressed to the situation of cavalry command at Athens, about which we are given more precise information in a treatise of *c.* 330 on the Athenian democratic constitution, whose author (Aristotle or a pupil) had certainly read Xenophon. If

Cavalry Commander can be given a fairly precise date in the mid-360s (see chapter 1 note 11), it may have been intended to have a directly practical impact, especially as Xenophon's two sons, who had been raised partly in Sparta, returned to Athens in the 360s to fight in alliance with Sparta against the common enemy Thebes; one of them, Gryllus, perished in a cavalry engagement shortly before the major confrontation at Mantinea in 362, which the Boeotian side under Epameinondas won.

However, too much should not be made of these possible specific references and applications. As usual in Xenophon's works, the primary emphasis is placed on morality, in this instance on the moral and religious qualities required to lead men as a cavalry commander in any situation, place or time. The work assumes, no doubt autobiographically, that it is the individual skills and actions of the commanders that determine the overall efficiency of the cavalry. The next treatise in this selection, *On Horsemanship*, may or may not have been written by Xenophon as a companion piece. But it is in any case by no means the only other work in the Xenophontic corpus that attempts to make horse sense. Some parts of *Cavalry Commander* closely resemble *Memoirs of Socrates* 3.3, for example, and Ischomachus, the gentleman-farmer hero of *Estate-manager*, is naturally an excellent horseman who has his horse led to and from his farm, where he mounts and performs military exercises (9.17–20).

HOW TO BE A GOOD
CAVALRY COMMANDER

CHAPTER I

Before doing anything else, you should offer up a sacrifice and ask 1
the gods to ensure that the way in which you conduct your command – your thoughts, words and deeds – not only may afford them
particular pleasure, but also may be particularly effective in bringing
yourself, your friends and your state alliances, honour and general
benefit. Once you have secured the favour of the gods,[1] you next 2
have to recruit horsemen, making sure that you do not fall short of
the legal quota and that the cavalry is at full strength. Additional
recruits are needed to stop the numbers dwindling because men are
always leaving for some reason or another, such as getting too old to
carry on.[2]

While the quota is being filled, you should take care that the horses 3
are being fed sufficiently to guarantee their ability to endure hard
physical work. After all, any horses that are too weak to exert themselves will not be able to catch up with a fleeing adversary or escape
from pursuit. You must also make sure that they are tractable, because
disobedient horses are a help to the enemy rather than their own side.
Any horses that kick while being ridden must be weeded out, because 4
horses of this type often do more harm than the enemy. You must also
make sure that, as far as their feet are concerned, the horses are capable
of being ridden even over rough ground,[3] because you can be sure that
they will do you no good at all anywhere it hurts them to ride.

Once the horses are satisfactory, you should next train their riders. 5
The first thing you have to ensure is that they are capable of jumping
up on to a horse's back, because that has saved many a life; the second
skill to develop is the ability to ride over all kinds of terrain, because
the enemy will not always be found on the same kind of ground.

6   Third, once your men have acquired deep seats, you have to train them until as many of them as possible can throw a javelin from horseback[4] and until, generally, they have all the skills of expert horsemen. Fourth, you must equip both the horses and riders with the kind of arms and armour that will enable them to inflict the maximum amount of harm on the enemy while sustaining as little as 7 possible themselves. Fifth, you must see that the men are capable of taking orders, because a good horse, a deep seat, and fine arms and armour are completely useless without obedience.

It is of course the cavalry commander's job to see that all these things 8 are properly ordered, but at the same time the state has recognized that it is hard for him to do it all by himself, and so it also elects commanders for each of the tribal regiments,[5] and has ordained that the Council is jointly responsible for the cavalry.[6] It is therefore advisable, in my opinion, for you to get your regimental commanders to share your desire for the efficiency of the cavalry, and to have suitable people address the Council with speeches designed to frighten your men (fear will make them better soldiers) and assuage any inopportune resentment the Council may feel.

9   Anyway, these are just notes[7] to remind you of your areas of responsibility; I will now take them one by one and try to explain how to obtain the best possible result in each case.

Starting with your men, then, the law makes it plain that you have to recruit them from among those who are, thanks to their wealth and physical condition, best qualified to serve in the cavalry, and that you are either to obtain a legal ruling about their qualification[8] or to 10 persuade them to join up. The people you should take to court, in my opinion, are the ones who might otherwise be suspected of having bribed you to waive the legal procedure in their case. After all, if you fail to press the best qualified people into service first, the less well qualified ones will immediately have an excuse for not joining up.

11   I am also sure that there are young men who can be filled with enthusiasm for serving in the cavalry if one describes the splendour of a cavalryman's life, while their fathers' or guardians' resistance can be weakened by pointing out that thanks to their wealth they will be forced to maintain a horse in the cavalry some time, by someone else

if not by you. You can then add that if their boys join up during your period of command, you will deter them from their extravagant craze for buying horses and you will make sure that they rapidly become expert horsemen. And you should do your best to keep these promises. 12

The Council should, to my mind, decree that in future any lazy horses* are to be ridden twice as much and that any horse which is incapable of keeping up is to be rejected. This would force them to feed and look after their horses better. I think the Council should also rule that vicious horses are to be rejected, because this threat would encourage the men to spend longer breaking their horses in and to be more sensible when buying them. It is also worth arranging for the rejection of any horses that kick during the riding-exercises, because it is impossible to get such horses to serve alongside others; they are bound to bring up the rear in any movement against the enemy, and therefore the horse's vicious behaviour makes the rider ineffective too.[9] 13 14 15

If anyone knows an easier and cheaper way of getting a horse's feet in prime condition, by all means use it. Otherwise, my experience leads me to recommend collecting stones from the road, each more or less a mina in weight,[10] and spreading them on the ground as a surface on which to give the horse its rub-down and for it to stand on every time it leaves its manger. The point is that the horse will constantly make walking movements on the stones when it is being rubbed down or bothered by flies. Once you have tried this method and seen how well rounded your horse's feet become, you will have confidence in the rest of my advice. 16

Assuming that the horses are now satisfactory, I will explain how to get your men up to scratch. I would convince the young ones to learn for themselves how to jump up on to a horse's back, but there is also nothing wrong with laying on an instructor. If you get the older ones used to being helped up by others in the Persian fashion, you will be doing them good too. 17

What about enabling your men to have deep seats whatever the terrain they are riding over? It is probably too much of a nuisance to take them out on frequent rides when there is no war on, but you should get them together and advise them to practise leaving the roads 18

and riding at speed over all kinds of ground, when they are riding out to the country, for instance, or elsewhere. This does almost as much
19 good as taking them out, without being so much of a nuisance. It is worth reminding them as well that the state endures expenses of almost forty talents a year on the cavalry in order to have them ready for immediate use and not have to hunt around for cavalrymen in the event of war.[11] Bearing this in mind will probably make them take their equestrian training more seriously, so as to avoid the possibility of having to fight for their country, glory and lives in an unprepared
20 state. You would also do well to warn them that you will take them out in person one day and will lead them over all kinds of terrain. And it is a good idea – better for the horses as well as their riders – to vary the kinds of terrain to which you conduct them before simulated battle manoeuvres.

21 I think the way to get as many of your men as possible learning how to throw the javelin from horseback is to tell the regimental commanders that you will be asking them to take personal charge of the javelineers from each regiment when they ride out to display their expertise. The chances are that they will then vie with one another to see which of them can produce the largest number of expert javelineers for the state.

22 The regimental commanders can also contribute hugely towards seeing that the men are properly armed, in my opinion, once they have taken on board the idea that the state gains far more, in terms of reputation, from a whole regiment being smartly turned out, than
23 if it is just their own equipment that is eye-catching. They will probably not be hard to convince of this, since it was lust for glory and honour that led them to want to hold the office of regimental commander in the first place, and since they can obtain the equipment required by law without in fact incurring any expenses themselves, given that the law allows them to compel the men to arm themselves out of their pay.

24 As for the men under your command knowing how to obey orders, it is important to explain to them all the benefits obedience entails even in theory,* as well as arranging things so that the disciplined ones prosper in actual fact, while the undisciplined ones lose out.

The most effective way, to my mind, of encouraging each of your 25 regimental commanders to take pride in heading up a well-turned-out regiment is to equip the scouts under your direct command with the finest arms and armour, compel them to practise javelin-throwing as much as possible, and take personal charge of them during their javelin-throwing displays (once you have put in plenty of practice yourself).[12]

If you were in a position to offer the regiments prizes for expertise 26 in all the accomplishments people expect to see rehearsed in the exhibitions put on by the cavalry, I am sure this would go a very long way towards introducing a competitive spirit throughout Athens.[13] Look at what happens in the choral competitions, where a great deal of effort and money is spent in the hope of gaining trivial prizes. However, you would have to find judges of such impeccable character that their verdict would be a source of pride for the winners.

CHAPTER 2

Let us suppose that your men are now fully trained in all these respects; 1 it is of course also necessary for them to know a formation which will enable them to look their most magnificent in religious processions and out on the riding-grounds, fight their best if called upon to do so, and make their way along roads and across rivers with the least difficulty and disorder. I will now try to explain which formation they should adopt, in my opinion, to achieve all this.

In the Athenian system, the cavalry is divided by tribe into ten 2 regiments. I think you should begin by appointing, with the approval of the relevant regimental commander, fit, ambitious men, who long for success and glory, as officers to lead each section of ten men within these regiments. These are the men you should post in the front rank. Next you should choose some of your most level-headed veterans – 3 the same number as the section leaders – to occupy the rear rank of each section of ten. To use an analogy: iron best cuts through iron when the cutter's leading edge is strong and is backed up by sufficient impetus.

4   As for the ranks between the front and the rear, the section leaders should select whom they want to stand behind them, and then every rank in turn should do the same; this would make it likely that everyone would have behind him someone he particularly trusted.

5   However, you must make absolutely certain that a capable man backs up each file, because it takes a brave man to stiffen the resolve of the men in front of him if they are ever called on to attack an enemy position, and such a man is also more likely to provide sound leadership

6   and save the lives of his fellow tribesmen if it is time to retreat. Of course, having an even number of section leaders makes it possible to divide each regiment into equal parts in more ways than if there were an odd number of them.

There are two reasons why I like this formation. In the first place, all the men in the front rank are officers, and men are more likely to think they ought to strive for success if they are in positions of responsibility than if they are ordinary rank-and-file soldiers. In the second place, passing an order on to officers rather than ordinary soldiers is a far more efficient way of getting something done.[1]

7   With this formation, the regimental commanders should post each of the section leaders as* they want them for an outing, just as it is the cavalry commander who stations the regimental commanders as he wishes before an expedition. If orders are given in advance like this, matters proceed in a far more disciplined fashion than they would if the men imitated the chaos of people leaving the theatre and getting

8   in one another's way. Moreover, faced with a frontal assault, the men in the front rank are far more willing to fight when they know that is where they have been stationed, and the same goes for the men in the rear in the event of a surprise attack from behind, since they know

9   better than to abandon their post. If they take up positions at random, however, they impede one another on narrow roads and when crossing rivers, and none of them is prepared to put himself in a position that would involve fighting the enemy.

Every single one of your men must receive thorough training in all these matters if they are to give their leader unswerving support.

CHAPTER 3

What about the responsibilities of the cavalry commander himself? 1
In the first place, it is his duty to sacrifice to the gods, seeking favourable
omens for the cavalry. Secondly, he has to see that the cavalcades
during religious festivals are spectacular. Thirdly, he has to ensure that
all the other public displays – in the Academy, the Lyceum, Phalerum
and the Hippodrome – are as magnificent as possible.[1]

Again, these are no more than notes; I shall now go on to explain
the best way for the cavalry commander to carry out each of these
functions.

It seems to me that the way to make the processions particularly 2
enjoyable for gods and spectators alike is to have the cavalry make a
circuit of the city square,[2] starting at the Herms, and pay their respects
to *all* the gods whose shrines and statues are to be found. So during
the Dionysia the choruses' dancing pays homage to other deities as
well as the Twelve. Once they have completed the circuit and are
back at the Herms, I think it would be nice if they charged their
horses by regiments up to the Eleusinium. I should also say something 3
about how the riders should stop their spears getting tangled up with
one another. If every man carries his spear so that it points between
the ears of his horse, the spears will create a fearsome impression and
be sharply delineated, and the overall appearance will be of a multitude
of spears. After this galloped cavalcade, they should ride slowly back 4
along the same route towards the shrines. This programme will allow
both gods and men to enjoy the spectacle of all the pleasing sights a
horse being ridden can afford.

I am aware that our cavalrymen are not used to this kind of 5
manoeuvre, but I feel that it is beneficial and worthwhile, as well as
being enjoyable for the spectators, and it has not escaped my notice
that our horsemen have in the past put on other novel forms of contest
in the days when the cavalry commanders were capable of getting
people to comply with their wishes.[3]

When the Lyceum is the venue for the parade, before the javelin- 6
throwing it is advisable to have them divide into two contingents of

five regiments each and deploy in an extended line, so that they occupy the entire width of the course, with the cavalry commander and the regimental commanders leading them as if they were going 7 into battle. Once they have passed the highest point of the theatre facing them, it would serve a useful purpose, in my opinion, if you also displayed the men's ability to gallop downhill in moderately sized 8 groups. I am sure they will not be reluctant to show off their ability to ride at the gallop, as long as they are confident that they can do it; anyway, it is not the kind of thing that should be omitted from their training, in case their first experience of it comes when the enemy force them to it.

9 I have already described the formation the cavalry should adopt during the reviews to make the best impression. If his horse is up to it, the leader should keep to the outside file during the troop's circuits, because then he will always be galloping, accompanied by those of his men who are taking the outside at the time. And so there will always be galloping for the Council to watch, and the horses will not get tired because they will be taking turns to rest.

10 When the cavalry display takes place in the Hippodrome, it would be nice, in the first place, to have the men deploy in an extended line so that the entire width of the Hippodrome is filled with horses and 11 they can drive the men in the middle out of the area. During the mock battle, which involves the regiments galloping away from and after one another, with the cavalry commanders leading their contingents of five regiments, another good idea is to have each of the two contingents ride through the other one. Imagine the scene: the lively advance of the two opposing lines towards each other, the splendour as they stand facing each other again after riding the length of the Hippodrome, the thrill as the trumpet sounds and they charge once 12 more, faster this time. Once they have come to a halt for a third time, the trumpet should sound again, and the two lines should charge each other flat out; after they have crossed, every single man should rest in battle order and await dismissal, and then ride up to the Council 13 in the customary fashion. It seems to me that these manoeuvres will look more warlike than the usual programme and will also have the appeal of novelty. But for a cavalry commander to ride more slowly

than the commanders of the regiments, and to play the same part in the manoeuvres, seems to me to be unworthy of his rank.

My advice for when your men have to ride on the hard ground of 14 the Academy is that they should lean back as they ride to avoid being thrown from their horses and should check their horses at the turns to stop them falling. They should gallop down the straights, however. If you follow this advice, the Council will have a safe as well as an attractive spectacle to watch.

CHAPTER 4

During expeditions a cavalry commander constantly has to think ahead 1 and plan to have his men alternate reasonable periods of riding with reasonable periods of going on foot, because their walking gives not only them but the horses' seats a rest. It is easy to form a correct notion of what constitutes a reasonable period, because every individual is himself a measure whereby you can observe when they are getting exhausted. However, if you cannot tell, while you are on your way 2 somewhere, whether or not you will meet the enemy, you should have each regiment take turns to rest, since it would be awkward to encounter the enemy with *all* your men dismounted.

On narrow roads, you should order your men to form a column 3 and then lead them on; on any broad highways you come across, you should instruct every regiment to form an extended front; when you come to a plain, you should <arrange>* all the regiments in line of battle. This not only provides valuable training, but also helps to make the journey more pleasant for the men, as they do not spend whole expeditions in a single monotonous formation.

When you are riding off the beaten track through difficult country- 4 side, it is very useful, no matter whether you are in enemy or friendly territory, to have a few of your light cavalry ride ahead of each regiment, to find easy ways around any impassable glens they come across and then show the rest of the men where to go; otherwise you might get whole regiments wandering around aimlessly.

In hostile territory, a sensible cavalry commander will have some 5 of his skirmishers posted in advance of the rest as scouts, because the earliest possible notice of the enemy is useful both for attack and for defence. Another sound principle is to wait after fording a river, because otherwise the men bringing up the rear will have to wear out their horses trying to catch up with the front man. Although these rules will come as a surprise to hardly anyone, few people are prepared to go to the bother of observing them.

6   It is a cavalry commander's job to make sure that he is familiar with both hostile and friendly territory even in times of peace. If he lacks first-hand knowledge, he should enlist the help of those of his men who are best acquainted with various places. A leader who knows the routes has a huge advantage over one who does not, and in planning tactics against the enemy a commander who knows the region is far better off than one in the opposite situation.

7   It is also a cavalry commander's job to have recruited spies, before the outbreak of war, from citizens of neutral states and from merchants – the latter because every state always welcomes people importing
8   goods. False deserters can occasionally be useful too. However, he should never rely on spies so much that he neglects to post guards; on the contrary, he should constantly be in the same state of readiness as he would be if he had received a report that a hostile force was on its way. After all, in wartime it may very well be difficult for even the most trustworthy spy to get a message through at the critical moment.[1]

9   The enemy will be less likely to become aware of the cavalry leaving the camp if the order is given by word of mouth rather than by crier or by posted notices. So it is advisable, to help the transmission of the command to move out, to appoint not only leaders for every section of ten, but also leaders for every half section of five, so as to reduce to a minimum the number of people to whom each of these officers
10   has to pass the message. Another function these half-section leaders can perform is to facilitate the extension of the regiment's line, when it is time for this formation, by deploying the men smoothly in their new posts.

What about when you need to post guards? I for one always recommend keeping your lookouts and sentries hidden,* because then they can serve a dual purpose: they can ambush the enemy as well as

guard their friends. At the same time, their invisibility makes them 11
less vulnerable to a surprise attack and more frightening to the enemy.
I mean, knowing that there are guards somewhere, but not knowing
exactly where or how many of them there are, not only saps the
enemy's morale, but also inevitably makes every location a source of
suspicion. Visible guards, however, show him which places are safe
and which are unsafe. Besides, hidden guards create the possibility of 12
posting a few men on patrol out in the open in front of their concealed
comrades and trying to lure the enemy into an ambush. Another trick
for ensnaring the enemy is sometimes to post guards out in the open
behind the hidden ones; this can prove just as effective a way of taking
the enemy in as the trick I have just mentioned.[2]

It is also a mark of a sensible commander never to take risks, if he 13
can help it, except when it is obvious that he will have the enemy at
a disadvantage. Doing the enemy favours should be regarded as a
betrayal of one's side rather than as courage. Another sound principle 14
is always to aim for the weak point of the enemy's position, even if
it is a long way off. After all, pushing yourself to make a great effort
is less risky than engaging a superior force. However, if the enemy 15
has managed to come between you and a friendly stronghold, then
even if they are the superior force, the right thing to do in this situation
is to attack them, either on the flank where your presence has gone
unnoticed, or on both flanks at once, because as one of your contingents
is retiring, the other one can charge the other flank, throw the enemy
into chaos and rescue your friends.

The value of spies as a means of trying to get information about 16
the enemy has long been recognized, but I am sure that the best plan
of all is for the cavalry commander to try to observe the enemy himself,
if he can find a safe vantage-point, and watch out for any mistakes
they might make. You should send suitable men to pilfer anything 17
that can be stolen and dispatch raiders to seize anything they can make
off with. If the enemy is on the march somewhere and a part of his
force which is weaker than your own becomes detached or rashly
fans out from the main body, you should not let this escape your
notice, either; but remember that the hunter must always be stronger
than the hunted.

18   This is not a difficult principle to grasp if you think about it. Even wild animals, which are less intelligent than human beings, put it into practice. Kites, for instance, have the ability to seize anything left unprotected and withdraw to a place of safety before being caught; wolves prey on anything which has been left alone and unguarded

19   and steal things from nooks and crannies. And suppose a dog sets out after a wolf and catches up with it: if the wolf is stronger it attacks the dog, but if it is weaker it tears off as much of its haul as it can and retreats. Again, sometimes, when wolves are not put off by watch-dogs, they organize themselves into two groups, one of which drives off the watch-dogs, while the other carries out the raid. That is how they

20   get their provisions. If wild beasts can plunder with such intelligence, surely a human being may be expected to display greater skill, given that animals themselves actually fall victim to human expertise.

CHAPTER 5

1   A true horseman should know how long it takes for a horse to overtake a man on foot and how much start slow horses need to escape from fast ones. It is also the job of a cavalry commander to be able to recognize terrain which suits infantry rather than cavalry and vice

2   versa. In addition, he should be so resourceful that he can make a small body of cavalry seem large and a large one small, give an impression of presence when he is not there and of absence when he is, and know how to achieve stealth not only when pilfering the enemy's property, but also when concealing his own men in the course of making a surprise

3   attack on the enemy. Another good ploy is for him to be able to undermine the enemy's confidence when his own position is weak, and so deter them from attacking, and give them grounds for hope when he is in a strong position, so that they make an assault. This will enable you to minimize the losses sustained by your own men, while taking maximum advantage of the enemy's mistakes.

4   In case you think that my instructions are impossible to put into practice, I will next take the ones that are apparently the most difficult and explain how they can be implemented.

It is experience of horses and what they are capable of that guarantees the success of operations such as the pursuit and retreat. But how do you gain this experience? By paying careful attention during friendly mock battles to the state of the horses after they have practised the pursuit and retreat.

When you want to give the impression that you have a large body 5 of cavalry, the first principle to adhere to if you can is never to try to trick the enemy when they are near by. Distance affords greater safety and increases the illusion. Secondly, a useful piece of information is that when bunched together horses look numerous, but when spread out they become easy to count; this phenomenon is due to a horse's size. Another way of increasing the apparent size of your force is to 6 get the grooms to stand among the actual cavalrymen with spears or, failing that, with fake spears.[1] You can do this not only when your men are halted for inspection, but also when you are bringing them up into a new formation. This is bound to exaggerate the apparent size and density of your troop.

Suppose, on the other hand, you want to make a large force appear 7 small. If the countryside offers hiding-places, the obvious course of action is to conceal the number of your men by keeping some of them out in the open while hiding the rest. However, if the area is completely exposed, you should first form the sections of ten into rows and then deploy them, with gaps between each section; during this manoeuvre the men from whichever section is nearest the enemy should keep their spears upright, while everyone else keeps them low down and out of sight.[2]

You can undermine the enemy's confidence by laying false 8 ambushes, making false sorties and creating false intelligence; and nothing raises his hopes like hearing that his opponents are experiencing problems and complications.

So much for my suggestions, but a cavalry commander should also 9 devise tricks of his own, suitable for his situation. The basic point is that deceit is your most valuable asset in war. Even children playing 10 'How Many?' prove themselves capable of trickery: they hold out their hands in a way that makes it seem as though they have quite a few pebbles* when they have hardly any, and make it look as though they have few when they are actually holding out a lot. So surely grown men can devise equivalent tricks when they put their minds

11 to it. If you think about it, you will find that the majority of important military successes have come about as a result of trickery. It follows, then, that if you are to take on the office of commander, you should ask the gods to allow you to count the ability to deceive among your qualifications, and should also work on it yourself.[3]

12 If you have access to the sea, a good trick is to get a fleet ready for battle and then make an assault by land, or alternatively to launch an attack by sea while pretending that you are planning a land attack.

13 It is the job of a cavalry commander to instruct the state in the relative weakness of a cavalry unit unsupported by infantry, compared to the strength of a combined force of both infantry and cavalry – and once he has got his infantry, it is a cavalry commander's job to make use of them. Infantry soldiers can be concealed both among and behind mounted horsemen, since a rider is much taller than a man on foot.[4]

14 Whatever you do to defeat your enemies – whether it takes force of arms or skill, and whether you use the tactics I have mentioned or come up with additional stratagems – I would advise you to enlist the help of the god,[5] because if the gods are well disposed towards you, fortune will favour you as well.

15 Another trick that proves very effective at times is to pretend to be over-cautious and totally disinclined to take risks. This may well tempt the enemy to make a fairly serious error in a fit of recklessness. Alternatively, once you have gained a reputation for risk-taking, you can also confuse your opponents by staying in one place and pretending to be about to do something.

CHAPTER 6

1 No craftsman would be able to shape things as he wished without plastic material in a condition to comply with his will.[1] You will not be able to do anything with your men either unless, with the god's help, they have been conditioned to feel loyalty for their leader and

to consider him more knowledgeable than themselves when it comes to fighting the enemy.

Subordinates come to feel loyalty, of course, when their leader is considerate towards them – that is, when they can see him making sure that they have food, that they are in no danger while they withdraw after a pursuit, and that they are guarded when they rest. When the unit is on garrison duty, the commander should be seen to be concerned about essentials like fodder for the horses, tents, sources of water,* and firewood, and to be attentive and alert to his men's requirements. When he has more than he needs of something, it is in a commander's best interests to share the surplus with his men.[2]

Briefly stated, there is the least chance of a commander being despised by his men if he shows himself to be better than them at the tasks he sets them. He therefore has to practise every aspect of horsemanship, from mounting onwards, so that they can see that on horseback their commander can clear a ditch safely, scramble over a wall, jump down from a bank and throw a javelin competently. All these things improve his chances of avoiding their contempt. If they recognize that he is an expert tactician as well, who knows how to deploy them so that they can get the better of the enemy, and if they also come to realize that he is not going to lead them against the enemy carelessly, or without having solicited the gods' goodwill, or when the sacrificial omens are unfavourable, this all helps to make the men in a commander's unit more ready to obey his orders.

CHAPTER 7

While intelligence, then, is a desirable quality in every leader, an Athenian cavalry commander needs to excel in two respects – in his homage to the gods and in his expertise at military matters – since his opponents just across the border have almost the same numbers of horsemen and large numbers of heavy-armed foot-soldiers.[1] If he tries to invade enemy territory without the rest of the community's armed forces he will come up against both divisions of their armed forces with only his cavalry, which is hardly safe. At the same time, if the enemy invades Athenian territory, the first point to note is that he is bound to do so with extra horsemen over and above his own cavalry and also with as many heavy-armed foot-soldiers as he thinks are required to defeat the whole Athenian army. If the whole community comes out to defend their land against an invading force of this size, there are grounds for expecting a favourable outcome. I mean, given the help of the god and proper management, the cavalry will prove better than the enemy cavalry, while the heavy infantry will match their opponents' numbers and, with the help of the god and proper training, will have the advantage both physically and mentally – in their fitness and their desire for victory. Besides, Athenians are just as proud of their lineage as Boeotians.[2]

4   However, during the invasion of the Spartans (supported by contingents from all over Greece) Athens relied on its navy and was content to do no more than defend the city walls.[3] If it did this again, and expected the cavalry to defend everything beyond the walls and to run the risk of taking on the entire enemy force all alone, there would, in my opinion, be two indispensable requirements: the staunch support of the gods and a thoroughly accomplished man for cavalry commander. After all, when faced with vastly superior forces plenty of intelligence is needed, and plenty of daring at the critical juncture.

5   He must also be a good strategist, I would say. If he took the gamble of engaging the army facing him – an army which not even the whole community was willing to confront – he would obviously be entirely at the mercy of the superior force and incapable of any significant

6   action. However, suppose he left the protection of property outside the city walls to just as many men as were needed to look out for the enemy and also to remove essentials to a place of safety from as wide an area as possible. A small force is as good as a large one at taking care of this; moreover, men who lack confidence in themselves and their horses are rather well suited to the job of guarding and removing

7   the property of people on their own side, because fear is apparently a formidable ally for a guard. So it may well be a good idea for him to select men of this kind for his pickets, but the rest of the men under his command – the ones not chosen as pickets – will turn out to be too few to be regarded as an army, in the sense that open combat will

be completely beyond their capacity. However, there will probably be enough of them for him to use them as a force of marauders.[4]

What he has to do, in my opinion, is keep these men in a state of 8 constant readiness to strike and, without exposing himself, watch out for any mistakes the enemy army might make – and the greater the 9 number of soldiers, the more liable they are to make mistakes. For instance, they might spread themselves thin in search of provisions and booty,* or while on the march, some of them might forge ahead in disarray, while others lag too far behind. The cavalry commander 10 should not let mistakes like these go unpunished, or the whole country will be occupied by the enemy; but he has to plan his strategy carefully, and withdraw straight after a strike before hostile reinforcements can arrive in strength.

It is also not uncommon for an army on the march to come to 11 roads where numerical superiority is no real advantage. The same goes for when it is crossing rivers too: this affords an opportunity for an alert commander to harass an army without endangering his own men and to control events so that he can choose how many enemy troops to attack. It is also a good idea sometimes to fall on the enemy 12 when they are in their camp, at their morning or evening meal, or just as they are waking up, because these are all occasions when soldiers are unarmed for a while – a longer or shorter while depending on whether they are horsemen or foot-soldiers.

Lookouts and sentries, however, should be the constant target of 13 the cavalry commander's plans, because there are never more than a few of them posted together at one time, and they may be at a considerable distance from the main body of troops. Once the enemy 14 is taking proper precautions against this kind of attack, the cavalry commander should, with the god's help, steal into enemy-held territory, taking care that <he has found out in advance>* how many men they have stationed at various points and whereabouts their patrols are. The reason for doing this is that if he can overpower one of their patrols, there is no finer booty in the world. And patrols are easy to 15 trick; they go after any small band of men they spot, in the belief that this is their function. However, it is important for our commander to check that he has an escape-route which does not take him straight into the path of any reinforcements that might be coming to help the patrol.

CHAPTER 8

1 Clearly, if your men are to succeed in inflicting losses on a far superior force without incurring losses themselves, the difference between them and the enemy has to be such that they make the enemy seem amateurish compared to their own expertise at horsemanship and its 2 military applications. The first prerequisite for this is that the men detailed to be marauders become so completely used to riding that they can exert themselves as much as their military role might require, because to send into battle horses and men whose training in this respect has been inadequate would in all probability be like pitting 3 women against men.[1] However, those teams of horses and men which have been drilled and schooled in jumping ditches, clearing walls, leaping up banks, scrambling safely down gullies and riding at speed downhill, will make those which have not learnt all these techniques seem as clumsy as land animals compared to winged creatures.* Or again, when it comes to rugged terrain, the difference between those who have and those who have not put considerable time and effort into toughening up their feet is like the difference between healthy and disabled people. And when it comes to pursuing the enemy and retreating back from his lines, if we say that those who have familiarized themselves with the terrain are like people who can see, then those who have not are like blind people.

4 You should also be aware that for a horse to be in good condition, it has to be well fed and to have been exercised until it can exert itself without getting short of breath. In addition, since bridles and horse-cloths are fastened with straps, a cavalry commander should never run out of them. They do not cost much, and without them your men will be useless.

5 You might think that having to train at horsemanship in the way I have been recommending is very laborious; if so, you should reflect on the fact that athletes preparing for a competition have much more

work to do, and of a more demanding kind, than those who practise horsemanship, however assiduously they do so. After all, most athletic 6 training involves working up a sweat by hard work, whereas pleasure is what nearly all cavalry training involves. It is the closest a man can get, as far as I know, to flying, and that is something people long to be able to do.[2] Then again, a military victory brings with it far more 7 glory than winning a boxing-match. The point is that although in either case the state gains in glory from the victory, yet in the case of a military victory the gods invariably also crown states with prosperity.[3] Speaking for myself, then, I cannot think of anything that deserves to be practised more than the arts of war.

It is worth bearing in mind that sea-pirates too are able to make a 8 living at the expense even of people who far outnumber them, because they have inured themselves to hard work. If your men are short of food, it is all right for them to turn land-pirates, even though the crops they gather belong to others. After all, there are two sorts of people: those who work the land and those who live on the products of others' work. And without recourse to one or the other of these practices, it is hard to find the means to stay alive, and the goal of peace becomes more remote.

You should also remember never to charge a superior force if you 9 leave behind you ground which is awkward for horses to cross. It is quite a different matter to become unseated during the pursuit than during the retreat.

Next, there is something else I want to remind you to be on your 10 guard against. It is true that some people use a totally inadequate force to charge an enemy who is perceived to be superior (and the upshot often is that the attackers have done to them what they were expecting to do to the other side), but others throw all the resources they can muster against an enemy who is known to be superior. In my opinion, 11 this is quite the wrong way to go about it: it is when you are proceeding against an enemy you expect to defeat that you should draw on all available resources. After all, an easy victory never gave anyone cause for regret. However, when you are attacking a considerably superior 12 force and you know in advance that you are going to have to pull back after doing your best, *this* is the situation, in my opinion, when

it is much better to use only a fraction of your total manpower, rather than the whole lot, for the assault. You should pick your best horses and men, however, because then they will be able to have some effect
13 and withdraw in relative safety. On the other hand, if you use *all* your men to attack a superior force and then decide to pull back, the ones mounted on the slower horses are bound to be captured, poor horsemanship will cause some to become unseated, and the difficulty of the terrain will result in others being cut off, since you will hardly come across a sizeable stretch of ground which is as good as one might
14 wish for. Moreover, there will be so many of them that collisions will take place among them, their progress will be hampered, and they will play havoc with one another in all kinds of ways. But good horses with competent riders will manage to escape even from hopeless situations,* especially if the cavalry reserves are used to threaten any
15 contingents that set out after them. False ambushes are advisable for this too, and another valuable plan is to find the best place to have some men from your side suddenly appear to slow the pursuit down.
16 Besides, there can be no denying that when it comes to making an effort and turning in a burst of speed, a smaller number has the advantage over a larger number rather than vice versa. I do not mean that a small band of men will be able to exert themselves more and will be quicker just because there are, merely in terms of number, a few of them, but that it is easier to find a few rather than a lot of men who will not only look after their horses properly, but also practise their own horsemanship with intelligence.[4]
17   If it so happens that your men are taking on another cavalry unit of more or less the same size, I think it advisable to divide each regiment into two squadrons. One of these squadrons should be headed up by the regimental commander, the other by whoever
18 strikes you as the best man for the job, which would be for him to follow for a while in the rear of the regimental commander's squadron, but then, when the enemy was close at hand and he received the command, to bring his men up against the enemy. These tactics would, I am sure, increase the force of the shock delivered by your
19 men to the enemy and make them harder to resist.[5] If each squadron was also accompanied by foot-soldiers, who suddenly appeared from

where they had been hiding behind the cavalry and closed with the enemy, I am sure that this would greatly increase your chances of victory. The point is that, in my experience, nothing cheers people up so much as unexpected good fortune, and nothing destroys their morale more effectively than an unexpected fright.[6] If you want evidence of this phenomenon, you need only bear in mind the dismay felt by those who fall into an ambush, even when they greatly outnumber their adversaries, and the terror felt by opposing armies for the first few days after they take up positions facing each other. The division of your men into squadrons is unproblematic, but it does take a good cavalry commander to find men to come up from behind and charge the enemy in an intelligent, reliable, committed and courageous fashion. Why does this require a good commander? Because he has to have the ability to make it clear to the men in his command, by his words and his actions, that obeying orders, following their officers and closing with the enemy are desirable, and to fire them with a longing for glory and the capacity to see their intentions through to the end.

Another possible scenario is that there are two armies drawn up in battle lines facing each other, or at least two areas of ground held by opposing sides, so that the cavalry does its wheeling, pursuing and retreating in the intervening space between these two forces. In this situation, the cavalry units from both sides tend to come out of their turns* slowly and then ride flat out in the unoccupied space in the middle. However, if you were to make it look as though you were going to do this, but then come quickly out of the turn and into pursuit or retreat, so that you pursue the enemy at speed while you are near your own lines, and pull back at speed away from his lines, this would enable you to inflict heavy losses on the enemy, while in all probability escaping with minimum losses yourself. Moreover, if you can manage to leave behind four or five of your best horses and men from each contingent concealed somewhere near the enemy lines, they will be very favourably placed to fall on the enemy unit as it is wheeling around to resume pursuit.

CHAPTER 9

1 Even a few readings will suffice for this treatise, but you need to have a constant awareness of what is going on around you, so that you can follow the best course of action in the light of prevailing circumstances. It is no more possible to write down everything a cavalry commander has to do than it is to know everything that is going to happen in the

2 future. The best piece of advice I can offer, I think, is to make sure that once you have decided on a particular plan of action it is carried out. Sound plans bear no fruit for a farmer, a shipowner or a commander unless care is taken to ensure that, with the gods' help, they are seen through.[1]

3 I am also convinced that the process of finding a thousand men to fill the quota for the cavalry would be hugely speeded up and simplified if the people of Athens were to commission a regiment of two hundred foreign mercenary horsemen. The point is that the presence of these men would, in my opinion, increase the loyalty of the whole cavalry unit and promote rivalry, on the issue of courage, between the

4 Athenians and non-Athenians. I know that the prestige of the Spartan cavalry dates from when they started to recruit foreign horsemen, and I see that foreign units are respected everywhere else, in all the other states which have them. After all, need stimulates a great deal of enthusiasm.[2]

5 The cost of the mercenaries' horses would, I think, be met partly by people who would be delighted to get out of serving in the cavalry (after all, they are prepared to pay even those who are trying to raise recruits for the cavalry* enough to keep them out of the service), partly by people who are prevented from serving by their poor physical condition, despite the fact that they fulfil the high property

6 qualification, and partly, I expect, by orphans with large estates.[3] I also think that some resident aliens[4] have the requisite ambition to be enrolled in the cavalry, because I know of several cases where a resident alien has been given some other privileged job to do by the Athenian citizen body and has been glad to take up the challenge and

7 carry it out. Similar considerations go for the infantry unit attached

to the cavalry: I think it would be particularly effective if it was made up of men who were especially bitter enemies of whomever you were at war with at the time.[5]

If the gods give their sanction, all these things will become realities. [8] If anyone is surprised at how often I have stressed the importance of working 'with the god's help', I can assure him that his surprise will diminish the more he finds himself in danger.[6] He should also reflect on the fact that during a war each side makes plans for the other side's destruction, but they rarely know how their plans will turn out. In a [9] situation like this, then, there is no one else to consult except the gods, who are omniscient and can communicate the future to whomsoever they choose through entrails, birds, oracles and dreams.[7] And it is plausible to think that they are more likely to recommend a course of action to someone if he worships them wholeheartedly when he is doing well, and does not ask their advice solely when he is desperate.

ON HORSEMANSHIP
(De Re Equestri)

INTRODUCTION

Plato's Socrates once implied that a man whose nature was functioning as harmoniously and purposefully as a horse's would be an excellent man (*Republic* 352e ff.). Xenophon, never entirely unmindful of practicalities, would have added that for a horse to fulfil its natural function required the addition of the human touch. Whether Xenophon himself wrote *On Horsemanship* is more than a little doubtful, but in content and sentiment it is no less certainly Xenophontic. Indeed, an attempt is made to represent the two treatises as companion pieces (12.14). But whereas *How to Be a Good Cavalry Commander* is written ostensibly for the attention of the publicly appointed official, *On Horsemanship* is written for the *idiotes*, or layman. A similar contrast of readership may be drawn between the more privately oriented *Estate-manager* and the publicly addressed *Ways and Means*.

A passing reference is made here (11.10) to a commanding phylarch or hipparch, but leadership is not this treatise's key theme. Successful, that is orderly and disciplined, management of military horseflesh is. The arrangement and exposition of the treatise render the medium in complete harmony with its message. In order to appreciate the finer points, the present-day reader needs to keep in mind throughout certain essential differences between ancient and modern equitation. Greek horses were smaller (by perhaps some two hands on average than the average cavalry charger early this century), stockier, more cob-like than those we are used to seeing or riding. Stallions were not gelded, which did nothing to assuage their tendency – shared by the mares – to bite. Nor did the rider operate with such seemingly indispensable modern aids to balance and control as stirrups and saddle. The horses for their part went unshod.

The nature of the beast meant that the horse was a hugely expensive commodity; the price most commonly paid for a horse in the fourth century was up to three hundred times the average daily wage of a skilled worker. The expense was especially magnified by a climate and terrain generally lacking in extensive lush pastureland. Only the seriously rich could hope to maintain a horse, let alone a stable or stud, and the horse correspondingly functioned as an obvious status symbol marking out the elite and often aristocratic few. It followed that even fewer Greeks could afford to own let alone breed racehorses – hence the quite prodigious extravagance implied by Alcibiades' boasting that he had entered no less than seven teams of four-horse chariots at the Olympics of (probably) 416: this was the 'blue-riband' event of the Games (cf. *Hiero* 11.5), and Alcibiades not only won the first prize but had four of his teams in the first seven finishers. Small wonder that he commissioned Euripides to write a commemorative and celebratory ode, besides exploiting his triumph shamelessly for political purposes. The young Xenophon must surely have been hugely impressed.

Most Greek horses were utilitarian workhorses, doubling up in peace and war (the same Greek word, *hippeus*, did service for both 'cavalryman' and 'horseman'). The closest a Greek came to riding a horse for pleasure was when he went hunting – but he rode only to, not during, the hunt, which took place on foot (see the next treatise, *On Hunting*). The author of this treatise therefore, like Agesilaus (*Agesilaus* 9.6), was interested chiefly in what went towards making a good war-horse – and a good cavalryman. At the same time, the horse's peacetime functions are not neglected, not least because ceremonial parades of horses and riders were an integral part of certain religious processions, for example that which distinguished the Panathenaia festival at Athens. This annual festival was celebrated with especial magnificence every four years, when the Panathenaic Games including horse-races were also staged. In the Parthenon frieze there could be seen (but only just – they are far more easily visible in their current place of display) a uniquely elevated depiction of the sort of ideal horse and rider that the author of *On Horsemanship* had it in mind to produce.

ON HORSEMANSHIP

CHAPTER I

I have, in fact, been riding for many years now, and I think that as a result I have become a competent horseman; I would therefore like to explain to my younger friends what I consider to be the most correct way for them to deal with horses. It is true that there already exists a handbook on horsemanship, written by Simon (the man who dedicated as a votive offering the bronze horse in the Eleusinium at Athens, with scenes of his achievements depicted in relief on the base); nevertheless, I shall not expunge from my own treatise those points on which I happen to agree with him.[1] No, the fact that on these matters my views coincide with those of such an expert horseman makes me regard them as all the more reliable and makes me far happier to transmit them to my friends. At the same time, I will try to explain any matters he failed to cover.

I shall first discuss how best to avoid being cheated when buying a horse. When scrutinizing a colt which is still unbroken, you must obviously base your assessment on its body, because a horse which has yet to be ridden will not give you any particularly clear indications of its temperament. You should start your examination of the body, in my opinion, with the feet. After all, however admirable the upper parts of a house may be, if its foundations have not been properly laid, it is no good. The same goes for horses as well as houses: there is nothing to be gained by a war-horse[2] with bad feet, however excellent it may be in all other respects, because it will not be able to make use of its good points.

You should start your assessment of the feet by checking the hoofs, because the horn may be thick or thin and the quality of a horse's feet is greatly improved if it is thick. The next point to observe is

95

whether both the fronts and the backs of the hoofs are raised or close to the ground. The reason for doing this is because on horses with raised hoofs there is a considerable distance between the frog,[3] as it is called, and the ground, whereas low hoofs put pressure on both the toughest and the softest part of the foot simultaneously, as bow-legged people do. According to Simon the sound of a hoof also shows whether or not a horse has good feet, and he is right, because a concave hoof gives off a sound like a cymbal when it strikes the ground.

4   Having made the feet my starting-point, I will continue, on the same principle, upwards to cover the rest of the body. The bones above the hoofs and below the fetlocks should not be too straight – too goat-like – because their excessive rigidity makes for a bumpy ride, and legs like this are more liable to inflammation. Nor should these bones come down too close to the ground, because then if the horse is ridden over clods of earth or stony ground the fetlocks might lose their protective hair and become grazed.

5   The cannon bones should be thick, since they are the body's supports, but they should not be padded out with veins or flesh. Otherwise, when the horse is ridden on hard surfaces, its lower legs are bound to become suffused with blood and the veins will turn varicose, the legs will swell and the skin will fall away from the bone. With this loosening of the skin, the pin[4] too often gives way and makes the horse lame.

6   As for the colt's knees, if they are supple and bend nicely as it walks, you can infer that its legs will be supple when it is ridden too, because with time all horses develop greater suppleness and flexibility in the knees. The approbation given to supple knees is justified, because they make the horse less likely to stumble or tire than inflexible legs do.

7   As with a man, thick thighs (the ones below the shoulder-blades) indicate greater strength and a better appearance.[5]

The broader the chest, the more handsome and strong the horse. Moreover, a broad chest means that the legs are kept a good distance apart, rather than getting in each other's way.

8   Its neck should imitate that of a cock rather than a boar; that is, the

neck should not droop but form a straight line from the chest to the top of the head. However, it should be hollow at the junction with the head, and the head should be bony and small-jawed. In this way, the neck will protect the rider and at the same time the horse will be able to use its eyes to see what is directly in front of it. Moreover, with this build any horse – even a very lively one – is extremely unlikely to be capable of bolting, because horses set about bolting with their necks stretched out rather than bent.

You must also check to see whether both sides of the mouth are 9 soft or hard or different from each other.* The point is that horses with dissimilar jaws in this respect tend to be less responsive to the bit on one side than on the other.

Prominent rather than sunken eyes indicate an alert animal and also allow the horse better vision.

Widely flared nostrils are better than narrow ones for free breathing 10 and for making a horse look more spirited. After all, when one horse is angry with another, or gets excited while being ridden, it flares its nostrils.

The larger the poll and the smaller the ears, the more like a typical 11 horse the creature appears.

High withers afford the rider a safer seat and a firmer grip on the horse's shoulders.[6]

A double spine[7] is not only more comfortable to sit on, but also better-looking than a single one.

The deeper the sides and the more they swell out as they approach 12 the belly,[8] the safer the seat the horse provides, the stronger the creature is, and also, in general, the better it eats.

The broader and shorter the loins, the more easily the horse raises its forequarters and follows through with its hindquarters. Besides, nothing diminishes the apparent size of the flanks more than loins like these, while large flanks not only disfigure the horse somewhat, but make it rather more weak and ungainly.

The haunches should be broad and well covered with flesh, so that 13 they are proportionate to the sides and the chest; if all these parts are firm, they will be lighter for running and the horse as a whole* will therefore be faster.

14   If the thighs (the ones below the tail) are well separated along with a broad line,[9] then when the horse brings up its hind legs there will be a good gap between them. This will also make it a more spirited and stronger creature to sit on and ride, and it will maximize its potential in all respects. We can deduce this from the case of human beings: when we want to lift something up from the ground, we always set about doing so with our legs apart rather than together.

15   A horse should not have large testicles, but this is not something you can observe on a colt.

As for the lower parts of the hindquarters – the hocks or lower legs, the fetlocks and the hoofs – what I have already said about the forequarters applies to them too.

16   I would also like to explain how one may most accurately estimate a horse's size. The tallest horses come from those foals which are born with the longest lower legs. For as time goes by – and this applies to all quadrupeds – although the lower legs do not grow very much, the rest of the animal's body grows until it matches the size of the lower legs.

17   It seems to me that by assessing a colt's physique in this way one is most likely to get a horse with sound feet, physical strength, firm flesh, a fine build and a good size. Some colts may change as they grow, but you can still apply these tests with confidence, because it is far more common for ugly colts to turn into useful horses than the other way round.

CHAPTER 2

1   There is no need, as far as I can see, for me to describe how to break a colt, because in our communities horses are ridden by people of the greatest wealth and highest public standing.[1] Also, the value of horse-breaking is far less, for a young man, than cultivating his own physical fitness and, once he knows how to ride, practising horsemanship; as for an older man, it is far more important for him to attend to his household, his friends, government and warfare, than it is for

2   him to spend time breaking in colts.[2] Obviously, then, anyone who

shares this opinion of mine regarding horse-breaking will give the job to someone else. Nevertheless, before giving the colt away, he should first draw up a contract stating what he expects the horse to know by the time it is returned; after all, this is what he would do if he were apprenticing a slave of his to a craft. And then the horse-breaker can refer to these notes to see what he has to do if he is to be paid.[3]

However, it is still your responsibility to see that the colt the horse-breaker receives is gentle, tractable and good with people. After all, these characteristics are invariably the result of what is done to the colt at your home by your groom, assuming that he knows how to ensure that the colt associates being alone with hunger, thirst and bothersome flies, and the company of people with food, drink and relief from distress.[4] Under these circumstances, colts are bound not just to be good with people, but actually to yearn to be with them. Then again, one should run one's hands over those parts of the horse's body which it especially enjoys having handled – which is to say, the parts with the most hair, and where the horse finds it particularly difficult to take care of any irritation by itself. You must also tell your groom to take the colt through crowds and to familiarize it with all kinds of sights and sounds; and if the colt finds any of this alarming, the groom must not lose his temper with it, but should calm it down and gently teach it that there is nothing to be afraid of.

I think that these are all the instructions I need to give a non-professional on the matter of horse-breaking.

CHAPTER 3

It may be, however, that you are buying a horse that has already been ridden. I will jot down all the information a buyer needs to avoid being swindled when buying such a horse.[1]

In the first place, it is important to note the horse's age. Any horse that has lost its milk teeth is an unpromising prospect and by the same token will be hard for you to dispose of.

Having ascertained that the horse still has its youth, the next point to note is its behaviour when taking the bit in its mouth and the headstall around its ears. The best way for the buyer to do this is to watch the bridle being put on and removed.

3 Next, he must pay attention to the horse's behaviour in accepting a rider on its back, because many horses hate letting anything come near them when they know perfectly well that the inevitable consequence for them is hard work.

4 He must also check on the horse's willingness, once mounted, to leave the vicinity of other horses, and make sure that when it is ridden past a group of stationary horses it does not head off towards them. Also, some horses have been so badly trained that they tend to bolt for the paths that lead home instead of keeping to their course.

5 The exercise known as the 'chain'[2] will show whether or not a horse is equally responsive to the bit on both sides of its mouth, but an even better way of detecting this is to change the direction of your ride, because it is often the case that a horse will not try to head for home unless the weak side of its mouth and the path for home coincide.

Further essential pieces of information are whether the horse can quickly be pulled up to a halt from a gallop, and whether there is any difficulty in getting it to turn.

6 It is worth testing whether alerting the horse with a blow makes any difference to its willingness to obey a command. Although a slave or an armed force which is incapable of taking orders is useless, a disobedient horse is worse than useless: it often even has the same effect as a traitor.

7 Now, I have been assuming that the horse is being bought for use in war, and it should therefore be put through all the tests that actual warfare will put it through. In other words, it should be made to jump across ditches and over walls, and leap up and down banks, and it should also be tested by being ridden uphill and downhill and along the faces of slopes.[3] All these tests will prove whether or not it has a

8 strong character and a sound body. However, a horse that does not perform very well at these trials need not be rejected, because it is often not incapacity but lack of experience of these hazards that makes it fail. Once it has gained the training, conditioning and practice, it might perform well, as long as it is basically sound and not simply a

9 bad horse. But you need to exercise caution in the case of horses

which are temperamentally nervous, because you will never be able to do any harm to the enemy from the back of an over-timid horse; often, in fact, such horses throw their riders and get them into the most terrible trouble.

You must also find out whether the horse is intolerant either of 10 other horses or of people, and whether it is skittish, because all these things prove troublesome for an owner.

An even better way, by far, of determining whether the horse 11 exhibits signs of wilfulness, such as refusing to take the bit or let itself be mounted, is to try to carry out the preliminaries of a ride all over again, after the horse has already completed its work. Any horse that willingly submits to further exertions when tired is giving a clear indication of strength of character.

In short, then, if a horse has good feet and a gentle disposition, if 12 it is fairly fast, if it is willing and able to endure hard physical work, and above all if it is obedient, this is a horse one may reasonably expect to give the least possible trouble and to be particularly good at keeping its rider safe in battle. However, those which are either so sluggish that they often need urging on, or so high-spirited that they often need careful coaxing, make constant demands on a rider's hands and adversely affect his morale in times of danger.

CHAPTER 4

So now you have bought a horse you like and brought it home. The 1 stable there should be located so as to afford the owner the maximum number of opportunities of seeing the horse. It is also worth having the stall constructed in such a way that it is just as impossible for the horse's food to be stolen from its manger as it is for the master's to be stolen from his storeroom.[1] Carelessness in this respect is carelessness about oneself, to my mind, for the obvious reason that in times of danger an owner entrusts his life to his horse. A secure stall is advisable 2 not just to prevent the theft of the horse's food, but also to make it clear when the horse is not finishing its food.* If you notice this happening, you can be sure that the horse either needs treatment for an excess of blood in its body, or is exhausted and needs a rest, or is coming down with barley-colic or some other ailment. Horses are no different from human beings in the sense that it is always easier to cure an ailment when it is just beginning than when it has taken hold and not been properly treated.[2]

3   It is just as important to care for the horse's feet as it is to ensure its general physical fitness by seeing that it is fed and exercised. Even naturally good hoofs are damaged by damp and slippery conditions in the stable. To avoid dampness, stables should have a drainage-channel,* and to avoid slipperiness, they should have tight-fitting paving-stones, each about the size of a hoof, on the ground; stables with these features also harden up horses' hoofs as they stand in them.

4   The next points to note are that the horse should be taken somewhere out of the stable by the groom to be rubbed down, and should be untied from its manger after the morning feed, so that it has a greater appetite for its evening meal. The way to make the best kind of yard outside the stable – the one which would most effectively toughen up the horse's feet – is to spread on the ground four or five cartloads of round stones, each big enough to fit in your hand and about a mina in weight,[3] and surround them with a border of iron to stop them dispersing. Standing on this would be as good for the horse's feet as spending a portion of every day walking on a stony road,

5   because* when it is being rubbed down, and when it is being bothered by flies, it inevitably makes the same movements with its hoofs as it does when walking. This kind of scattered-stone surface also toughens up the frogs on its feet.

Just as much care should be taken to ensure the softness of a horse's mouth as is taken to ensure the hardness of its hoofs. Whatever softens a person's flesh also softens a horse's mouth.[4]

CHAPTER 5

1   In my opinion, it is also a sign of a true horseman to have taught his groom the proper way to manage a horse. In the first place, then, the groom should know never to knot the halter by which the horse is

tied to its manger at the point where the headstall is worn. The reason for this is that if the halter irritates the horse's ears, the horse will be inclined to rub its head against the manger. This often produces sores, and if these parts are sore the horse is bound to be more difficult when it comes to having its bridle put on and being rubbed down.

Another sound instruction for the groom is to remove the horse's 2 dung and bedding to a single spot every day; this will make dumping it less arduous and at the same time will help the horse.[1]

It is also important for the groom to be aware that when taking the 3 horse out for a rub-down or a roll he should put a muzzle on it. In fact, the horse has to be muzzled whenever it is taken anywhere unbridled, because a muzzle stops it biting without impeding its breathing, and also goes a long way towards eliminating even its propensity to bite.

The horse has to be tied to a point higher than its head, because 4 its instinctive response to any irritant in the region of its face is to toss its head upwards, and so, if it is tied up in the way I have recommended, the rope will simply go slack rather than snapping when the horse tosses its head.

The rub-down should start with the head and mane, since there is 5 no point in cleaning the lower parts of its body if the upper parts are still dirty. Next, in rubbing down the rest of the horse's body, the groom should use his set of instruments first to make the horse's coat stand up* and then to brush the dust out following the lie of the hair. However, he must not use any instrument for the hair on the spine, but just rub and smooth it down with his hands, following the direction in which the hair naturally grows; this method will avoid impairing the horse's seat. Also, a horse's head is bony, so it would hurt the horse to have its head cleaned with anything made out of metal or wood; the groom should therefore thoroughly wash its head with water.

The forelock should be rinsed with water as well. Despite the length 6 of these hairs, they do not stop the horse seeing; their function is to brush pests away from its eyes, and we should appreciate that the gods have given horses these hairs instead of the long ears they gave donkeys and mules to protect their eyes. The tail and the mane should be 7

washed too, since it is important for these hairs to grow. The tail hairs need to grow so that the horse can reach as far as possible to brush pests away, and the mane so that the rider has plenty to grab hold of
8 when mounting. The other reason the gods gave horses manes (and the same goes for forelocks and tails) was for display. Proof of this is that brood mares with long manes generally refuse to be covered by donkeys. This in fact is why it is the universal practice of mule-breeders to cut the mares' manes to prepare them for being mated.[2]
9 I do not recommend washing down the horse's legs; so far from doing any good, its hoofs are impaired by daily soaking. It is a good idea to cut down on cleaning the underside of the belly as well, which not only causes the horse a great deal of distress, but also the cleaner
10 these parts become, the more pests gather under the belly. And even if a lot of trouble has been taken over cleaning these parts, no sooner has the horse been led out than there is no difference between it and any other dirty horse. These parts should be left alone, then; and rubbing down the legs with just the hands is enough.

CHAPTER 6

1 I will now go on to explain how to rub down a horse with the least danger to oneself and the most benefit to the horse.* The point is that if you face in the same direction as the horse while cleaning him, you run the risk of being struck in the face by both the knee and the
2 hoof. However, if you face in the opposite direction when cleaning the horse and rub it down while sitting clear of its legs, on a level with its shoulder-blade, this will enable you to avoid being hurt, and you can also attend to the frogs by turning up the hoof. A similar method should be employed in cleaning the hind legs.
3 The man who takes care of the horse should be aware that when carrying out this and all the other jobs that need doing he should as much as possible avoid approaching the animal from a position directly opposite the animal's head or tail. For if the horse means mischief, these are the two points at which it can get the better of a human being. Approaching it from the side, however, is not only the least

risky way to go about it, but also the way to get the largest number of jobs done.

Walking with the horse behind you when it is on a leading-rein   4 seems to me to be a bad idea, because it makes it almost impossible for one to protect oneself, while at the same time it allows the horse almost total freedom to do anything it wants. However, I also   5 disapprove of training the horse to go out a long way in front of the leading-rein, because it allows the horse to get up to mischief on either side, as it pleases, and also to turn around until it is facing the person holding the leading-rein. Moreover, if several horses are   6 involved, how could one stop them getting in one another's way? No, a horse should get used to having the person with the leading-rein by its side, because in this position it has little chance of doing mischief either to other horses or to people, and is also conveniently placed for the rider to mount up, should he ever suddenly need to.

The correct way for the groom to put the bridle on is as follows.   7 First he should approach the horse from the left; next he should pass the reins over the horse's head and let them rest on its withers, and then take the headstall in his right hand and offer the bit with his left hand. If the horse accepts the bit, he should obviously put on the rest   8 of the bridle at this point; if it refuses to open its mouth, he must present the bit to the horse's teeth and push* the thumb of his left hand into the horse's mouth. Most horses open their mouths under these circumstances, but if it still refuses to take the bit, he should press the horse's lip against its tush; it is extremely rare for a horse not to take the bit when treated like that.

There are other matters for the groom to learn. First, he should   9 never lead the horse by just one rein, because this makes it less responsive to the bit on one side of its mouth than the other. Second, he should know the correct height of the bit in the mouth. If the bit presses against the corners of the mouth, it hardens the mouth and desensitizes it; if it falls too close to the front of the mouth the horse can take the bit between its teeth and refuse to obey.

The groom should also take careful note of whether or not the   10 horse accepts the bit easily when it realizes that it is going to have to exert itself. Willingness to take the bit is so crucial that a horse which

11 refuses the bit is completely useless. If the horse wears a bridle not just when about to work, but also while being led to its feed and being brought home after a ride, it would not be at all odd to find it seizing the bit of its own accord when it is offered.

12 It is also worth the groom knowing how to give a leg-up in the Persian fashion,[1] not just so that the actual owner has someone to get him up on to the horse's back easily if he is rather old or is ever weak from illness, but also so that the owner can help out anyone else who needs a man to give him a leg-up.

13 The single most important precept and lesson is never, in any of one's dealings with the horse, to get angry with it. The point is that anger and foresight do not go together, and so we often do something

14 that we are bound to regret later.[2] Suppose the horse is nervous of something and refuses to go near it; then you have to teach it not to be frightened of this thing. The best way to do so is to have a stout-hearted horse set an example,* but failing that you should touch the supposedly frightening object yourself and gently lead the horse

15 towards it. Compulsion and blows only make the horse more afraid, because any harsh measures that are inflicted on a horse in such a situation are thought by the horse to be caused by whatever it is that it is wary of.

16 When a groom hands a horse over to a rider, I do not think there is anything wrong with his knowing how to get the horse to crouch, to make it easy for the rider to mount, but I do think that a rider should practise and acquire the ability to mount without the horse making it simple for him. After all, different horses will come his way on different occasions, and the same horse will not always serve him in the same way.

CHAPTER 7

1 So now the groom has handed the horse over and you are poised to mount.* I shall next describe how a rider should go about his horsemanship to make things most comfortable for both himself and his horse. First, then, he should take the lead-rope, which is attached

either to the chin-strap or to the cavesson,[1] in his left hand, and hold it ready with enough slack so that whether he intends to mount by grasping the mane near the ears or by vaulting on with the help of a spear, he will not jerk the horse. With his right hand he should take hold of the reins at the withers, along with a handful of mane too, to make absolutely sure that as he mounts he does not jerk the horse's mouth with the bit.

In taking off from the ground to mount, the left hand should be used to pull oneself up, while the right arm is kept at full stretch and helps the upward movement. This method of mounting will enable a rider to avoid presenting an unsightly figure even from behind by bending his left leg. The knee of the right leg should not touch the horse's back, but the lower leg should pass cleanly over to the right side of the horse. Once the foot has been brought over, the buttocks can come to rest on the horse.

It may be that the horseman is using his left hand to lead the horse and his right hand to hold his spear, and so it is advisable, in my opinion, to practise vaulting on to the horse from the right as well. There is nothing extra to learn for this; he just has to use the left side of his body for what his right side did before, and his right side for what his left side did before. The reason why I recommend learning this method of mounting as well is that he would be fully prepared as soon as he is up on the horse's back, in case he needed suddenly to engage the enemy.

Once seated, whether he is riding bareback or using a horse-cloth, it seems to me that the typical posture of sitting in a chair is to be avoided. The position to take is as if he were standing upright with his legs apart. This position will enable him to get a firmer grip on the horse with his thighs, and since he has a straight back he will be able, should the need arise, to put more power into throwing a javelin or delivering a blow from the back of the horse.

The lower leg, along with the foot, should hang slackly from the knee. A stiff leg could get broken if it was struck by anything, but a flexible lower leg will simply be pushed back by anything it encounters without altering the position of the thigh. A rider should also acquire the habit of keeping the upper part of his body, from his hips upwards, as relaxed as possible, because this will enable him to exert himself for longer and he will be less likely to fall off if someone pulls or pushes him.

8   So now our rider is seated. The first thing for him to do is teach his horse to stand still while he draws out from under himself, if he needs to, any bunched-up clothing,[2] makes the* reins of equal length and finds the most comfortable grip on his spear. The next point to note is that he should keep his left arm close in to his side, not just because in this position a rider is as trim as possible, but also because

9 there is no more powerful position for his hand. The best reins, to my mind, are of equal length, and are not weak or slippery or so thick that the rider cannot when necessary hold his spear in his hand as well.

10   Now the rider gives the horse the signal to move forward. He should start the horse at a walk, because then the transition is as smooth as it may be. If the horse lets its head droop, the rider should make the reins shorter; if it holds its head too high, he should lengthen the

11 reins. That way he will allow the horse to look its most elegant. When the horse moves up from a walk to its natural trot it will do so with hardly any distress, its body will be supple and relaxed, and it will proceed comfortably to a pace where it can be urged into a gallop. Now, the approved way is to lead with the left, and the best way to make sure this happens is to use your stick to move the horse up from

12 a trot to a gallop* just when it is rising with the right,** because the next thing it is going to do is raise its left foreleg, so that is the side it will lead with; it will take the initial step of the new gait just when it turns back to the left. For a horse naturally leads with the right when turned to the right and with the left when turned to the left.[3]

13   I set a great deal of store by the exercise called the 'chain', since it gets the horse used to bending to both the left and the right. It is also a good idea to change the direction of your ride, so that both sides of the horse's mouth are worked equally in the course of taking first

14 one and then the other direction. If the ends of the chain are squared off rather than rounded, it is even more valuable, because the horse will be happier to turn a corner when it has had enough of a straight line, and one and the same exercise will provide it with practice both

15 at following a straight course and at turning. You will have to check

the horse at the turns, because it is neither easy nor safe for it to make a tight turn at speed, especially if the ground is hard or treacherous. When checking the horse, the rider should make absolutely sure that 16 his use of the bit does not make the horse lean at all, and that he does not lean over himself either, because otherwise I can assure him that it will take hardly anything to bring both himself and his horse to the ground. As soon as the horse has come out of the turn and is facing 17 the straight, you should get it to speed up, because during a battle, obviously, such turns precede either the pursuit or the retreat. So it is worth having the horse practise taking a fast pace once it has completed a turn.

When you feel that the horse has had enough exercise, it is advisable 18 to let it rest for a while and then suddenly take it up to its top speed – away from other horses, of course, not towards them. Next you should rein it in from its gallop and bring it to a standstill again in as short a space as possible, and then wheel it round and urge it forward once more from the standing position. The point is that you are bound to meet with situations which call for either one or the other of these procedures.

When you come to dismount, you should never do so in the 19 vicinity of other horses or near a group of people or outside the area where you ride. The horse should be allowed to rest in the same place where it has to work.

CHAPTER 8

There will be occasions when the horse has to gallop downhill, uphill 1 or along the face of slopes; there will be hazards it has to jump across or out of or down. It follows, then, that you have to teach and train both yourself and your horse in all these procedures, to enable horse and rider to keep each other safe and, generally, because that seems to be the way for them to increase their usefulness to each other. You 2 may think that I have discussed this before and am therefore repeating myself,[1] but that is not so: what I was suggesting previously was that at the time of buying a horse you should test its ability to perform these manoeuvres, whereas now I am talking about the importance of training a horse you actually own. And I will now describe the correct way to go about this training.

3   If the horse you have acquired is completely unfamiliar with jumping across ditches, you must lead the way across yourself with the horse on a loose leading-rein and then pull on the leading-rein to make it 4 jump across. If it refuses, someone with a whip or a switch should give it as hard a whack as he can, which will make it clear the required distance and a lot more besides! And from then on you will never need to do that again; it will take the mere sight of someone coming up behind it to make the horse jump.

5   Once it has got used to jumping across ditches with the leading-rein, you should mount up and introduce it first to narrow ditches and then gradually to wider and wider ones. Just as it is about to make its jump, you should spur it on. The same use of the spur is recommended for training it to jump up and down banks. The point is that the horse will perform all these actions – jumping across ditches or up or down banks – with a greater degree of safety both to itself and to its rider if it does them with its whole body rather than trailing its hindquarters.

6   You should start the horse's downhill training on soft ground; eventually, by the time it has got used to it, it will prefer taking downward slopes rather than upward slopes at speed. The worry some people feel that riding a horse downhill might cause it to dislocate its shoulders can be dispelled by the knowledge that although the Persians and Odrysians[2] always race their horses downhill, their horses are just as healthy as ours in Greece.

7   It is also important for me to mention the part the rider plays in assisting each of these manoeuvres. When the horse makes a sudden forward motion, the rider should lean forward, because then the horse is less likely to slip from under the rider and throw him backwards. When the horse is being pulled up short, however, the rider should 8 lean back, because then he will experience less of a jolt. When the horse is jumping a ditch or going uphill, it is advisable to grip the mane, because the terrain is already giving the horse enough problems without your pulling on the bit as well. When the horse is going downhill, you should lean a good way back and help the horse with

the bridle, to avoid a situation where both you and the horse are hurtling downhill out of control.

The correct way to go about your rides is to vary their length and the kind of terrain you cover. Apart from anything else, this is less disagreeable to the horse than always covering the same ground[3] and going out for rides of a similar length.

Since the rider has to have a deep seat when riding flat out over all kinds of terrain, and since he has to be able to manipulate his weapons properly from horseback, I recommend hunting as a method of improving your horsemanship, if you have access to suitable country-side and wild animals.[4] Otherwise, a good exercise is for two horsemen to come to an agreement whereby one of them flees on horseback over a variety of terrains and the other gives chase; the fugitive holds his spear reversed as he retreats, with the head pointing to his rear, while his pursuer wields blunted javelins and a spear which has been similarly treated. When the pursuer gets within javelin range, he lets fly at the fugitive with his blunted javelins, and then, once he has caught him up and is within striking distance, he stabs at him with his spear. If they get to close quarters, it is a good idea for one of them to pull his opponent towards himself and then suddenly push him away, because this is the way to unseat him. The correct response to being pulled is to get one's horse to move on, because by doing so the person being pulled is more likely to unseat the one doing the pulling than to fall off.

Imagine a situation where a skirmish is taking place between the cavalry of two opposing forces, with one side pursuing their opponents up to the enemy lines, while the other is retreating back to their own army. Under these circumstances, it is worth knowing that as long as you are close to your own side, the proper and safe course of action is to be among the first to wheel round and charge the enemy, but that when you are near the enemy lines, you should keep your horse under control. This tactic makes it possible for you to inflict heavy losses on your opponents while in all probability avoiding losses yourself.

Whereas the gods have given us human beings the ability to use reasoned argument to teach other people what to do, you can

obviously not use reasoned argument to teach a horse anything. The best way for you to teach a horse what it is supposed to do is to reward
14 it when it does what you want and punish any disobedience. It does not take long to state this rule, but it applies to every aspect of horsemanship. For instance, a horse will be more prepared to take the bit if something good happens whenever it does so; and it will not let you down when jumping across or out of obstacles, or in anything else, if it knows that after it has done its duty it will be allowed to rest.

CHAPTER 9

1 So far I have covered how to avoid being swindled when buying a colt or a horse, how to treat a horse so as to avoid spoiling it, and how, if necessary, to produce a horse with all the qualities a cavalryman needs in battle. This is probably the right moment to discuss the further topic of the best way of managing a horse in case it turns out to be either excessively lively or excessively sluggish.
2 The first thing to appreciate is that spirit in a horse is the equivalent of anger in a human being. So just as the best way to avoid infuriating someone is not to say or do anything that will irritate him, you are least likely to arouse a high-spirited horse if you avoid annoying it.
3 You should begin, then, right from the moment you mount up, by taking care not to do so in a way that will upset the horse. And then, once mounted, you should let it stand for longer than you would an ordinary horse before giving it the gentlest of aids to walk on. Next, you should start it off at a particularly slow walk before moving it so gradually up to a faster pace that the horse hardly notices that it is
4 going more quickly. But any abrupt aids, whether communicated by sight or hearing or touch, upset a spirited horse no less than they would a person.*
5 Again, suppose a lively horse is starting to speed up too much and you want to check it; you should not give it a sudden wrench, but
6 gently rein it in, calming it down rather than forcing it to a halt. Long rides, not exercises involving frequent turns, calm horses down; a peaceful, extended ride quietens and calms a lively horse, rather than

exciting it. But the idea that a long, fast ride will tire the horse out 7
and make it calm is quite wrong. In fact, this is exactly the situation
in which a spirited horse tries its hardest to seize control, and the
upshot of such an outburst – as with short-tempered people – has
often proved fatal for both horse and rider. You should stop a spirited 8
horse from ever* reaching its top speed, and of course you should
never let it race against another horse (remembering that the most
high-spirited horses are also the most competitive).

Another point is that smooth bits are more suitable for lively horses 9
than rough ones.[1] If you do put a rough one in the horse's mouth, a
slack rein must be used to make it simulate a smooth bit. It is also a
good idea, especially for a lively horse, to get oneself used to sitting
quietly and to making as little contact with the horse's body as possible,
beyond the contact we need to ensure a secure seat.

You should be aware of the precept that a horse can also be calmed 10
down by making kissing noises with the lips and roused by making
clicking noises with the tongue. However, if right from the start you
stroke the horse while clicking and treat it roughly while making
kissing noises, the horse will learn to be roused by the kissing noise
and soothed by the clicking noise.

By the same token, then, when surrounded by clamouring voices or 11
the sound of the trumpet, it is important not to let the horse see you
discomposed and not to do anything to disturb it either. Instead, in a
situation like this you should let the horse halt, if you can, and bring it
its morning or evening meal, if possible. But the best piece of advice 12
I can give, if you need a horse for war, is not to get one that is too
high-spirited.[2]

All I need say about managing a lazy horse, I think, is this: always do
the opposite of what I have suggested for a lively horse.

CHAPTER 10

The usual way of getting a good war-horse to put on a grander and 1
more imposing display as it rides by is to pull at its mouth with the
bit, spur it on and use a whip on it. These measures actually produce

the opposite of the desired splendid effect, so you should avoid them.
2 I mean, when the horse's mouth is pulled up, it cannot see where it is going, the spur and whip startle it, and the upshot is that the horse gets all agitated and writhes about* – which is the way a horse behaves
3 when it hates being ridden, and is ugly rather than attractive. However, if you teach it to ride on slack reins, to hold its head up high and arch its neck, you will be getting the horse to do exactly what gives it
4 pleasure and delight. You can tell that it enjoys this because when a horse wants to show off in front of other horses (especially female horses) it holds its head up high, arches its neck with a great deal of spirit, prances with supple legs raised high off the ground and lifts its
5 tail. So by making your horse hold itself exactly as it does when it is displaying itself at its best, you are giving people an impression of a horse that enjoys being ridden, and you are making it seem a grand, spirited and imposing animal. I shall now try to explain how, in my opinion, these results are to be obtained.

6   In the first place, you should have at least two bits.¹ One of them should be smooth and have good-sized discs, while the other should be rough and have heavy, small discs. The pimples of the rough bit should be sharp enough to hurt the horse when the bit is inserted into its mouth and make it drop the bit into place; when it is given the smooth one instead, then, it will be such a relief that it will carry out on the smooth bit everything it has been trained to do on the rough
7 bit. A possible problem, though, is that it may find the smoothness of a smooth bit too easy and keep leaning on it; that is why the smooth bit is equipped with large discs, which are designed to force the horse to open its jaws and let the bit drop into place. It is also possible to adapt the rough bit to other kinds of bit so that it acts by either compression or tension.²

8   Whatever kind of bit you use, it must be flexible. The trouble with a stiff bit is that whichever part of it is actually gripped by the horse, the whole of it is held against the horse's jaws. Imagine a person picking up a spit: it is the whole spit he picks up, never mind at what
9 point of its length he actually takes hold of it. The other kind of bit, however, behaves like a chain in the sense that the only part of it to remain unbent is the part which is actually gripped, while the rest

hangs loosely off this part. The horse constantly tries to retrieve the parts of the bit that are evading its grip in its mouth, and in so doing it lets the bit drop from its jaws. That is also why there are rings fixed in between the axles, so that as the horse goes after these rings with its tongue and teeth it does not think of taking the bit up against its jaws.

In case anyone does not know what the terms 'flexible' and 'stiff' mean when applied to bits, I had better explain this as well. A bit is flexible when the links on its axles are broad and smooth enough to bend easily; moreover, if all the parts that are fitted on to the axles have wide rather than restricted apertures, the bit is even more flexible.* However, if it is hard for all the various parts of the bit to communicate and interlock, the bit is stiff.

Whatever kind of bit you have, there is not the slightest difference in the use to which it has to be put if you want your horse to look impressive in the way I have described. The pressure on the horse's mouth should neither be so harsh that it tosses its head or so gentle that it does not notice it. As soon as it has raised its neck in response to the pressure, you must give it its head – remembering the general instruction, which I have given plenty of times already, that you should reward any instance of obedience on the part of the horse. So when you can see that the horse is enjoying the upright carriage of its neck and the slackness of the reins, you should avoid the kind of harsh measures you use when you are forcing it to exert itself and just coax it as if you were planning to go for a normal ride. This is the best way to encourage a horse to move up to a fast pace.

It is easy to see that a horse relishes a fast pace, because there is not a horse in the world that, given its freedom, ambles along at a walk rather than running. A horse instinctively enjoys a gallop, provided that it is not forced to gallop too much. After all, the same goes for a horse as for a human being: excess is never enjoyable.³

So suppose our horse now has the ability to bear itself in a stately manner. In the early stages of its training, as you will remember, we got it used to increasing its pace after coming out of turns.⁴ If you rein in a horse that has been trained to do this and at the same time use one of the various signals to urge it forward, it finds itself restrained by the bit and yet roused by the signal to go forward. In irritation, the horse throws out its chest and raises its legs high off the ground (but not in a supple manner, because a horse's legs lose most of their suppleness when it is disgruntled). If you let it have its head when it is in this excitable state, the relaxation of the bit will make it think you are no longer restraining it, and it will be so pleased that it will prance forward with a stately carriage and with supple legs, putting on exactly the same kind of display it would before other horses. The sight of a horse behaving like this makes people think of it as a dignified creature, hardworking, a good ride, lively, proud, a joy to see and yet obviously full of spirit.[5]

Anyway, that is enough on this topic for anyone who is interested in getting their horse to behave in this way.

CHAPTER 11

What if someone wants a flamboyant, prancing horse which is suitable for use in processions? You certainly should not expect every horse to be able to develop these attributes, but only one which starts off with a proud temperament and a strong body. The idea that all it takes for any horse to be able to raise its body off the ground is supple legs is wrong; it is closer to the truth to say it takes loins that are supple, short and sturdy, and then a horse can bring its hind legs up a good distance under its forequarters. (Note that by 'loins' here I do not mean the part by the tail, but between the side and the haunches, and by the flank.) So if you rein the horse in just when it is bringing up its hind legs, it will sink its haunches back on to its hocks and raise its forequarters until its belly and sheath are visible to anyone directly in front of it. At this point you should let it have its head, and then the onlookers will get the impression that the horse is performing this wonderful trick all by itself – and there is no more wonderful trick that a horse can perform.

Now, some people train a horse to do this by hitting it with a switch under the hocks, and others get a man to run alongside the horse and hit it with a stick under the gaskins. However, to repeat myself yet again, I think the best form of training is if every occasion when the horse does what the rider wants it to do is followed by him allowing it to rest. The point is, as Simon says too, that when a horse 6 acts under compulsion it does not understand what it is doing, and the action is just as inelegant as a dancer's movements would be if he were trained by whip and spur. Under that kind of regime the same goes for a horse as a human being: both of them are far more likely to look ugly than attractive. No, however dazzling and attractive a display the horse is required to put on, it always has to do so of its own accord, acting only on the aids the rider gives it. So if you 7 take the horse out for a hard ride, until it has worked up a good sweat,* wait for the moment when it has adopted a beautiful prancing movement and then quickly dismount and remove its bridle, I can assure you that the horse will progress on to prancing of its own accord.

When artists portray gods and heroes on horseback, this is the 8 posture they give the horses,[1] and it makes a splendid impression when men can get their horses to adopt it. In fact, the sight of a prancing 9 horse is so fine, or perhaps frightening or wonderful or amazing,* that people of all ages can only stop and stare at it. I mean, no one can tear himself away or gets tired of watching a horse, as long as it is giving such a dazzling display.

If it so happens that the owner of a magnificent horse like this 10 becomes a commander of a tribal regiment or a commander of the whole cavalry, it is far more important for him to ensure that all the troops under his command create an eye-catching spectacle, rather than concentrating on making himself the only smart one.[2] So if a 11 cavalry regiment is being led by a horse which perfectly exemplifies all the qualities for which people praise this kind of horse* – that is, a horse with a particularly high and frequent prancing step, which covers hardly any distance at all – obviously all the rest of the horses will follow it at a walking pace as well. Now, would there be anything impressive in such a sight? However, if you urge your horse on and 12 lead at a pace which is neither too fast nor too slow – that is, if you adopt the pace which shows off spirited horses at their liveliest and best – there will be such consistent clopping behind you, and such solid neighing and snorting, that the whole regiment, rather than just you alone, will make a remarkable spectacle.

13   If you go about buying horses properly, if you bring them up so that they are capable of enduring hard physical work, and if you manage them correctly during their battle-training, when exercising them for parades and during actual warfare, nothing but supernatural intervention[3] could stop you increasing the value of your horses beyond what they were worth when you got them, and could prevent you from owning famous horses and becoming a famous expert at horsemanship yourself.

CHAPTER 12

1   I would like to add some words on what arms and armour you should have if you intend to face danger on horseback.[1]

In the first place, then, you should, I think, have a breastplate made for your trunk. Now, a well-fitting breastplate can be supported by the whole trunk,* but all the weight of one that is too loose falls on the shoulders, and one that is too tight is a straitjacket rather than a piece of armour.[2]

2   Since the neck is one of the vital parts of the body, you should have a covering made for it as well, in my opinion. It should emerge out of the breastplate and conform to the contours of the neck. That way it will not be merely decorative and, if properly made, it will encase the rider's face all the way round to his nose, should he want it to.

3   The best kind of helmet, to my mind, is the Boeotian type, because while it too covers the parts above the breastplate – in fact, does so better than any other type – it does not restrict the wearer's vision.[3]

The breastplate too should be made in such a way that it does not
4 stop you either sitting down or bending over. The flaps should be large enough and of a suitable material to afford the region of the lower abdomen, genitals and thereabouts* protection against missiles.

5   A wound even to the left hand will incapacitate a cavalryman, so I recommend the piece of armour which is known as the 'arm' and

is specially made for the left arm. The value of this piece of armour is that it protects the shoulder, the upper arm, the forearm and as much of the hand as is involved in holding the reins, and it can be stretched and bent. It also covers the gap in the breastplate under the armpit.

The right arm has to be raised in order to throw a javelin and 6 deliver a blow. So the part of the breastplate which impedes this should be removed and replaced by hinged flaps designed to open up when the arm is raised and close when it is lowered. For the arm the 7 kind of armour which is separately fastened on like a greave seems to me preferable to the kind that is attached to another piece of armour.* The part of the body that is exposed when the right arm is raised should be covered near the breastplate by either calf-skin or metal, or else the body will be unprotected at its most vital point.

Since a wound to the horse endangers the rider's life too, the horse 8 must be protected by armour as well. It should have a head-piece, a chest-piece and side-pieces* (which will also act as thigh-pieces for the rider). But the most important part of the horse's body to protect is the flank, which is simultaneously the most vital part and the most vulnerable. The horse-cloth can be made to cover the flanks as well, 9 but the design of any blanket that is used in this way should be such that it affords the rider a safer seat and at the same time does not hurt the horse's back.

So nearly all of both the horse's and the rider's bodies will be protected by armour. The rider's shins and feet, however, will probably 10 stick out beyond the thigh-pieces, but they can be protected too, by buskins made out of the same kind of leather as boots, which can act at one and the same time as protection for the shins and as footwear.

As long as the gods are looking kindly on you, with this armour 11 you should avoid injury. As for offensive weapons, I recommend a sabre rather than a sword, because from the height of a horse's back the cut of a sabre will serve you better than the thrust of a sword. And instead of a cane-shafted spear (which is weak, and awkward to 12 carry as well), I recommend two cornel-wood javelins, because once you know how to use them it is possible to have hurled one and to use the other against adversaries in front or behind or to either side of you. They are also less fragile than a spear, and easier to carry too.[4]

13   It is a good idea, to my mind, to throw your javelin from as far away as possible, because this gives you more time to wheel your horse around and take hold of the other javelin. Here, in a few words, is the best way of throwing a javelin: thrust your left arm forward, draw your right arm back, raise yourself up off the horse's back from your thighs and then throw the javelin. If you throw it with the point at a slight upward angle it will fly furthest and with the most power, and you will of course achieve the greatest accuracy if you keep the point directed at the target at the moment of release.

14   The notes, instructions and exercises I have written down here are intended for the use of a non-professional. I have explained in another treatise what information and practices are relevant for a cavalry commander.

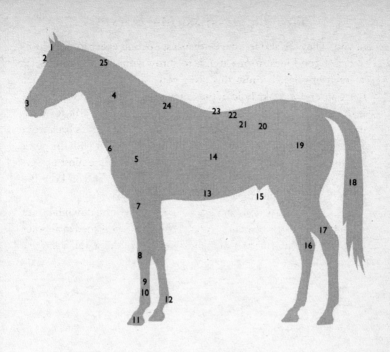

1. Poll
2. Forelock
3. Nostril
4. Neck
5. Shoulder
6. Chest
7. Thigh below the shoulder
8. Knee
9. Shank
10. Cannon bone
11. Hoof
12. Fetlock
13. Belly
14. Side
15. Sheath
16. Hock
17. Gaskin or thigh below the tail
18. Tail
19. Haunch
20. Flank
21. Loins
22. Spine
23. Seat
24. Withers
25. Mane

The points of a horse mentioned by Xenophon

ON HUNTING
(Cynegeticus)

INTRODUCTION

Hunting to many of us today is not a sport, as defenders of 'bloodsports' maintain, nor an integral part of a complex modern food-producing regime, but merely an indulgence of unnecessary and unacceptable cruelty to wild creatures, chiefly foxes, deer and rabbits. That judgement would apply also with especial force to the 'hunting' of migratory birds with guns that is practised in many parts of southern Europe, including Greece. An alternative, almost metaphysical view (witness William Golding's *Lord of the Flies*) holds that at heart we humans are all hunters, a tribute perhaps to the huge percentage of the time span of *homo sapiens* that depended on his successfully being Man the Hunter.

The ancient Greeks were not exercised by moral anxieties of this kind, although Euripides' *Bacchae* is a spectacularly vivid illustration of their concern with the metaphysics of the bestial in man. Not that hunting lacked opposition on any grounds, as we shall see; but Xenophon and his fellow devotees were untroubled by saboteurs from any ancient Greek League against Cruel Sports. Besides, hunting for them was not only a secular leisure pursuit. It was also an act of religious devotion performed under the sign of Artemis, a huntress herself (1.1, 6.13) and goddess of the wild margins. It was complementary to, not in competition with or opposition against, the Greeks' fundamental ritual of animal blood-sacrifice, since the animals they typically sacrificed were domestic not wild (even if some aspects of the ritual may perhaps allude to the prehistoric palaeolithic era when humans depended for their livelihood on wild game, not agriculture). The charming autobiographical description in *The Persian Expedition* (5.3.7–13) of Xenophon's estate at Scillous near Olympia makes hunting's religious connotation explicit:

. . . he [Xenophon] used to take a tenth of the season's produce from the land and make a sacrifice to the goddess [Artemis]. All the townspeople, and the men and women of the district used to take part in the festival, and the goddess provided those who camped out there with . . . a share both of the animals sacrificed from the sacred herds and also of the animals caught in hunting. There were plenty of them as Xenophon's sons and the sons of other townspeople used to go hunting specially for the festival, and anybody else who liked joined them in the hunt. Pigs, antelopes and stags were caught . . .

On the other hand, the present treatise is by no means politically innocent. In a passably egalitarian age and within a democratic society, hunting, which required extensive wealth and leisure time, attracted the stigma of aristocratic self-indulgence. To that somewhat envious charge the author replied implicitly by urging young men to regard hunting as educational (1.18). Here, the author was able to exploit the imagery of hunting central to the transition-to-manhood myths and rituals that at Athens contributed to the eventual formalization of an ephebic training programme in the 330s (see Chapter 2 note 1). He stressed too, more controversially, that hunting was not only politically correct but even politically beneficial. Huntsmen, as he represented them, made brave, inventive and strong-willed soldiers, ready and able to fight on behalf of the community. Hunters, indeed, being noble, true and bold, were – it is claimed – morally superior to politicians, especially democratic ones, who as a breed were treacherous, cowardly and corrupt. The extended hunting metaphors that one finds in other Xenophontic works (e.g. *Memoirs of Socrates* 3.11), as in Plato, served therefore not merely to illustrate but also to reinforce an elite style of life and code of morality.

The wild animals that typically found themselves on the wrong end of a hunter's missile or spear were either hares (though whether the Greeks used their blood as an exfoliant in the manner of the elegant Roman ladies of Ovid's day, we do not know) or wild boar. The hare formed an essential item in the repertoire of pederastic courtship among the Greek social elite. Its presentation by the would-be lover to his desired beloved symbolized both the element of erotic chase necessarily involved in the transaction and the lover's prowess as a hunter. The wild boar, however, weighing perhaps 100 kg. and with a hide so thick that today it can be pierced only by high-calibre bullets, was an altogether different proposition, strong meat not only as food but also as a gendered symbol: hunting a wild boar in Xenophon's Greece carried something like the same masculine (or masculinist) overtones as does bullfighting in Spain (or rather, did – there are now female matadors).

As noted in the introduction to *On Horsemanship*, a huntsman might ride to the hunting ground on horseback, but the actual hunting would be done on foot. Key to his success was the management of his hounds – the Greek for huntsman was literally a 'driver of dogs'. If the present treatise is anything to go by, those hounds would normally or always be the females of the species. And indeed subspecies: one of the many marks of the author's cynegetical expertise is his elaborate attention to breeds and breeding.

I have been careful so far in this introduction to speak vaguely of 'the author' – in manner (jerky style, loose grammar, awkward arrangement) *On Hunting* differs so greatly from works that are certainly Xenophon's that many modern scholars have found it impossible to believe its attribution to him. (It should be said, however, that Arrian, the 'new Xenophon' of the Roman era, accepted the whole work as genuine when composing his own *Cynegeticus*.) The problem of authenticity is doubly vexed in that the concluding chapter not only is explicitly autobiographical – 'I am just a layman . . .' – but also delivers a sustained and passionate profession of pedagogical faith – '. . . but I know that the best place to look for instruction in goodness is one's own nature, and that the second best course is to go to people who really know something good rather than to professional deceivers' (13.4), that is the sophists, whom the author affected to despise no less than did the professional anti-sophists Isocrates and Plato. At least – and at most – we may fairly claim that Xenophon would have endorsed wholeheartedly sentiments of this sort, if not necessarily the manner of their expression.

ON HUNTING

CHAPTER I

Hunting with hounds was invented by the gods Apollo and Artemis.[1] They presented it to Cheiron in recognition of his virtue, and he, delighted with the gift, put it to use. Now, his pupils, who came to learn hunting and other noble pursuits from him,[2] were Cephalus, Asclepius, Meilanion, Nestor, Amphiaraus, Peleus, Telamon, Meleager, Theseus, Hippolytus, Palamedes, Menestheus, Odysseus, Diomedes, Castor, Polydeuces, Machaon, Podaleirius, Antilochus, Aeneas and Achilles, each of whom was honoured by the gods in his time. It should not occasion surprise that most of them died, despite being favourites of the gods, because that is what it is to be human; in any case, they have become widely celebrated.[3] Nor should it be thought odd that they were not all contemporaries: Cheiron's lifetime covered all of theirs, because he was in fact a half-brother of Zeus, since they had the same father, but different mothers – Rhea for Zeus, the nymph Naïs for Cheiron. And so, although Cheiron was born before any of his pupils, he was the last to die, for he tutored Achilles.

As a result of their devotion to hounds and hunting, and of course of the rest of their education, they gained heroic stature and became admired for their virtue. Cephalus was abducted by a goddess, but Asclepius met with the even greater good fortune of raising the dead and curing the sick, and for this he has undying fame among men as a god.[4] Meilanion was so outstanding for his diligent determination that although the best men of the time were his rivals for the prize of the greatest marriage of the time, it was he and he alone who gained Atalanta.[5] The excellence of Nestor has been brought to the attention of the Greeks already, so there is no need for me to speak of it.[6]

8 Amphiaraus won extraordinary acclaim in his campaign against Thebes,[7] and was then honoured by the immortal gods.*

Even the gods were moved by Peleus to desire his marriage to
9 Thetis and to celebrate the wedding in Cheiron's home. Telamon proved worthy to win from the most important state the woman he had resolved* to marry, Periboea the daughter of Alcathous, and when the foremost of the Greeks, Heracles the son of Zeus, was handing out the prizes for valour after his capture of Troy, he awarded Telamon
10 Hesione.[8] Meleager received conspicuous honours, and the misfortune that followed when his aged father forgot the goddess[9] was not his fault. Theseus singlehandedly killed the enemies of the whole of Greece, and is still admired even today for having vastly increased the
11 size of his city's territory.[10] Hippolytus was honoured by Artemis and even spoke face to face with her; by the time of his death his self-restraint and piety had earned him general recognition as a blessed man.[11] Palamedes, during his lifetime, was by far the most intelligent person of his day,* and after his death – a death he did not deserve – the gods granted him the right to take revenge, to a degree never permitted any other human being. (One version of the story of his death is wrong, because it assigns responsibility to two men, one of whom was almost the greatest hero there has been, while the other was a match for anyone in bravery and virtue. No, the deed was done by bad men.)[12]

12 As a result of his devotion to hunting, Menestheus became so outstanding for his diligent determination that, by general agreement, none of the leading Greeks came close to him in military prowess, except Nestor, who, however, is said merely to rival him, not to
13 surpass him. Odysseus and Diomedes never failed on any occasion to cover themselves with glory; in short, the fall of Troy may be attributed to them. Castor and Polydeuces became so famous for what they achieved in Greece on the basis of Cheiron's education that they are
14 now immortal.[13] As a result of this same education, Machaon and Podaleirius became skilled craftsmen, speakers and warriors.[14] Antilochus is so famous for his splendid death in defence of his father that he is the only one to whom the Greeks have given the name 'the
15 devoted son'.[15] By rescuing not just the gods of his father's and

mother's families, but his actual father, Aeneas gained such a reputation for piety that his enemies went so far as to allow him alone of all those they conquered in Troy not to be stripped of his armour. Achilles has 16 bequeathed to posterity such admirable and impressive memorials of what he gained from this education that no one tires of telling his tales or hearing them.

Such was the calibre of these men (who* even today are loved by 17 all good men and envied by the bad) as a result of their studies with Cheiron that whenever a state or a king within Greece was threatened with disaster, it was they who removed the threat, and whenever there was conflict or war between Greece as a whole and all foreign peoples, it was they who won victory for the Greeks and so made Greece invincible.[16] So I would advise young men not to despise 18 hunting and education in general,[17] since they are the way for them to become good at warfare and at everything else which is a sure route to excellence in thought, speech and action.

CHAPTER 2

Hunting, then, is the first activity a young man just out of childhood[1] 1 should take up, before turning also to other subjects which will enhance his reputation.* He should consider his means and pursue it, if he can afford to, in a manner commensurate with the benefit** he will gain from it; if he is less well off, he can at least commit his enthusiasm to the pursuit and so not fall short of his own capacity.

I shall now describe what and what kind of equipment he needs in 2 order to take up hunting. As well as listing each item, I will also explain it, to enable a potential hunter to understand the business before setting his hand to it. I would not have anyone belittle these details: they are the prerequisites of achievement.

The net-keeper must be wholehearted about his job and speak 3 Greek.[2] He should be about twenty years old, physically light but strong, and mentally competent, so that he can use these qualities to master the physically demanding aspects of his job and to enjoy it.

4   Short nets should be made out of fine Phasian or Carthaginian flax,[3] and so should road-nets and game-nets. A short net should be nine-threaded, in three strands, with each strand consisting of three threads; its total length ought to be five hand-spans, with its meshes two palms wide; the surround of a short net must be free of knots, to avoid snags.[4]

5   Road-nets should be twelve-threaded, and game-nets sixteen-threaded. The length of a road-net should be two, three, four or five fathoms, and of a game-net ten, twenty or thirty fathoms – no more, or it becomes unwieldy. Both road-nets and game-nets should be
6   thirty-knotted, with the same size mesh as that of a short net. At the corners, a road-net should have eyelets and a game-net rings; the surround of both kinds is best made out of twisted cord.

7   The stakes for a short net should be ten palms long, but there should also be some shorter ones. Stakes of different lengths are to be used on sloping ground, to keep the net an even height off the ground, while stakes of the same length are to be used on level terrain. Stakes must be smoothed down at their tips so that they are easy to disengage from the net. The stakes for a road-net must be double the height of those for short nets,* while those for game-nets should be five hand-spans long, with short tines (i.e. shallow notches). The stakes for every kind of net should be sturdy, of a thickness that is commensurate with
8   their height. A greater or lesser number of stakes may be used with a game-net; if the net has been set up at a very tight stretch, fewer stakes
9   are needed than if it is slack. Another important piece of equipment is a calfskin sack in which to keep the short nets, road-nets and game-nets for the hunt,* and also the sickles which will be needed so that undergrowth can be cut down and used to block up gaps where necessary.

CHAPTER 3

1   There are two kinds of hounds,[1] the Castorian and the Vulpine. Castorian hounds are so called because it was Castor, a keen hunter, who kept the breed pure.* Vulpine hounds are named after the fact that

they are a cross between dogs and foxes; in the course of time the nature of these two parent species has become completely intermingled.

Here is how to recognize inferior specimens, which are in the majority: they are undersized, with noses turned downwards, dull-eyed, squinting, graceless, stiff-jointed, weak, thin-coated, long-limbed, badly proportioned, listless, insensitive to scents and with unsound feet. The problem with undersized hounds is that they often fail to keep up with the work because of their small size; a downward-turning nose impedes the mouth, and stops such dogs holding the hare; dull-eyed and squinting dogs are less keen-sighted; graceless dogs also look ugly; stiff-jointed dogs end a hunt in bad shape; weak and thin-coated dogs are incapable of the necessary effort; long-limbed and badly proportioned dogs, with their physical irregularities, move heavily; listless dogs abandon their work, and even lie down in shady spots to avoid the sunlight;* those with insensitive noses find it hard to scent a hare with a high rate of success; and those with unsound feet cannot endure hard work even if they have the temperament to do so, but give up because they get footsore.

Moreover, hounds of the same breed go about their tracking in a wide variety of ways. When they pick up the scent, they may go on without giving any sign, so that there is no way of knowing that they are tracking; or move only their ears, but keep their tails still, or keep their ears still, but wag the tips of their tails. Some prick up their ears and run along the path of the scent with furrowed brows, their tails drooping and tucked safely away; plenty of hounds, however, do nothing of the kind, but rush madly around in the area of the hare's traces, barking their heads off, and when their path coincides with the traces, they stupidly trample out the scent.* Then there are others which are constantly circling around, making detours and picking up false traces way out ahead, with the result that they leave the hare behind; if they ever do run across the traces, they guess the direction they have to take, and if they catch sight of the hare they tremble and do not make a move for it until they see it bolt off.

Hounds which constantly interrupt their casting and sniffing about to run up and examine what the rest of the pack has discovered have no confidence in themselves; on the other hand, those which stop their more expert colleagues forging ahead, by causing a disturbance and impeding their progress, are over-confident. Some hounds find false trails attractive and get terribly excited by anything they come across, and so take the lead even though they know perfectly well that they are misleading the rest; others do exactly the same without even knowing that they are misleading the others. Those which never leave the beaten paths and fail to recognize a true trail are no good, 8 and those which ignore the trace of a hare that is making for its form and which overshoot the trace of a running hare are unsound.

Some hounds set out eagerly in pursuit at first but are too feeble to keep it up, others race ahead and then lose their way, and others foolishly get put off their mark by meeting a road, and more or less 9 refuse to come when summoned. Quite a number of hounds give up the chase and return because they detest hunting, and quite a number do so because they are fond of people. Some do their best to mislead by baying when they are off the scent, and so make false trails out to 10 be true ones. Conversely there are others which, even though they may be busy following a course, leave their own work and in an undisciplined fashion make for anywhere they have heard a shout coming from. Some set off in pursuit without any certainty about what they are doing, while others pick up a lot of false trails but their judgement is poor. Of those which spend their time sniffing about alongside the trail and circling around together, some are merely pretending to hunt, while others are acting out of malice.

11   Most of these faults are innate, but there are also cases of hounds becoming unmanageable as a result of unscientific training. Hounds with these defects may well put a person off hunting, however enthusiastic he was, but I will now go on to explain what hounds of the same species should be like physically and otherwise.

CHAPTER 4

1 In the first place, a good hound ought to be large, and then her head should be light, flat-nosed and well defined. She should have a sinewy lower forehead, with prominent, black, bright eyes; the forehead

ought to be broad, with a deep dividing line; she should have small, thin ears,[1] with little hair behind them, a long, supple, rounded neck and a broad chest with some padding of flesh. The shoulder-blades should project a little way from the shoulders,* the forelegs should be short, straight, round and firm, and the elbows straight. Her ribs should not have vertical depth, but should extend horizontally. It is best for the loins to be fleshy, neither long nor short, and not too supple or too stiff. Her sides should be medium-sized, the haunches rounded, well covered with flesh at the back, not compact at the top and tightly drawn in on the inside. The lower parts of the flanks should be hollow, as should the main flanks too; the tail should be long, straight and whippy, the thighs firm, the lower legs long, rounded and solid. Her hind legs ought to be considerably longer than her forelegs, and wiry, and her feet should be rounded. A hound with these points will be physically strong, light, well proportioned and fast on her feet, and will have eager features and a good mouth.

When trying to pick up a scent, it is best for them to leave the beaten paths quickly, with their heads held obliquely down to the ground, and when they come across a scent to smile and lower their ears. After circling around for a while,* the whole pack should advance towards the form along the hare's traces, with their eyes constantly moving and tails wagging. When they get close to the actual hare, they should run about more quickly than usual to show its whereabouts to the hunter, and should increase the level of their communication by their eagerness, by moving their heads and eyes, by changing their stance, by looking back at the hunter and then staring into the undergrowth, by returning to the hare's lair, by sniffing about in front, behind and to the sides of the spot, and by their genuine excitement and delight at being at last near the hare.

They should give chase strongly, baying and barking loudly all the time, and following the hare over whatever ground it takes. They should be fast and flamboyant in pursuit, capable of frequent changes of direction, and they should give tongue again and again, whenever it is right to do so. They ought not to abandon the trail and return to the hunter.

So much for a hound's physique and how she should go about her work. In addition, she should also have a good temperament, a good sense of smell, sound feet and a good coat. The sign of a good temperament is that the hound does not abandon the chase in the heat of the day; the sign of a good sense of smell is that she can catch the scent of a hare even when the ground is as bare, dry and sun-baked as it can be at the approach of the dog-star; the sign of sound feet is that her pads do not get torn to pieces by a run in the mountains at the same time of year; the sign of a good coat is light, thick and soft hair.

7 It is best for a hound not to be entirely tan, black or white in colouring, because that indicates a poor pedigree – a wild dog with
8 no cross-breeding. So tan and black hounds should have white hair sprouting on their foreheads, while white ones should have a patch of tan hair there. At the top of the thighs, on the loins and on the underside of the tail, the hair should be straight and thick, but on the upper part of the tail it should be only moderately thick.

9 It is a good idea to take the hounds to the mountains more often than the fields, because it is possible for them to track and follow a hare without distractions in the mountains, whereas that is impossible in both cases in areas of cultivated land because of the beaten paths
10 there. It is also a good idea to take them out to rough terrain even if they fail to find a hare, because this sort of terrain strengthens their
11 feet and it does them good to exercise thoroughly there. In the summer-time they should be taken out only in the morning, in the winter at any time of the day, in the autumn at any time except the middle of the day and in spring at any time before the late afternoon, because the temperature is not excessive at these times.

CHAPTER 5

1 A hare's traces are long in the winter-time because of the length of the nights, and short in the summer for the opposite reason. In the winter no smell arises from their traces early in the morning when there is frost or ice on the ground, because frost sucks up the warmth of the traces with its strength and holds it within itself, and ice puts a

freezing layer down on top of the warmth. Also, in these conditions, the hounds' noses become numb with the cold, which ruins their sense of smell. It is only once the sun or the advancing day has released the traces that the hounds can smell and the traces return to the surface and emit a scent.

A heavy dew also obliterates a hare's traces by carrying the scent down into the earth, and occasional storms draw scents out of the ground* and make it a poor medium for carrying scents until it has dried. South winds also make scents deteriorate, because the moisture they carry disperses them. North winds, on the other hand, concentrate and preserve scents if they have not already been dissolved. Rain and showers overwhelm scents, and the heat of the moon – especially of a full moon – obscures them.[1] Traces are particularly broken at the time of a full moon, because hares enjoy the light of the moon and frolic with one another by hurling themselves up into the air and leaping considerable distances. Traces can also become confused when foxes cross them before the hounds get there.

Spring with its temperate weather is good at making scents stand out, except when the ground has a sprinkling of flowers and hinders the hounds by muddling up the scent of the flowers and that of the hare. In summer scents are tenuous and unclear, because the heat of the ground obliterates the delicate warmth of the hare's traces; besides, the hounds do not detect scents so well at that time of year, because their bodies are relaxed.[2] In autumn scents are clear, because cultivated crops have been harvested and wild plants have grown old and died back, so that there is none of the earth's produce left to emit smells which might get muddled up with the hare's scent and so confuse the hounds.

In winter, summer and autumn a hare's traces usually follow a straight line, but in spring they are complex, because although the creature mates throughout the year, it does so especially during this season. The upshot is that they cannot help roaming around together, and so complicate their traces.

The smell arising from the traces of a hare making for its form lasts longer than the smell arising from the traces of a running hare, because a hare halts on the way to its form,* but makes rapid progress when it is on the run. So the ground is thickly covered with scents in the first case, but not in the second. There is more smell in places with undergrowth than on bare ground, because as the hare runs through the undergrowth and sits up there it makes contact with a large number of objects.

8   Everything growing or covering the earth provides hares with their resting-places; they lie underneath, on top, inside, next to, near, at some distance from or between things. Sometimes they even leap as far as they can into the sea or a stretch of water, if there is anything sticking out of the surface or growing there.

9   A couching hare usually makes its form in a sheltered place in cold weather and in a shady spot when it is hot, but in the spring and autumn it chooses a sunny location. When a hare is on the run, however, its behaviour is different because it is so frightened by the

10   hounds. When a hare rests it places its lower legs under its sides, and invariably puts its forelegs together, stretched out in front of its body, with its chin resting on the tips of its feet, and its ears spread over its shoulders. This position enables it to protect its tender parts. Since its

11   coat is thick and soft, this too serves as a protection. Hares blink during their waking hours, but when they are asleep their eyelids are wide open and motionless, and their eyes stay perfectly still. While asleep, their nostrils twitch constantly, but less often when they are awake.

12   When the ground is thick with vegetation, they keep to the fields rather than the mountains. A hare stays in its form, wherever that may be, while it is being hunted, unless it becomes frightened for its young,* in which case it bolts off.

13   The species is so prolific that a female hare may have given birth to one litter, be in labour with another and be pregnant with a third. The scent of young leverets is stronger than that of older ones, because while they are still soft and tender their whole body trails on the

14   ground. Extremely young leverets are ignored by hunters and left in the goddess's care,[3] but yearlings set off at a very fast run, until after their first pause, when they slow down. They are light on their feet, but weak.

15   To pick up the traces of a hare a hunter must gradually lead his hounds beyond the fields and up to wherever they eagerly follow the

traces – that is, on to uncultivated hillsides,* into meadows, glens and stream-beds, and among rocks and shrubs. If a hare bolts off, the hunter must not shout, or else the dogs will go crazy and find it hard to recognize the traces. Sometimes, when a hare has been uncovered 16 by hounds and is being chased, it crosses streams and doubles back and takes refuge in cracks and holes, because it is not just dogs they are afraid of, but eagles as well, since young ones, up to a year old, tend to get snatched up by eagles as they are crossing hillsides and bare stretches of ground, and the older ones are run down and killed by hounds.

Mountain-dwelling hares are the fastest runners, then the ones that 17 live on the plain, and the slowest are those which live in marshy ground. The ones that roam over every kind of terrain are hard to chase,* because they know all the short cuts, in the sense that they usually run uphill or over even ground, tend to avoid uneven ground, and keep off downhill slopes altogether.

When being chased, the fact that their bodies reflect the sun means 18 that hares are particularly easy to see, if they have some red in their coat, as they are crossing ploughed fields and running through stubble. They are also easy to see on beaten paths and on roads (as long as they are level), because the bright parts of their coat reflect the light. But they are hard to see when they run for cover among rocks, on hillsides or on stony or wooded ground, because they are the same colour as their surroundings.

When a hare is out in front of the pack of hounds, it may stop, 19 raise itself into a squatting position, listen for any baying or noises indicating the presence of hounds near by and then set off in the opposite direction from any noise it does hear. Sometimes, even 20 though there is nothing for it to hear, it imagines or convinces itself of some threat, and runs for cover, doubling back past the same objects and over the same ground, leaping this way and that, and confusing its traces with further traces. The longest runners are those which are 21 discovered on bare ground, because they can see where they are going, whereas the shortest runners are those discovered on wooded ground, because the darkness frustrates them.

There are two species of hare. The larger variety is dusky in colour, 22

and the white patch on their foreheads is big; the smaller ones are
23 tawny and have a small white patch. The first kind are dappled all the
way around their tails, while the second kind are dappled on either
side of their tails. Large ones have bluish-grey eyes, small ones have
greyish eyes. Large ones usually have quite a bit of black at the tips
24 of their ears, while small ones have only a little. The smaller variety
is to be found on most of the islands, whether uninhabited or inhabited.
The reason more of them live on the islands than on the mainland is
that on most of the islands there are no foxes to attack and kill the
hares and their young, and no eagles either, which keep to the high
mountains rather than low ones, and the mountains on the islands are
25 generally smaller than on the mainland. Besides, uninhabited islands
are rarely visited by hunters, inhabited islands are only sparsely
inhabited, and by people who tend not to be hunters, and one is not
allowed to take dogs over to sacred islands.[4] So where only a few
mature or young hares are killed by hunting, there are, of course,
huge numbers of them.

26 Hares do not have good eyesight, for a number of reasons. In the
first place, their eyes bulge outwards[5] and their eyelids are too small
to afford them proper protection, with the result that their vision is
27 weak and diffuse. The same features also mean that although the
creature spends a great deal of time asleep its eyesight is not helped
by this. Its speed also makes a significant contribution towards its poor
eyesight, because a hare lets its vision slide rapidly over each object
28 before identifying it. Then its fear of the hounds when it is being
chased combines with all these factors to rob the creature of its ability
to plan ahead. The upshot is that it accidentally collides with all sorts
of things and dashes into the net.

24 If hares took a straight line when trying to escape, they would be
very hard to catch. As things are, however, they double back around
and stick close to the places where they were born and raised, and so
they get caught. They are invariably fast enough to outrun hounds,
and if they are caught, it is because they have met with an accident
that has cancelled out their natural physical abilities, because there is
nothing in the world of their size which can match them in terms of
their construction. A hare's body consists of the following components.

A head which is light, small, downward-pointing and narrow at [30] the front;* a neck that is narrow, rounded, supple and quite long; shoulder-blades that are upright and not compact at the top; front legs which are light and close set; a narrow chest; light, symmetrical ribs; rounded loins; a fleshy rump; sides that are supple and quite loose; haunches which are round, well covered with flesh all around, and the right distance apart at the top; small, solid thighs, with taut muscles on the outside, and not too much of a bulge on the inside; lower legs that are long and firm; forefeet which are especially supple, as well as being narrow and straight; hard, broad hind feet; feet that can endure any kind of rough terrain; hind legs that are much longer than the forelegs and are bent slightly outwards; and a coat that is short and light. Since its frame consists of these elements, there is no [31] way for it not to be strong, agile and very light on its feet.

Evidence to show how light hares are on their feet is given by the fact that their normal quiet progress involves taking off from the ground. No one has seen or ever will see a hare walking. It brings its hind feet up beyond its forefeet, and to the outside of them: that is how it runs along. This is unmistakable in the snow.

A hare's tail is too short to be able to guide its body, and so plays [32] no part when the hare is running. It uses one or the other of its ears for this function. When it is started into flight by the hounds, it lets one of its ears droop and hang at an angle – whichever ear is on the side where the threat is coming from – and then it quickly swivels round, using this ear to guide it, and before long has left its assailant far behind. A hare makes such a charming spectacle that the sight of [33] one being tracked, found, chased and caught would make anyone forget all his passions.[6]

If the hunter is hunting on cultivated land, he should avoid any [34] fields with crops in them, and leave springs and streams alone. It is wrong and bad to tamper with them, and encourages onlookers to contravene normal practice.[7] On days when hunting is forbidden,[8] he should suspend all hunting-related activities.

CHAPTER 6

1 The dogs' equipment consists of collars, leashes and girths. A collar should be soft and broad, so as not to spoil the hound's coat. A leash should have a noose to hold on to, but nothing else: people who have their leashes double up as collars are not looking after their hounds correctly. Girths should have broad straps so as not to chafe the dog's sides, and should have spikes sewn on to them, to safeguard one's breeding programme.

2 Hounds should not be taken out hunting when they are off their food, since this is a sign that they are not well, nor when a strong wind is blowing, because this disperses the traces, making it impossible for the hounds to pick up the scent, and blows over the short nets

3 and game-nets. If neither of these obstacles exists, one should take the dogs out every other day. Do not let them get used to chasing foxes: there is nothing worse for them, and they are never there when

4 you need them. They should be taken out to a variety of different hunting-grounds, to enable them to become experienced hunters, and to familiarize the hunter with the land. Go out early in the morning, to give the dogs an opportunity for proper tracking; the scent is by nature tenuous, and does not last all day, so a late start robs the hounds of the chance of coming across a hare, and the hunter himself of his benefit.

5 The net-keeper should wear light clothing when he goes out hunting. He should set up his short nets at bends, in overgrown thickets, on hillsides, in hollows, shady places, streams, gullies and watercourses with permanent streams, because these are the places

6 where a hare is most likely to try to take refuge. A list of all the other possible places would be endless. <He should block up>* the approaches to these places and the pathways through them, whether open or faint, and should do so in the morning, but not too early, so that if the net-station is near the places to be beaten, the hare does not take fright at hearing the noise close at hand; however, if there is quite a distance between the places to be beaten and the net-station,

7 it does not matter so much if this job is done early. He must clear the

net-stations of anything that might get in the way, and fix the stakes at an incline, so that they can take the strain when pulled. He is to loop an equal number of meshes over the top of each pair of stakes and provide them with a corresponding degree of support, in order to raise the belly of the net in the middle. A long, heavy stone is to 8 be attached to the net's surround, to stop the net straining in the opposite direction once there is a hare inside. He must set the stakes in a long row, and high enough to stop the hare jumping over the top of the net.*

The net-keeper is to set up the game-nets on level ground, and 9 the road-nets on roads and at suitable points on beaten paths. The procedure is to attach the surround to the ground, bring the corners together, fix the stakes between the guys, put the surrounds on the tips of the stakes and block up any gaps on either side of the nets.

Then he should go around checking the nets. If the short net is 10 pulling the row of stakes out of line, he should re-establish them. When a hare is being chased into a net, he is to let it carry on forward,* and then race after it, shouting out loud. When a hare has been trapped in a net, he is to calm the hounds' frenzy; he should do so without touching them, just with soothing words. He should also call out to the hunter, to let him know what is going on – that a hare has been caught or has run past on one side or the other of the net, or that he has not seen a hare, or at least not had a clear sighting.**

When he goes out hunting, the hunter should wear unpretentious, 11 light clothing and footwear, and carry a club; the net-keeper should accompany him. He should not bide his time when tracking a hare; true hunters do not delay, and to do one's utmost to capture a hare quickly shows determination.* The hunting-ground should be approached in silence, in case any hare that happens to be near by bolts off at the noise. The hounds should be tied to the undergrowth, 12 each one to a separate shrub, so that they are easy to set free, and the short nets and game-nets should be set up according to the directions I have given. Next the net-keeper should go and check the nets, while the hunter should take the hounds and go to the point from where he will initiate the hunt. After praying to Apollo and Artemis 13 the Huntress,[1] and pledging a share of the catch to them, he is to unleash a single hound. She should be the most skilful tracker of the pack, and should be released at sunrise in winter, before daybreak in

14 summer and some time in between in spring and autumn. When the hound has picked up a true scent from among all the confusion of smells, he should let slip another hound. If the trace carries on, he should let the rest of the hounds go as well, one by one, at short intervals. He should then follow them, but without urging them on, and once in a while call out to each of them by name, to stop them

15 getting worked up too soon. On they go, out of sheer enjoyment and will, separating out their quarry's traces – which may be double or treble, intersecting* past or over the same spots, confused, roundabout, straight or crooked, concentrated or tenuous, distinct or indistinct – running past one another, with tails wagging fast, ears down and eyes flashing.

16 When they have closed in on a hare, they will let the hunter know by the shaking of the whole of their bodies (not just their tails), by their aggressive forward surges, by trying to outrun one another, by determinedly running along together and by quickly forming up as a pack and then separating, only to charge forward again. Finally they

17 will reach the hare's form and make a rush for the creature. The hare will dart up and away, making the hounds bark and bay at the sight. Now, with the dogs in pursuit, the hunter should call out, 'Good dogs! Good! Well done! Clever dogs!' He should wrap his cloak around his arm, pick up his club and run with the pack after the hare,

18 without trying to head it off, which is impossible. In its hasty flight, the hare vanishes from sight, but then it invariably doubles back to where it was discovered. At this point, with the hare still on the move,* he should call out to the net-keeper, 'Hit it, slave! Go on, hit it!'[2] And the net-keeper is to let the hunter know whether or not the hare has been caught.

19 If the hare is caught on its first run, the hunter ought to recall his hounds and start looking for another hare. If not, he should keep on running with the pack at top speed, without giving up on the hare, but determinedly carrying right on after it. If the chase leads the hounds to make contact with the hare again, the hunter should call out, 'Well done! Well done, dogs! Go on! After it, dogs!'

Suppose the pack gets such a long way ahead of him that not only is it impossible for him to run and catch up with them, but he has actually gone off course, and cannot see whether they are wandering about somewhere near by or have stopped or are keeping on the hare's traces, he can still ask anyone he meets by calling out as he runs past, 'Hello there! Have you seen my dogs?' Once he has found out 20 where they are, if they are on the trace, he should rejoin them and give them encouragement, speaking to each of them in turn by name, and using as many variations in pitch and tone of voice as he can manage – high and low, soft and loud. Whatever other kinds of encouragement he gives, if the chase is taking place in the mountains he should call out, 'Good dogs! Well done, dogs!'* If they are not on the trace, but have run on too far, he should call out, 'Come back, come back here, dogs!'

If they have got ahead of the trace,* the hunter should wheel them 21 round and get them to describe numerous circles; wherever the scent is indistinct for them, he should plant a stake as a marker for himself, and should use this as a starting-point from which to send the pack out in a line, with cries of encouragement and reassurance, until they come across a distinct trace. As soon as the trace is unmistakable, the 22 hounds will set off in pursuit, hurling themselves at it, leaping along beside it, clustering together, picking up false scents, pointing them out to one another and orienting themselves against familiar landmarks. When they are racing like this along the trace, all bunched together, the hunter should run with them at full stretch, to stop them over-shooting the scent in their eager rivalry.

Once the hounds have closed in on a hare, and show the hunter 23 plainly that they have, what he has to watch out for is the hare being so frightened of them that it bolts off ahead. With their tails waving to and fro, with their collisions and frequent leaps over one another, with their constant baying, as they raise their heads and look at the hunter to let him know that now this is the real thing, they will start the hare off by themselves and run baying after it. Whatever happens 24 – whether the hare dashes into the nets or runs past them to one side or the other – the net-keeper must call out to let the hunter know. If the hare has been caught, moreover, the hunter should go and look for another one; if not, he should carry on running after it, while employing the same methods of encouragement for his hounds.

25   When the hounds are tired from their pursuit and it is getting late in the day, the hunter must go in search of the hare, which by now will be suffering from exhaustion. He should search every plant and feature of the terrain, often retracing his steps to make sure that he has not missed anything, because the hare does not take up much space when it is lying down, and it is too tired and frightened to get to its feet. He should bring his hounds along with him, keeping their spirits up with frequent words of encouragement to any that are fawning on him, few to the independent ones and a moderate number to those which fall between these two states, until he has either killed the hare on the run or driven it into the nets.

26   Then he should collect his short nets and his game-nets, rub down the dogs, and leave the hunting-ground, after waiting a while, if it is a summer afternoon, in case the dogs' feet get blistered as they make their way home.

CHAPTER 7

1   He should let his hounds off work during the winter and mate them, so that they can have the leisure to produce a thoroughbred litter towards spring, which is the best season for dogs to develop in.[1] There
2   are fourteen days during which the mating frenzy grips them.* He should introduce them to good male dogs towards the end of this period, because they are more likely to conceive quickly then. When they are close to term, it is best not to take them out hunting all the time, but only once in a while, or else their determination might cause a miscarriage. The period of gestation is sixty days.

3   He should leave the new-born puppies in the care of the mother rather than any other bitch, because the attentions of a bitch which is not their mother do not promote growth, whereas the mother's milk and breath are good for them, and her protection is welcome to
4   them. Continue to give the puppies milk for a year after they start to walk, and the food which is going to form their regular diet, but

nothing else, because overfeeding deforms a puppy's legs, makes its body liable to disease and impairs its insides.

Give them short names which are easy to call out, such as, for instance: Spirit, Pluck, Handle, Spike, Lance, Raider, Guard, Picket, Trooper, Sword, Killer, Blaze, Butch, Battler, Ringwood, Wily, Striker, Hasty, Fury, Growler, Upstart, Peppy, Brawn, Bloomer, Prime, Happy, Joy, Sharpeyes, Brighteyes, Rover, Force, Soldier, Earnest, Glory, Bryony, Steadfast, Barker, Slayer, Merry, Mighty, Sky, Sunbeam, Spearhead, Crafty, Prudence, Tracker, Dasher.

The hunter should introduce female puppies to hunting at eight months and males at ten months. He should not let them loose on the trace of a couching hare, but keep them on a long leash, following hounds which are on the scent, and let them run to and fro over the trace. If they are physically well formed for running, he should not let them go as soon as a hare is sighted, but should wait until the hare is so far ahead that they can no longer see it. For if he releases dogs which are both physically and temperamentally well adapted for running when they are close to the hare, the sight of it will make them strain and rupture themselves, since their bodies are still unformed. So this is something for the hunter to be careful about. If they are not so well built for running,* however, there is nothing to stop the hunter letting them loose, because they have no chance of catching the hare, and so will not come to the kind of harm the others would.

When the hare is on the run, however, he should let them chase it as long as they are prepared to stay on the trace,** and if they succeed in catching it he should give them it to tear apart. If after a while they prove reluctant to stay together, but scatter instead, he should call them back, until they have got used to finding a hare by running after it, because if there is never any discipline[2] to the way they look for a hare, they will eventually become conditioned to the bad habit of sniffing around off the trace.

While the hounds are young, they should be fed in the vicinity of the nets, at the time when the nets are being taken up, so that any hounds which have wandered off during the hunt as a result of their inexperience will return for their meal and can be safely recovered. This practice can be discontinued once the hare has become their

firm enemy, because then they will be more concerned with the hare
12 than worried about their food. The hunter should generally feed them
himself when they ask for it, because even though they do not know
the cause of their hunger,* when they are hungry and they get food
they feel affection for the person who gives it to them.

CHAPTER 8

1 It is a good idea to track hares when the snow is thick enough to
cover the ground, but if there are still patches of bare ground, they
will be hard to find. When it is cloudy and the wind is from the north,
the traces remain visible on the surface for a long time, because the
snow is slow to melt; but when the wind is from the south and the
sun is shining, the snow soon melts and the traces quickly disappear.
When it is snowing constantly, however, you should not bother to
go out hunting, because the snow covers up the traces. The same
goes for when there is a strong wind, because the drifting snow covers
them up.

2 The hunter certainly should not go out hunting with hounds under
these conditions because the snow blisters their noses and their feet,*
and the extreme cold makes the hare's scent impossible to find. Instead
he should collect his game-nets and go out with an assistant to the
mountains, leaving the fields behind, and make his way along any
3 traces he finds. If the traces are confused, he should circle around,
following single sets of traces back to a single point, in an attempt to
find any which break out of the confusion. Hares often roam around
in search of a place to rest, and a life of pursuit has also given them
4 the habit of employing artifice when they are on the move. When,
as a result of this kind of search,* a trace becomes visible, the hunter
should press on forward. The trace will take him either to a place
with plenty of cover or to a steep slope, because the wind carries the
snow over such places and leaves plenty of resting-places there.

5 Once the traces have led the hunter to this kind of spot, he should
not go too near, in case the hare bolts off, but should circle around
the area. The chances are that the hare is there, and he will find out

by checking that the traces nowhere emerge from the place. Having 6 determined that the hare is there, he should leave it alone, because the hare will stay there, and look for another one before the traces become indistinct, bearing in mind what season of the year it is, and therefore making sure that, if he does find other hares as well, there will be enough time for him to surround them. In due course he 7 should hang his game-nets around each hare that he has found (the method being no different from that used on ground which is bare of snow), enclosing everything the hare may be near, and once the nets have been set up, he should approach and start the hare moving. If the hare extricates itself from the nets, he should run after it, 8 following its traces. The hare will end up in another similar location, unless it crouches in the actual snow. Wherever the hare ends up, the hunter should investigate the spot and surround it. If it does not stay there, he should continue his pursuit, because he will eventually catch the hare even without the help of the nets, since the depth of the snow and the amount that sticks to the hair on the lower parts of its feet combine to tire the creature out.

CHAPTER 9

The best hounds for hunting fawns and hinds are Indian hounds, 1 because they are strong, large, fast and not lacking in courage – a combination of qualities which makes them capable of hard work.[1] New-born fawns should be hunted in spring, which is the season when they are born. The hunter should go out into the meadowland 2 and find out where there are the largest numbers of deer. He should then go to this spot, wherever it may be, before daybreak, with the dog-handler and* the hounds and javelins. He should tie the hounds to trees some way off, so that they will not catch sight of any deer and bark, and then keep a lookout. At daybreak he will see the hinds 3 taking their fawns to the various places where each of them is going to bed her fawn down. Once they have settled them down and given them milk and looked around to make sure that they are not being observed, each hind moves off to one side to watch over her fawn.

4 When the hunter sees this happen, he should untie the hounds from the trees, pick up the javelins and approach the place where he saw the nearest fawn bed down, carefully noting all the features of the terrain to avoid making a mistake, because from close at hand their appearance is considerably different from what it was at a dis-

5 tance.* When he has spotted the fawn, he should approach it; it will flatten itself to the ground and keep still, and will let itself be picked up, bleating loudly, unless it has been exposed to the rain, in which case it will not stay where it is, because the moisture in its own body

6 is quickly congealed by the cold and this makes it set off.[2] But it will be caught by the hounds after a hard chase. When he has the fawn, he should give it to the net-keeper. It will bleat, and this sound, as well as what she has seen, will bring the hind running over to whoever

7 has the fawn to see if she can rescue it. This is the time to set the hounds on her and to make use of his javelins. Once he has secured this first fawn, he should make his way to the others and use the same method of hunting on them too.

8 This is how young fawns are taken. Older ones are not so easy, because they graze with their mothers and with other deer, and when chased they take up a position in the middle of the fleeing herd –

9 occasionally in the front, rarely at the back. Moreover, the hinds lash out with their hoofs against the hounds in defence of their young. All this makes the fawns hard to capture, unless one immediately makes an assault on the herd, scatters the hinds and isolates one of the fawns.

10 Having made this sudden burst, the hounds fall behind in the first run, because the absence of the hinds makes the fawn terrified, and there is nothing to compare with fawns of this age for speed. It will not take long for them to be captured, however, on the second or third run, because they are still too young to be physically capable of sustaining the effort.

11 Traps are also set for deer in mountainous regions, around meadows, streams and springs, on paths and in any cultivated fields they visit.

12 The traps should be made out of plaited yew (with its bark removed to prevent rotting), with a circular crown and spikes of alternate iron and wood woven into the plaited part; the iron spikes should be longer, because while it is the job of the wooden spikes to yield to

the deer's foot, the iron ones should stick into it.[3] The noose which 13
is to be placed on top of the crown, and the rope itself, should be
made out of plaited esparto,[4] which is particularly slow to rot. The
actual noose, as well as the rope, has to be sturdy, and the log which
is tied on to the end of the rope should be oak or holm-oak, three
hand-spans long, still with its bark on, and one palm in diameter.

To set the trap, dig a round pit five palms deep, with its rim the 14
same size as the crown of the trap, and gradually narrowing down
towards the bottom, and also dig out enough soil to accommodate
both the rope and the log. Next, put the trap a little way down in 15
the pit, so that it ends up level with the surface of the ground, and
lay the noose on the top of the trap. Once the trap and the log have
been laid in their respective places, put thistle stalks on the top, without
letting them project beyond the trap, and then a layer of light leaves,
from whatever plants are in season. Next sprinkle some soil on the 16
leaves, beginning with the topsoil dug out of the pits, and then on
top of this lay some clods of earth, which should be taken from some
distance away, to make it as difficult as possible for the deer to spot
the emplacement. Carry any soil that is left over far away from the
trap, because if the deer smells newly turned earth, it will become
cautious – something it is always liable to do at short notice.

The hunter should take his hounds and inspect the traps he has set 17
in the mountains at dawn without fail, and at other times of the day
as well, and the traps he has set in the fields early in the morning. For
in the remoteness of the mountains deer are caught during the daytime,
as well as at night, whereas in the cultivated fields they are caught
only at night, because during the day they are frightened of the human
beings there. When he finds a trap upset, he should let the hounds 18
off their leashes with a word of command and set out at a run along
the path left by the log. He should keep an eye out for the direction
the deer has taken, which will usually be perfectly clear, because there
will be disturbed stones, the marks made by the log will be easy to
spot in cultivated fields, and if the deer traverses rugged terrain, there
will be bits of bark torn from the log sticking to the rocks, which will
make a fairly easy trail to run along.

If it is the deer's foreleg that has been caught in the trap, it will 19

soon be taken, because every part of its body, including its face, gets struck by the log as it races along. If it is one of its back legs, its whole body labours under the disadvantage of dragging the log, and it might dash into the forked branches of a shrub and get stuck there, if it does
20 not snap the rope. But whether the hunter catches it in this way or by wearing it out, he must not go near it, because stags butt with their horns and kick with their feet, and hinds use their feet. So he should throw his javelins from some distance away.

In summer deer may also be caught by being chased without the aid of traps, because they get so exhausted that they come to a standstill and can be hit with javelins. They also get so confused when they are cornered that they leap into the sea or into pools. Sometimes they collapse from shortness of breath.

CHAPTER 10

1 For hunting wild boar, the hunter must have Indian, Cretan, Locrian and Laconian hounds, short nets, javelins, pikes and traps.[1] The first point to note is that the hounds of each species must be outstanding
2 enough to be prepared to battle the creature. The short nets should be made out of the same kinds of flax as are used for the hares' nets; they should be 45-threaded, in three strands, with each strand consisting of fifteen threads, and be ten knots in height, from top to bottom, with each mesh one cubit deep. The surrounds should be one and a half times as thick as the netting, with rings at the corners; they should run under the meshes and project, at the ends, beyond the rings. Fifteen rings are enough.*
3 He should have a thorough assortment of javelins with broad, razor-sharp heads and sturdy shafts. The pikes should have blades five palms long, with stout bronze barbs halfway down their sockets, and with cornel-wood shafts as thick as the shaft of a spear.[2] The traps should be of the same design as those used for deer.[3] He should have several fellow hunters, because it is not easy to capture a boar, even for a large number of people. I will now explain how each of these pieces of equipment should be used for hunting.

First, then, they should make their way to a place where they expect 4
the hunt to get started. There they should let one of the Laconian
hounds go, and make a circuit of the place along with her, while
keeping the rest of the pack on their leashes. When she finds a boar's 5
traces, they must form up in single file and follow the tracking hound*
as she gives clear signs as to which way the train is to follow. The
hunters too will find plenty of evidence of the boar – traces in soft
ground, broken branches in any thick undergrowth and, where there
are trees, scars made by its tusks. By following the traces, the hound 6
will usually end up at a thicket, because that is the kind of spot
generally chosen by boars as resting-places, since they are warm in
the winter and cool in the summer.

On reaching the boar's lair, the hound will bark, but only in 7
exceptional cases will the boar get to its feet. So the hunters should
take the hound and tie it up along with the others a good distance
away from the lair, and then have the short nets set up at the boar's
places of refuge, by hanging the meshes on forked branches in the
undergrowth, and forming out of the net itself a long, extended recess,
using sticks to prop it up inside on both sides, so that the maximum
amount of daylight can penetrate into the recess through the meshes,
and the interior will consequently be as well lit as possible when the
boar runs into it. The surround should be attached to a strong tree,
not to a shrub, because bushes catch on the threads of the net.* Use
undergrowth to block up even unlikely places of refuge in the case
of each net, so that the boar runs straight into the nets.

Once the nets are in place the hunters should go to the hounds and 8
untie them all; then they should take their javelins and pikes in
their hands and advance towards the boar's lair. One man, the most
experienced among them, should tell the dogs what to do, while the
rest follow in due order, spread out at a considerable distance from
one another, to allow the boar enough room to pass between them,
because if they are all bunched together and the boar dashes into them
as it tries to escape, there is a risk of someone being gored, since it
vents its fury on anyone it meets.

When the hounds are close to the lair, they will hurl themselves 9
into the attack. The uproar will make the boar get to its feet. It will

toss aside any of the hounds that attack it face on, and dash off at a run into a net. If it avoids the nets, the hunters must chase it. If the ground where it is held by a net is sloping, it will not be long before it is back on its feet, but on level ground its immediate reaction will
10 be to stay still, thinking things over within itself. This is the moment for the hounds to attack, and the hunters should carefully let fly with their javelins, and pelt it with stones too, standing in a semicircle around its rear, but a good way off, until it pushes itself forward enough to stretch the surround of the net tight – which is the cue for the most experienced and self-disciplined of the hunters to approach the boar head on and spear it with a pike.

11   If despite all the javelins and stones the boar refuses to stretch the surround tight, but slows down, wheels round and confronts any hostile approach, in these circumstances a hunter must take his pike in hand and advance, holding the pike with the left hand in front of the right, because it is the job of the left hand to guide the pike while the right hand drives it in. The left foot should accompany the left
12 hand forward, with the right foot following the right hand.[4] He should make his approach with the pike held out in front of him, with his legs only a little further apart than in a wrestling stance[5] and his left side turned towards the left hand, looking the beast in the eye and assessing what movements it might make by taking note of what it does with its head.* He should bring the pike to bear, taking care that the boar does not knock it out of his hands with a jerk of its head,
13 because it will follow up the impetus gained from the jerk. If the pike is knocked out of his hand, he should throw himself on his face and cling on to the lower parts of the undergrowth, because if the beast attacks him when he is in this position, the curve of its tusks will prevent it from lifting him up. If he is off the ground when the beast attacks, however, he is bound to be gored. In any case, the boar will try to get him off the ground; if it cannot do so, it will stand over
14 him and trample him. There is only one way out of this desperate situation, and that is for one of the man's fellow hunters to approach the boar and provoke it by wielding a pike as if he were going to let fly with it; however, he must not in fact throw the pike, in case he
15 hits his companion on the ground. When the boar sees what is going

on, it will leave the man it is standing over and turn all its rage and
fury against the person who is provoking it. The man on the ground
must waste no time in leaping to his feet, remembering to retain his
grip on his pike as he does so, because there is nothing noble about
safety unless it is accompanied by victory.[6] He must bring the pike to 16
bear once again just as he did before, and plunge the pike within the
shoulder-blades, where he can get at the throat, with a firm thrust.
The boar will be so enraged that it will press on, and if it were not
for the barbs on the blade of the pike, it would impale itself along the
shaft until it reached the man wielding the pike.

A boar is so powerful that it has some surprising qualities. For 17
instance, if you put some hairs on one of its tusks just after it has died,
they shrivel up. That is how hot its tusks are. The tusks on a live
boar which has been provoked become blazing hot; this is the only
explanation for the fact that, when it misses in an attempt to gore a
hound, the ends of the hairs on the dog's coat become singed.

This is the least of what one has to go through to capture a male 18
boar. If it is a sow that has dashed into the nets, the hunter must run
up and thrust at it, taking care not to be knocked to the ground. If
this occurs, he is bound to be trampled and bitten, so he should do
all he can to avoid falling in its way. If it happens by accident, the
same means for getting to his feet are available as in the case of the
male. Once back on his feet, he must lunge at the beast with his pike
until he has killed it.

Another method for capturing boars is as follows. Short nets are 19
set up for them on the paths between glens and thickets, at bends, on
rocky ground and at the entrances to meadows, marshes and pools.
One of the hunters is given the job of guarding the nets, pike in hand,
while the rest take the hounds and search for the most likely spots.
As soon as a boar is found, it is chased. If it dashes into a net, the 20
net-keeper must take up his pike, go up to the boar and deal with it
in the way I have already described; if it avoids the nets, he must run
after it.

In stiflingly hot weather, simple pursuit by hounds can lead to a
boar's capture, because for all its enormous strength the creature gets
short of breath and tired.

21 Boar-hunting causes the death of large numbers of hounds, and the hunters themselves are at risk too, or at least they are when during a chase they have no choice but to approach a boar, pikes in hand, when the animal is tired or standing in water or has taken up a position by a cliff or is reluctant to leave a thicket, because under these circumstances there is no net or anything else stopping it from charging anyone who comes near. Still, a hunter does have to approach a boar in these situations; it is time for him to show the courage that led him
22 to choose this way of satisfying his desire to hunt.[7] He must wield his pike and thrust his body forward in the way I have described; then, if he does have an accident, it will not be because he was not doing things correctly.

Traps may be set for boar as for deer, and in the same places. The procedure is identical – inspection, chase, approach and use of the pike.[8]

23 A new-born boar does not allow itself to be captured easily. It is never alone when young, and when the hounds find it, or it sees something in the distance, it quickly vanishes into the undergrowth; it is usually accompanied by both its parents, which make formidable foes on these occasions, since they are even more aggressive in defence of their young than they are on their own behalf.

CHAPTER 11

1 Lions, leopards, lynxes, panthers, bears and other exotic animals are caught in foreign lands, on or around mountains which provide suitable habitats for such creatures, such as Pangaeum, Cissus north
2 of Macedon,[1] Olympus in Mysia, Pindus or Nysa east of Syria. Because the terrain is so difficult, one way of taking them is by using aconite as a poison. Hunters mix it with the animals' favourite food and leave
3 it near pools and other places they visit. When they come down off the mountain at night, they may be driven into a corner by mounted and armed men, and taken this way, although this method is dangerous
4 for the men involved. For some of these animals, people dig large, deep, round pits, leaving a pillar of earth in the middle. They put a

goat in the pit in the evening, tie it to the pillar and build a fence of undergrowth all around the pit, with no entrances, and high enough not to be looked over.* During the night animals hear the goat inside, run around the outside of the fence and, failing to find a way in, leap over the top and are caught.

CHAPTER 12

So much for the practical aspects of hunting.[1] A strong desire to hunt   1 can also lead to a great deal of profit. It makes for physical fitness, improves the sight and hearing, slows down the process of growing old, and above all it is good training for warfare.

They will not, for instance, get tired when marching under arms   2 across difficult terrain, because they will have built up their stamina by their habit of carrying weapons when hunting animals.[2] Secondly, they will be able to sleep rough and efficiently guard any spot they are assigned. When attacking the enemy, they will be capable of   3 carrying out their orders as well as the assault, because that is how they do things themselves when hunting game. If they have been posted in the front line, they will not break rank, because they are capable of maintaining a position in the face of danger. If the enemy   4 troops are in flight, they will pursue their opponents in the correct manner and without taking risks, across every kind of terrain, because they are perfectly familiar with this kind of activity. If their own force has suffered a setback in terrain that is wooded, precipitous or otherwise awkward, they will be capable of saving themselves in a respectable manner, and of keeping others alive too, because their familiarity with hunting will increase their level of expertise. In the past, in fact, even   5 with the main body of their allies in flight, a few such men have renewed the battle against the victorious enemy and have routed them, thanks to their fitness* and courage in difficult terrain which has caused the enemy to make mistakes. For those in prime physical and mental condition success is never far off.[3]

Our ancestors too were aware that this is the means of success   6 against the enemy, and that is why they made hunting part of a young man's course of studies. Even though they were always short of produce, it was the original custom, instituted by them, that hunters could freely follow game through fields bearing any kind of crop;

7 they also prohibited night-hunting within a radius of many stades from the city, so that those who possessed this skill would not deprive young men of their game.[4] They appreciated that hunting is the only thing young people enjoy doing which does them a very great deal of good, in the sense that it brings them up surrounded by reality,

8 and so gives them self-restraint and honesty; they realized that their successes in war and in other areas were due to these men. Moreover, whereas other enjoyable activities – the base ones, which should not be studied – debar young men from noble pursuits, hunting does not: they can undertake any other honourable occupation they like.[5] These, then, are the kinds of men who develop into fine soldiers and

9 military commanders. For men who have striven to rid their minds and bodies of all that is disgraceful and immoderate, and to instil instead a growing desire for virtue, are men of outstanding worth, because they will not let anyone get away with wronging their city or harming their land.

10 Some people claim that a passion for hunting is misguided, on the grounds that it makes one neglect one's domestic affairs. They do not understand, however, that every benefactor of his community and

11 friends is taking particularly good care of his domestic affairs. If hunters are training themselves to be of service to their country in the most important matters, they are not thereby deserting* their own affairs, because everyone's domestic affairs depend for their preservation or loss on the safety or destruction of the community, and therefore hunters safeguard the affairs of every private citizen in the community, as well as their own.[6]

12 The envious irrationality of those who make this claim is often such that they prefer to be ruined by their own badness rather than to be kept safe by other people's goodness. For the majority of pleasures are actually bad, and by succumbing to them these people are induced to choose the worse alternative in what they say or what they do –

13 and then their stupid words arouse antagonism, and their evil deeds bring disease, punishment and death down on themselves, their chil-

dren and their friends. Given that they are incapable of recognizing evil, but quicker than others to recognize a source of pleasure, who is going to make use of them when the community needs protection?[7] However, anyone who takes a passionate interest in the pursuit I am [14] recommending will steer clear of these troubles, since a good education teaches people to observe the laws, to speak about justice and to listen only to others doing the same. So these people, by their dedication [15] to a life of hard work and education, may provide themselves with nothing but arduous training and schooling, but they also provide protection for their communities; the others, however, the ones who refuse to submit to an arduous education and prefer a life of intense pleasures, have no redeeming moral features at all. They submit to [16] neither laws nor good advice, because as a result of their avoidance of hard work they have no idea what sort of qualities a good man should have.[8] Consequently, they are incapable of piety or intelligence, and their lack of education frequently makes them find fault with those who have submitted to an education. In short, then, these men [17] are never responsible for any good; every discovery and invention that has helped mankind is due to the better sort – that is,* to those who are prepared to make efforts.

There is convincing evidence to support this claim. After all, in [18] times past those students of Cheiron's who, as I mentioned,[9] started when they were young men with hunting, went on to acquire expertise in a large number of fine fields of endeavour; as a result they attained the high virtue for which they are still admired today. It is perfectly obvious that all men passionately desire virtue, but because it takes hard work to achieve it, the majority give up. The point is that the [19] attainment of virtue is never certain, whereas the hard work involved is all too obvious. Perhaps, if virtue had a visible body and people understood that they were just as visible to her as she was to them, they would neglect her less. For under the watchful eyes of his beloved [20] every man does better than his best and allows nothing disgraceful or bad to enter his words or deeds, in case he is seen by him.[10] But people [21] openly commit many shocking crimes on the assumption that, just because they cannot see her, virtue is not looking. She is omnipresent, however, because she is one of the immortals, and while she honours

those who are good to her, she has no respect for those who are bad.
22 If people knew that she was watching, they would commit themselves without hesitation to the arduous work and training needed for the hard task of catching her, and their reward would be virtue.

CHAPTER 13

1 What surprises me about the sophists, as they are called, is that although most of them profess to educate young men in virtue, they actually do exactly the opposite.[1] It is not just that we have never *seen* a man become good thanks to the sophists of today; their writings are also
2 not designed to improve people. Much of their writing is concerned with trivia, which can give young men vain enjoyment, but not virtue. To read it in the hope of learning something is a pointless waste of time; their treatises keep people from doing something useful
3 and teach them things that are offensive.[2] These are serious criticisms, but then the issue is serious; as regards the content of their treatises, my charge is that while they have gone to great lengths over style, they have eliminated the kind of sound views which educate the younger generation in virtue.
4 I am just a layman, but I know that the best place to look for instruction in goodness is one's own nature, and that the second best course is to go to people who really know something good rather
5 than to professional deceivers.[3] My language may perhaps be plain, but then it is not my purpose to embroider. I am trying to put into words sound opinions of the kind needed by those who have been brought up with the proper attitude towards virtue. After all, education is not afforded by language, but by opinions, provided they are good.
6 I am far from alone in criticizing the sophists of today – note that I am not talking about genuine lovers of wisdom – for using their skills on style rather than content. I am well aware that someone, probably one of the sophists, might point out the faults in something that is not a well-written, coherent treatise; after all, swift and ill-
7 founded criticism will prove no problem for them. I have written it the way I have, however, because my purpose is to produce a sound

treatise, and one which is designed to increase people's knowledge and virtue, not their sophistic skills. I want it to *be* useful, not just to *seem* useful, because then it will never be refuted. The sophists' 8 intention in lecturing and writing is to deceive others for their own gain; they do no one any good at all. There has never been in the past nor does there exist now a knowledgeable sophist; in fact, they are all perfectly happy to be called sophists, which to a right-thinking man is a term of reproach. My advice, then, is to be wary of the 9 instruction offered by sophists, but not to disregard the considered opinions of philosophers. For whereas sophists hunt wealthy young men, philosophers are prepared to associate with everyone, and they place neither too much nor too little weight on men's fortunes.[4]

One should also not envy those who seek their own advantage at 10 all costs, whether they do so in private or in public life. Bear in mind that whereas the best citizens* are well thought of and assiduous, the bad ones fare badly and have poor reputations. As a result of stealing 11 money from private citizens and embezzling from the community they are less valuable when the state's safety is at stake,* and they are disgracefully far from being physically fit enough for warfare, since they are incapable of exertion. Hunters, however, present themselves and their property in prime condition for the common good of their fellow citizens. Hunters go after wild animals, while the others go 12 after their friends. Moreover, attacking one's friends is universally disparaged, whereas hunting wild animals is universally acclaimed, because if hunters succeed they overcome a foe, and if they fail they win praise not only for striking at enemies of the whole community, but also because the purpose of their expedition was not to harm a man or to satisfy their own greed. Then again, the very attempt makes 13 them better and more intelligent people, for the following reason: they will never capture game unless they put in an extraordinary amount of effort and a great deal of thought and study. Their adversaries 14 are battling for their lives on their home territory, so they fight hard and all the hunter's efforts come to nothing if he does not use considerable determination and a high degree of intelligence to overcome them.

In other words, whereas those politicians who seek their own 15

advantage train to defeat their own side, hunters train to defeat public enemies; whereas this training makes hunters better equipped to meet enemies in battle, the others are made far worse in this respect by their training; for the one group hunting goes together with
16 self-control, for the other with immoral impetuosity; hunters can rise above moral corruption and sordid greed, the others cannot; they speak with elegance, the others with harshness; and as for the gods, there is nothing to check impiety in the one group, while the others are paragons of piety.[5]

17　　There exist old stories about the pleasure the gods find in hunting, whether they are doing it or watching it.[6] It follows that the young men who take up the pursuit I have been recommending are the favourites of the gods, and are also acting with reverent piety, because they think that some god is watching their hunting. These men, if any, are good to their parents and to their community as a whole, to
18 every one of their friends and fellow citizens. And hunting has imbued not just all its male devotees with virtue, but also all the women to whom the goddess has granted this gift, such as Atalanta and Procris.[7]

WAYS AND MEANS

(Poroi)

INTRODUCTION

Modern scholars have at least the benefit of hindsight. Using (or abusing) that advantage, some are pleased to claim that the Greek polis as a form of political community was an evolutionary dead end, doomed to extinction. That was emphatically not how either Xenophon or, yet more tellingly, Aristotle saw it. Xenophon did, once, allow the scope of his pedagogical vision to be enlarged to encompass the whole Persian Empire, but in *Cyropaedia* he was interested more in Persia's moral than in its financial economy, and in how the lessons in leadership embodied in his idealized Cyrus the Great (reigned *c.* 559–530) might be applied to the governance of the Greek city. Elsewhere, like his fellow Socratics, Xenophon measured his ambition to the scale of the polis and its constituent households. And in *Ways and Means* much more obviously than in any other treatise, apart from *How to Be a Good Cavalry Commander*, the polis he had centrally in mind was his own native Athens. Internal references and external indications make it extremely probable that the work was composed around the mid-350s, in direct and immediate consequence of Athens' defeat in a war against some of its major allies within what was left of its Second Sea-League. The temptation is therefore strong to associate the treatise's composition with Xenophon's actual or desired return to Athens towards the end of his life.

'Cities, like households, but to an even greater extent, are often in want of financial resources and in need of more ways of gaining them' (Aristotle, *Politics* 1259a40). Whether or not Aristotle had read the present work, that observation provides the context in which *Ways and Means* should be read within Xenophon's *œuvre*. For it is primarily valuable, not, as are several of the treatises, for Xenophon's views on leadership qualities or any other facets of individual moral virtue, but for how he envisaged practical Athenian 'political economy'. It is in fact the most overtly pragmatic of Xenophon's treatises, more so even than *Cavalry Commander*. As such, it is an oddity, not only within Xenophon's œuvre but in Greek literature as a whole. Whereas *The Estate-manager* fits seamlessly into what the Germans call *Hausvater-literatur*, that is homespun wisdom literature regarding domestic management, *Ways and Means* seeks to operate at the level of 'national' or state economy, that is, to be received as an exercise in political economy rather than domestic science. Whereas the central term of *The Estate-manager* is arguably *epimeleia* (care, concern), which has inescapably moral implications, the analysis and recommendations in *Ways and Means* are offered in a spirit of goal-oriented economic rationality.

In fact, so pragmatic in orientation is *Ways and Means* that it could be read – and perhaps was written – almost as a party-political pamphlet. Athens in the mid-350s was desperately short of public funds, so short indeed that certain forms of pay for public service which were normally distributed out of central funds had to be temporarily suspended. Desperate times demanded desperate measures. In advocating above all a large investment in publicly owned slave labour in the state silver mines, Xenophon was arguing radically against alternative, more conservative and conventional schemes: such as, at one extreme, deep cuts in public expenditure associated with a mild increase in indirect taxation, or, at the other extreme, aggressive overseas imperialism financed initially by hugely increased direct taxation of the very rich.

Its pragmatic orientation, however, does not of course mean that the treatise is value-free. It is noticeable that immediately after the long chapter on slave investment (4) Xenophon ceases to be a narrowly fiscal reformer and puts on again his political theorist hat, aiming to show his readers how to lead the good life of military and other public political service. Moreover, the treatise simply assumes the validity of slave labour, whereas an important part of the first book of Aristotle's *Politics* is given over to an attempted justification of a doctrine of natural slavery against the views of those philosophers or sophists who argued that all slavery, inasmuch as it was based on force rather than

166

rational persuasion, was morally indefensible. Aristotle's unconvincing rejoinder amounted to little more than an endorsement of the standard Greek view according to which all non-Greek 'barbarians' were by their nature morally and intellectually barbaric, and therefore 'naturally' suited for slavery in the Greek world. Xenophon too was presumably looking to the non-Greek periphery (Thrace and Asia Minor were the chief actual sources of slave labour) for the supply of his mine-slaves.

Perhaps it is needless to say, but Xenophon's scheme was not in practice adopted. In the real world of the mid fourth century Athens veered opportunistically between versions of the two extreme solutions to the problems of raising public revenues sketched above. Not that this was at all exceptional: other Greek cities habitually resorted to a variety of expedients that can rarely be dignified with a label other than 'scams'; many such examples are listed, in sometimes hilarious detail, in the second book of the Pseudo-Aristotelian *Oeconomica*. In a historical context like that, Xenophon's *Ways and Means* deserves more credit from us than his contemporaries were willing or able to accord it, as a bold and original intellectual construct.

WAYS AND MEANS

CHAPTER I

My view has always been that a state's political system reflects the characteristics of its leaders. However, it has in the past been claimed by some of the leading politicians in Athens that, although they recognize the principle of equity just as much as anyone else, the poverty of the citizen masses forces their political programme to fall somewhat short of total equity towards the allied cities.[1] I therefore undertook to see if there was a way for the citizens of Athens to sustain themselves from their own resources, which would be the fairest system, because that would, in my opinion, not only provide them with a remedy for their poverty, but also alleviate the mistrust in which they are held in Greece. As soon as I started to look into the project, I was struck by the realization that the land is naturally capable of providing a very good income. In order to demonstrate the truth of this, I shall begin by describing the natural properties of Attica.

In the first place, the plants themselves prove how exceptionally mild the climate is here; I mean, plants that cannot even grow in many parts of the world actually bear fruit here. In the second place, the sea off the coast of Attica is just as profusely productive as the land. Then again, whatever the season, all the good things supplied by the gods begin earlier and end later here than anywhere else.[2] Moreover, the excellence of this land depends not just on things that flourish and decline annually: it also bears good things that last for ever. For instance, there is an inexhaustible supply of stone[3] in it which is turned into wonderful temples, magnificent altars, and most fittingly beautiful statues of the gods, and is much in demand both in Greece and abroad; there is land which is unproductive when cultivated, but which when mined feeds far more people than the equivalent amount of arable land does. The land is shot through with silver – and who can doubt that this is the gods' doing, when not even the tiniest vein of silver ore reaches any of the states that border on Attica by land or sea?[4]

6   It is not unreasonable to hold that Athens was founded at the centre of Greece and therefore of the whole inhabited world,[5] considering that the further away from it one is, the more one encounters severity of cold or heat, and that everyone who undertakes the journey from one end of Greece to the other, by sea or by land, passes Athens, as if it were the pivot of a circle.[6]

7   Even though Attica is not actually surrounded by water, it resembles an island in the sense that anything it needs to import or wants to export is borne to and from the country by the winds from every quarter. This is because Attica lies between two seas, but it is also connected to the mainland, so there is a thriving land trade as well.

8   Moreover, most states have non-Greeks on their borders who make trouble for them, but Athens' neighbours are themselves far away from non-Greek lands.[7]

CHAPTER 2

1   As I said, all these things are due, in my opinion, to the land itself, but in addition to these indigenous advantages, let us start by also taking the interests of the resident aliens into consideration.[1] This group constitutes, I believe, one of the best sources of income Athens has, because they are self-supporting and help their states in a number of ways without receiving public pay for it; in fact, they pay a resident

2   alien's tax.[2] I think their interests would be adequately served if we were to abolish all the rules which apparently deprive resident aliens of status and honour without helping the state in the slightest, and also were to rescind their obligation to form a company of heavy-armed infantry to serve alongside the citizen units. After all, it is very risky for them to leave Athens, and no trivial matter for them to leave their

3   children and households.[3] Besides, it would help us if military service

were undertaken entirely by citizens rather than having citizens, as now, enlist alongside non-Greeks from far-flung places such as Lydia, Phrygia and Syria, where quite a few resident aliens come from.[4] In addition to the advantage gained by abrogating their duty to join the army, it would also be to the state's credit if Athenians were seen to rely on themselves rather than foreigners to fight their battles.

Also, if we granted resident aliens certain privileges, and in particular the right to serve in the cavalry,[5] I think we would make them more loyal and at the same time improve Athens' strength and importance.

Another point is that there are a number of abandoned houses and sites within the city walls, and if the state were to allow those applicants whom they judged suitable to take possession of these sites and build on them, I think this would greatly improve both the numbers and quality of people who wanted to live in Athens.[6]

Then again, if we made the custody of resident aliens an official post, along the lines of the custodians of orphans,[7] and rewarded in some way those who presented the state with the most resident aliens, this is another move that would increase the resident aliens' loyalty; the chances are that it would also make everyone who is currently not enrolled as a citizen of some state want to live in Athens, which would raise its revenues.

CHAPTER 3

I shall now explain why maritime trade is a particularly agreeable and profitable pursuit for Athens. In the first place, of course, there is nowhere that can rival the excellence of the havens it offers shipping, where ships can berth and ride out stormy weather in complete safety.[1] Moreover, in most states traders are more or less compelled to take on a return cargo, because the local currency is unusable beyond the borders of these states. In Athens, however, although it is usual for traders to export goods for which there is a demand in return for the merchandise they imported, they can also export silver instead, if they would rather not take on a return cargo – and this is good business because they will be able to sell the silver anywhere in the world for

3 more than the original purchase price.² Also, if the Controllers of the Peiraeus Emporium were to offer a reward for the fair and rapid resolution of disputes,³ so that the departure of traders was facilitated, this would make Athens much more attractive for traders, and they

4 would come in far greater numbers. It would also be a sound and good idea to give traders and shipowners the right to front seats in the theatre, and occasionally to invite to state banquets the ones whose ships and cargo seem so outstanding that they may be counted as benefactors of Athens. The point is that if they are honoured in these ways the prospect of prestige as well as profit will make them look

5 on us as their friends and flock to Athens.⁴ And obviously imports, exports, transactions, sales, rents and excise duties would increase along with the rise in the number of residents and visitors.

.6 The kinds of increase in revenue I have been discussing need involve no prior expenditure apart from considerate legislation⁵ and attention to detail. However, all the other sources of income that

7 occur to me would, I am sure, require an initial capital fund. Nevertheless, remembering how generous the citizenry was when we went to the assistance of Arcadia during Lysistratus' period of command, and again during Hegesileos' command,⁶ I am reasonably confident that the people of Athens will fund the kinds of projects I have in mind.

8 Also, I am aware how often war-ships are dispatched abroad, fitted out* at considerable expense, when it is unclear whether or not the expedition will be successful, and all that is certain is that those who paid for it will never recover their money in whole or even in part.⁷

9 However, they will never find any return as good as what they can get from investing in the state capital fund: given a return of three obols a day, the return on ten minas is almost a fifth (i.e. the same as the return on financing a ship's voyage), while the return on five

10 minas is a third, and most Athenian citizens will receive a larger return each year than their initial outlay, because their outlay of one mina will yield a return of almost two minas.⁸ What is more, these returns are provided by a state, and a state is held to be the most secure and

11 enduring of human institutions.⁹ I also think that if their names were to be included in the register of eternal benefactors of the state, plenty of non-Athenians would make a contribution, and even some foreign

states, attracted by the register. I would go so far as to expect even some kings, tyrants and satraps to want to share in this bounty.[10]

Once the capital reserve fund is in existence, it would be a sound 12 and good idea to construct extra hostels for shipowners in the vicinity of the harbour (in addition to the ones that already exist), purpose-built places for traders to do their buying and selling, and state-subsidized hostels for visitors. Also, if houses and shops were built in Peiraeus 13 and Athens for retailers, this would not only be to the state's credit, but would also generate a great deal of revenue.

I also think it would be a good idea to investigate the feasibility of 14 state ownership of a merchant marine, as already happens in the case of war-ships; these merchant ships could then be hired out against collateral, on similar terms to those which apply to state property in general.[11] If this proved to be feasible, it would turn out to be another rich source of revenue.

CHAPTER 4

As for the silver mines, it is my opinion that if they were organized 1 properly they would make an enormous amount of money for Athens, leaving aside any other sources of revenue it may have. I should explain what I mean for the sake of any readers who are not aware of the mines' potential, because once you have grasped their potential you will be in a better position to decide what to do with them.

Everyone knows that the mines have been worked for a very long 2 time; at any rate, no one even hazards a guess as to when the enterprise was first undertaken.[1] Yet although the mining and removal of silver ore have been going on for so long, you should consider how small a pile what has been removed so far would make compared to the untouched silver-bearing hills. Nor is it the case that the area with 3 deposits of silver is contracting: further reaches of it are constantly being discovered.

Now, for a while[2] huge numbers of men were to be found in the mines, and during that period no one was ever without work; in fact, there was always more work than there were workers. And even now, 4 if someone owns slaves who work in the mines, he never decreases the size of his work-force, but always adds as many men to it as he possibly can. The reason for this, I suppose, is that the quantity of the precious metal that is discovered is directly proportionate to the size of the work-force engaged in digging and searching for silver ore. The upshot of this is that it is the only work I know of where no one is envious of new entrepreneurs.[3]

5   Here is another point. Whereas farm-owners can always tell you the right number of teams of oxen and men to work their land, and count themselves worse off if they gain more than this optimum number, all you ever hear from people involved in the silver mines 6 is that they are short of workers.[4] The point is that mining is not like working with bronze or iron, for instance, where if there is a large number of smiths their products become cheap and the smiths are forced out of business. Likewise, when grain or wine is plentiful, the price of the crops falls, working the land becomes unprofitable and in the end large numbers of farmers abandon their work and become traders or retailers or money-lenders instead. However, the more silver ore that is discovered and the more silver there is as a result, the 7 more people turn to this line of work.[5] I mean, when someone has enough furniture for his house he stops buying it there and then, but no one has ever had so much silver that he did not feel the need for more; no, some people with silver in vast quantities derive as much pleasure from *burying* the amount that is surplus to their requirements as they do from putting the silver to use![6]

8   Another point is that times of national prosperity are accompanied by a strong demand for silver. Men want to spend money on fine arms and armour, good horses, and impressive houses and fittings; 9 women indulge in expensive clothes and golden jewellery. At the same time, however, in times of national crisis, brought on by crop failure or war, silver coin is even more in demand, to pay for supplies and mercenaries, given that the land is being left unfarmed.

10   Then again, while I do not wish to contradict the claim that gold is just as useful as silver, I do know that when gold is being discovered in large quantities, its value goes down, but it pushes up the value of silver.[7]

11   Now, my purpose in explaining all this is to encourage us to channel

as large a work-force as possible towards the silver mines and make arrangements for them, confident in the knowledge that the ore will never give out and that silver will never lose its value. In actual fact, 12 I think the state has anticipated me in this plan, because it permits any foreigner who wants to make mining his business to do so on the same conditions as citizens.[8]

I want to make my position on the subject of the state allowance 13 even clearer than I have so far. In order to do so, I shall now go on to describe how the mining of silver should be organized for Athens to derive the maximum benefit. I do not expect what I am about to say to occasion any astonishment, as if I had solved a difficult problem, because I will partly be doing no more than pointing out what is still plain for all of us to see even today,[9] and we have also all heard that in the past things were no different. However, what may very well 14 be surprising is that the state just watches all the private individuals who make money from the mines and does not copy them.

For instance, those of us who have bothered to pay attention to these matters have of course known for a long time by hearsay that Nicias the son of Niceratus once had 1,000 of his slaves working in the mines, and that he hired these men out to Sosias the Thracian for an obol each a day, after deductions, with any losses in the work-force to be made up by Sosias. Then there were Hipponicus,[10] whose 600 15 slaves, hired out on the same terms, brought him a clear mina a day, and Philemonides with 300 slaves bringing him half a mina a day. I imagine there were others too, each capable of realizing his own level of profit. But why should I bring up instances from the past? Even 16 today there are plenty of men in the mines hired out in the same way. If my proposals were put into practice, the only novelty would be 17 that the state would imitate those private individuals who have arranged things so that their ownership of slaves is a permanent source of income for themselves, and would acquire state-owned slaves, up to the level of three for each Athenian citizen.[11]

Is this plan viable? Every aspect of it should be examined separately 18 to decide whether or not it is. Taking first the cost of the slaves, it is perfectly clear that public funding is a far more realistic proposition than raising that kind of money from private citizens. And it would

be a simple matter for the Council to announce that people are
19 welcome to bring slaves for it to buy. Once the slaves have been
bought, why should anyone be more reluctant to hire from the state
rather than from private individuals, assuming that the conditions of
hire are the same? After all, people hire sanctuaries and houses from
the state, and buy the rights to levy taxes from it.

20 The slaves the state now owns can be insured by obtaining guarantees
from the people who hire them, just as the state does from those who
buy the rights to levy taxes. In actual fact, though, it is easier for a
21 tax-farmer to cheat than it is for a slave-hirer. I mean, the question
in the case of public money is how do you catch someone in the act
of exporting it, when it is indistinguishable from private money? But
the question in the case of slaves is how is anyone going to steal them,
when they have been branded with the official public tattoo and when
there is a stipulated penalty for anyone selling or exporting them?[12]

So far, then, there seems to be nothing to prevent Athens owning
22 and keeping slaves. But suppose someone wonders where all the hirers
are going to come from, to cope with the number of labourers. This
is not a problem, however. One need only bear in mind, first, that a
good proportion of those who are already established in the mines
are so well off that they will hire state-owned slaves to supplement
their own work-force; second, that a good proportion of the labourers
in the mines are getting on in age; and, third, that there are plenty of
people, from both Athens and abroad, who may not have the physical
strength to be either willing or able to do this kind of work themselves,
but who would be glad to make a living working in an administrative
capacity with their minds.[13]

23 Suppose, however, that the initial work-force consisted of 1,200
slaves. There can hardly be any doubt that within five or six years,
on the basis of just the revenue from this initial work-force, the
number would grow to at least 6,000. Then the annual income derived
from a work-force this size, assuming that each slave brings in a clear
24 obol a day, is sixty talents a year. If twenty talents of this are spent on
further slaves, the state will already have forty talents available for
other important projects. And once there are 10,000 men in all in the
work-force, they will generate an income of 100 talents.

In actual fact, though, the state will receive far more than that, as 25 any of my readers who still remember how much slaves cost before the Deceleian affair will verify.[14] Further evidence comes from the fact that throughout the period of the mines' existence countless thousands of men have worked in them, and yet there is no difference between the mines today and in the past, as we can tell from our ancestors' records. The whole current situation of the mines suggests 26 that the work will always require more slaves than can be found there at any given time, since however deep or far underground the mining operations extend, there appears to be no end to the silver;[15] and it is 27 just as possible to open new seams nowadays as it always was, so no one can say for sure whether there is more ore in the areas that have already been opened up or in those that have yet to be mined.

Why, then, it might be asked, are fewer slaves employed at present 28 on opening new seams than in former times? Because the people with an interest in the mines today have less money, since work has only recently restarted there.[16] Opening a new seam is, after all, highly risky: if you strike a good seam, you can make a fortune, but otherwise 29 you can lose all the money you have invested in the operation. So people nowadays are rather reluctant to take this risk. However, here 30 again I think I can offer some advice which will make the business of opening new seams entirely risk-free. There are, of course, ten Athenian tribes. If the state were to give each tribe the same number of slaves, and if they were to pool their fortunes as they went about opening new seams, it would take only a single successful strike for them all to profit, and if two, three, four or five tribes found rich 31 seams, the profits from these operations would obviously be even greater. Past experience shows that in all probability they would not all fail to make a lucky strike.

Private individuals can of course combine in this way too – that is, 32 they can pool their fortunes to reduce the risks – but there is no need to worry about either the state-run operation interfering with the private concerns or vice versa. No, just as every contingent that joins an alliance strengthens and is strengthened by all the others, so the more people who make mining their business, the more of value they will discover and extract.

33 So much, then, for the ways I suggest Athens' affairs should be organized for there to be sufficient money in the public treasury to
34 pay every Athenian his allowance. As a result of calculating the huge capital sum necessary to finance all these measures, some people might doubt whether enough money could ever be raised, but in fact even
35 so they should not lose heart. After all, it is not the case that these measures are necessarily advantageous only if they are implemented in their totality all at once. No, there will be instant benefit however
36 many houses are constructed, ships built or slaves bought. In fact, there is a sense in which it will be better to implement them step by step rather than all at once: if a whole lot of us go ahead and build houses at the same time, we will end up paying more for lower-quality products than we would on a gradual approach, and if we go in search of huge numbers of slaves we will be forced to buy inferior men at
37 inflated prices. If we let our resources dictate the pace at which we go about the business, however, we can repeat* those aspects of our
38 plans which were well conceived and avoid any mistakes. Besides, if everything happened at once it would be up to us to cover all the costs, whereas if we put some things in motion and postpone the rest for a later date, the revenue generated would contribute towards
39 the necessary expenditure. Then again, the chief worry everyone seems to have is probably the prospect of the mines becoming over-crowded if the state acquires too many slaves, but we can eliminate this worry by not putting more men in each year than the work itself demands.[17]

40 So it seems to me that the least troublesome way of implementing these measures is also the best way. However, if you think that the expenses of the recent war[18] have completely drained the state's resources, what you should do is make sure that the administration of the state in the year to come is covered by the amount of money raised by the taxes that were levied before the end of the war, and then invest the surplus so as to maximize your revenues – the surplus coming from the fact that there is peace, from looking after the resident aliens and the traders, from the expansion of import-export business now that more people can be involved in it, and from increased excise duties and market rents.[19]

Another fear might be that these measures would be nullified in 41 the event of war. It should be borne in mind, however, that with these measures in place a war would be much more frightening for the aggressors than for Athens. After all, could there be a more useful 42 asset in wartime than men? There would be enough of them to man a sizeable state-funded fleet, and a large well-tended land army too would make life difficult for the enemy.[20]

Besides, on my evaluation, it would be possible to keep the mines 43 open even in wartime. In the vicinity of the mines there are two strongholds about sixty stades apart: one at Anaphlystus to the south, and the other at Thoricus to the north. If there were a third fortress 44 halfway between these two at the highest point of Besa, the mines would be the focus of all the strongholds, and at the first hint of enemy activity no one would have far to retreat to safety. If the enemy came 45 in some force, they would obviously make off with any grain or wine or sheep they found out in the open, but silver ore would do them as little good as stones, so why would they seize it?

Moreover, how could the enemy launch a strike against the mines? 46 Megara is the enemy city nearest to the silver mines, of course, and it is rather more than 500 stades away; Thebes is the next closest, and it is rather more than 600 stades away. Now, an expeditionary force 47 coming from somewhere around there to attack the mines will have to pass Athens. A small force will probably be wiped out by our cavalry and patrols, and if they come in strength they will have left their own property unprotected, which will be problematic for them, because by the time they reach the mines Athens will be considerably closer to their home towns than they will be. Besides, even if they 48 do come, how will they be able to stay, given their lack of supplies? Sending a detachment off in search of food would endanger the object of the whole enterprise, let alone the foragers themselves, while if they all went off foraging they would have to end the siege and become the besieged instead.[21]

Now, Athens' allowance system will not find its finances improved 49 solely by the money raised by hiring out slaves; given the concentration of men in the vicinity of the mines a great deal of revenue will also be generated from the market there, from the state-owned houses in

50 the region, from the kilns[22] and so on and so forth. it would even become a densely populated community in its own right, if the measures I have suggested are implemented, and plots there would become as valuable to its owners as plots in and about Athens.[23]

51 So if my proposals are put into effect, I agree* that the state will become not only financially better off, but also more obedient, more

52 disciplined and militarily more effective.[24] After all, the people assigned to take exercise will train far more assiduously in the gymnasia once they receive a better* allowance for food than they do when they are being trained up for the torch races; and the units assigned to garrison duty, to the light infantry and to patrolling the countryside, will do all these jobs with more enthusiasm if in return they receive the maintenance due to each of these tasks.[25]

CHAPTER 5

1 There can hardly be any doubt that peace is a prerequisite for all the sources of revenue to realize their full potential. Surely, then, it is worth setting up a committee of Custodians of the Peace.[1] With these officers duly elected, Athens would become more attractive and more

2 frequently* visited by people from all over the world. Some people might think that Athens would pay for constant peace with loss of influence, prestige and fame in Greece, but in my opinion this is another distorted way of looking at things.* After all, it goes without saying that the longer the period of unbroken peace a state enjoys, the better off it is held to be.[2] And Athens is better placed to grow

3 during peacetime than any other state in the world. With the city at peace, it will be in demand by everyone – shipowners and traders to start with. And what about those with a surplus of grain, wine, oil or sheep? What about people with a good head for business and money

4 as well? Artisans, sophists and philosophers, poets and the producers of their plays, spectators and audiences who appreciate works of quality, whether sacred or secular?[3] Suppose you wanted to sell or buy a lot of goods in a short space of time: what better place could you find to do so than Athens?

Even if no one takes exception to this, it still remains the case that ₅ there are people who think it will take war rather than peace for Athens to regain its position of dominance, which is what they want to see happen. These people should first consider the Persian Wars and ask themselves whether we gained the leadership of the fleet and our position as treasurers of the Greek confederacy by force or by helping Greece.[4] Secondly, after Athens had been deprived of its ₆ rulership for having supposedly wielded power with excessive brutality, was it not only when we stopped perverting the course of justice that we had the leadership of the fleet restored to us by the Aegean islanders, of their own free will?[5] Thirdly, is it not the case that the ₇ Thebans chose Athenian leadership because they had been well served by Athens?[6] Fourthly, did we force the Spartans to allow us to dispose of the leadership as we wanted? No, they let us do so because they had been well treated by us.[7]

It seems to me that the current situation of chaos in Greece presents ₈ us with an ideal opportunity for recovering our control[8] over the Greeks easily, safely and cheaply. We could try to reconcile the warring states with one another and to make peace between the factions tearing various states apart. Also, if you make it clear that your concern is to ₉ regain for the temple at Delphi its lost autonomy and that you intend to do so by sending delegations everywhere in Greece rather than by military means, I for one would not be surprised if you found enough solidarity among the Greeks for them to enter into solemn treaties with one another and to band together against any nation that might try to gain control of the temple once it has been abandoned by the Phocians.[9] And if you make it clear that what you want to see is a ₁₀ complete end to war, on land and sea, I for one think that the safety of Athens would feature strongly in everyone's prayers,[10] second only to that of their own homelands.

It may be thought, however, that Athens profits more by war than ₁₁ by peace. Personally, I cannot think of a better way to assess whether or not this is true than by reviewing Athens' past history once again and seeing how things turned out. Anyone who does this will find ₁₂ that in times past the state's funds were enormously increased in times of peace and completely drained in times of war. This review will

also make him realize that things are no different today – that, thanks to the war, a number of sources of revenue dried up, while any money that did come in was used up on miscellaneous projects, and that only the end of the war at sea has stimulated growth of revenue and made it possible for the people of Athens to spend money on projects of
13 their own choice.[11] 'What about an unprovoked assault on our state?' I might be asked. 'Are you saying we should remain at peace even in the face of aggression?' 'No,' I would reply, 'but I am saying that a policy of not initiating unjust wars against others would enable us to punish our enemies far more quickly, because they would not find anyone to come and support their cause.'[12]

CHAPTER 6

1 Now, since none of my proposals is impossible or even hard to put into practice, since by doing so we will improve our relations with the rest of Greece, live in greater security and gain a more glorious reputation, since the general populace of Athens will never go short of subsistence and the wealthy members of society will no longer have to spend money to support the war effort, since a generous surplus will enable us to celebrate our festivals on an even more magnificent scale than we do now, to repair our temples, rebuild the walls and dockyards, and return our priests, Council, functionaries and cavalry to the traditional ways of doing things,[1] what could be wrong with setting this programme in motion straight away, in order
2 to see prosperity and security come to the state in our time? If you citizens of Athens were to decide to carry out my proposals, I for my part would advise you to send emissaries to Dodona and Delphi to ask the gods[2] whether the state would, both now and in the future,
3 profit and benefit by being organized along these lines. If the measures meet with their approval, we should in my opinion next ask which of the gods should be propitiated to ensure that we carry out these measures in the most expedient and advantageous manner. Only when they have told us the names of the appropriate gods and we have obtained good omens from our sacrifices to them should we set the

programme in motion. For if we act with the help of the god it is likely that all our actions will promote the profit and advantage of the state.[3]

NOTES

HIERO THE TYRANT

CHAPTER I

1. *festivals . . . at once*: This applies especially to the four major 'panhellenic' festivals: the Olympics, the Pythian Games (held at Delphi), the Isthmian Games (at the Isthmus of Corinth) and the Nemean Games (at Nemea in the north-east Peloponnese). Despite what follows, Dionysius I (see Introduction) did make an enormous personal splash at the Olympics of either 388 or 384.

2. *praise . . . criticism*: A tyrant might go to great lengths to secure a favourable 'press', as the real Hiero did by patronizing Pindar and Bacchylides as well as Simonides. See Pindar's *Pythian* I and II, in C. M. Bowra's Penguin *The Odes of Pindar* (1969); and Bacchylides *Ode* V. Simonides' surviving work is most conveniently read in D. A. Campbell's *Greek Lyric* III (Loeb Classical Library, 1991).

3. *flattery*: An entire homiletic literature grew up around the topic of *kolakeia*, 'flattery': see, e.g., Theophrastus' *Characters* II and Plutarch's 'How to distinguish a flatterer from a friend', in I. Kidd and R. Waterfield's Penguin *Plutarch Essays* (1992), pp. 61–112.

4. *find particularly attractive*: A married Greek man, unlike a married Greek woman, could indulge his sexual appetites outside marriage without necessarily incurring even social disapproval. Two of the outlets available at least to wealthier men were slave girls (1.28) and – far more prestigious – free, adolescent boys (1.29–38); note that our term 'pederasty' comes from the Greek *paiderastia*, desire for boys: see Dover, *Greek Homosexuality*. A large part of the humour in the plot of Aristophanes' *Lysistrata* depends on the fantasy that Greek husbands would and could look only to their wives for sexual satisfaction.

CHAPTER 2

1. *savouries*: The Greek diet was as a whole frugal – the Persians, according to Herodotus (*The Histories*, trans. A. de Sélincourt, rev. edn., 1996, 1.133), 'say that the Greeks leave the table hungry'. But Greek Sicily was famous for its gourmandizing, and for its cooks – the oldest European cookbook was composed by one Archestratus, a younger contemporary of Xenophon. Special side-dishes on top of the basic cereals (so basic indeed that *sitos* meant both grain and 'food' in general), pulses and fruits were called collectively *opsa*, translated here as 'savouries'; meat was rarely eaten, and even fish could count as a luxury. See A. Dalby, *Siren Feasts: A Study of Food and Gastronomy in Greece* (Routledge, 1996).

2. *reward your friends*: This was a standard tenet of Greek, pre-Christian ethics, though difficulties of application arose when it was not clear who one's (true) friends were, or when one's friends were themselves in conflict with each other. The sociological and theological dimensions of such difficulties were thoroughly aired in Greek tragedy, the philosophical in Platonic dialectic. See D. Konstan, *Friendship in the Classical World* (Cambridge University Press, 1997). Xenophon, characteristically, assumes the validity of the tenet but does not dig deep.

3. *armed escort . . . at all times*: It was taken as a mark of Greek civilization that – apart from some 'backward' exceptions – citizens of Greek communities no longer carried arms: see Thucydides 1.6 (*History of the Peloponnesian War*).

4. *protect himself there more than anywhere else*: The precautions allegedly taken by Dionysius I were elaborate in the extreme (only his daughters were allowed to shave him, or rather singe him with hot coals, etc.), but the evidence is largely anecdotal.

5. *war . . . have explained*: The paradigmatic instance is the advice of Thrasybulus, tyrant of Miletus, to Periander, tyrant of Corinth, supposedly *c.* 600, to cut off the tallest ears of wheat, that is, murder 'all the people in the city who were outstanding in influence or ability' (Herodotus, *The Histories* 5.92f–g). Xenophon's use of 'war' (also 4.11) is deliberately extreme.

CHAPTER 3

1. *any setbacks*: For the thought see Xenophon's *Cyropaedia* 1.6.24.

2. *remains inviolate*: The fact that the rape of a wife was considered a less heinous offence than her seduction (and in Athenian law might receive a

lesser penalty) is baffling and repugnant to us, but was a direct reflection of the Greek regime of patriarchy according to which the wife's interests and needs were safeguarded only in so far as they directly affected those of her 'lord and master'. The husband stood to lose more face by being consensually cuckolded than by failing to protect his wife from sexual violation by a man unknown to her (or him). Notice that at 3.7 the affection of wives for husbands is not necessarily reciprocated.

CHAPTER 4

1. *violent death*: This remarkably graphic image brings to the surface the underlying tension in Greek society between slave owners and slaves. Not that Greek slave owners typically lived in constant dread of insurrection and murder, as those in the United States Old South appear regularly to have done; but the murder of a master (or mistress) by a slave was by no means unknown (see 10.4) – whereas collective insurrection was almost unheard of, except in Sparta, where the Helots were not barbarian chattel slaves but a locally enslaved Greek people all too conscious of the birthright of freedom and self-rule the Spartans systematically denied them (see *Agesilaus*, chapter 1 note 6).

2. *are polluted*: Ritual pollution (*miasma*) could be incurred in several ways, but murder ranked high up the scale. The Spartans, with brutal legalism, formally declared the Helots to be enemies, outside the protection of laws against murder, so that Spartans who killed Helots would be cleansed in advance of the taint of blood guilt.

3. *statues . . . their sanctuaries*: The point is a somewhat rhetorical one, but Xenophon's Athens did set up statues of the so-called Tyrannicides Harmodius and Aristogeiton. They were displayed in the Agora or civic centre, which though not itself a religious sanctuary did contain religious shrines and was barred to certain types of convicted criminals.

4. *hates losing to his rivals*: For this motif, compare Alexander the Great's unwillingness to compete against anyone but kings: Plutarch, *Alexander* 4.5; *Moralia* 179d, 331b.

5. *a person's perceived needs*: This is a Socratic insight that Xenophon repeats elsewhere (especially *The Estate-manager* 1–2). According to ordinary Greek perceptions, wealth meant above all not having to work for one's living.

6. *steals from temples*: The crime of *hierosulia*, theft from sanctuaries or temples, was always a capital offence, since it was regarded as theft of a god's or hero's property; other types of theft might attract the death penalty depending on circumstances.

CHAPTER 6

1. *companions wanted*: The *symposium* or private drinking-party was a sophist-icated refinement of Greek upper-class life with its own developed code of practices. It was often associated with pederasty (see chapter 1 note 4). Sometimes, no doubt, the wine-assisted conversation attained a certain philo-sophical elevation, but *The Dinner-party* of Xenophon (see Penguin *Conver-sations of Socrates*, pp. 227–67), like Plato's more famous *Symposium*, were essentially literary-intellectual exercises.

2. *sleep . . . a trap*: Contrast the more relaxed attitude to sleep of 'Simonides' (1.6).

3. *slaves free*: Tyrants had a reputation for freeing slaves – either private slaves belonging to their opponents or communally owned slaves whose personal loyalty to themselves they wished to secure: see e.g. *A History of My Times* 7.3.8 (where the Penguin translation should read 'a man who not only liberated slaves but made them citizens' – a reference to the unusually democratic tyrant of Sicyon, Euphron).

4. *by fears*: Cf. *Cyropaedia* 3.1.27.

5. *harvest-time*: Most Greek farmers were more or less self-sufficient peasant agriculturalists most of the year, but extra labour – from one's neighbours on a reciprocal basis, or from hired free workers or slave gangs – might regularly be needed at any of the three main harvests: wheat and barley in May–June, vintage in July–August, olives in January–February.

CHAPTER 7

1. *regarded as men and not just as human beings*: For the sentiment cf. *Cyropaedia* 1.6.25. The real Simonides was of course a professional acclaimer or praise-singer. Note how the Greeks implicitly – and explicitly – ranked men in the gender sense above women.

CHAPTER 8

1. *social equality*: The original text is uncertain here – the present translation follows the manuscript that gives the noun *isotimia* in the genitive case, making this the earliest known attestation of a word meaning literally 'equality of honour or respect' (*time*). Greek culture generally, but more especially democratic Greek culture, was broadly egalitarian in spirit, despite obvious socio-economic inequalities, and the gap between a tyrant and his subjects violated that ethos.

CHAPTER 9

1. *the ruler*: The word translated 'the ruler', *archon*, could refer either to a sole ruler such as Hiero, or to an appointed official in a republican city such as the board of ten annual archons chosen by lot at Athens. The following reference to 'impresarios' (*choregoi*) could be particularly Athenian, since the choregic system was employed for the tribal competition in dithyramb at the annual Great Dionysia festival (see also note 5); but see next note.

2. *tribes . . . regiments . . . division*: 'Tribes' (*phulai*), not to be confused with the social units of some contemporary peoples, were an almost universal feature of Greek civic organization, in both peace and war; but the words Xenophon uses for 'regiments' (*morai*) and 'divisions' (*lochoi*) would seem to be specifically Spartan. Xenophon seems to be drawing here on his knowledge of both his native Athens and his adopted Sparta.

3. *farming*: For praise of husbandry in other Xenophontic works, see *The Estate-manager*, chapter 5 and *Memoirs of Socrates* 2.1.19, 3.4.7–12, 4.5.10.

4. *promote it and bring it about*: There may be an implicit self-reference here to the sorts of innovations Xenophon suggests in *Ways and Means*.

5. *horse-races . . . choral competitions*: Horse-racing was the sport of kings, or at least the Greek super-rich – see Introduction to *On Horsemanship*; and chapter 11 note 1 below. Most successful athletes seem to have come from well-to-do backgrounds, but instances of states sponsoring poor but talented competitors became increasingly common. Choral competitions, at Athens anyhow, were financed by *choregoi* – besides the tribal competition in dithyramb mentioned in note 1 above, these wealthy impresarios, who were performing a compulsory public service or 'liturgy', also financed choruses in tragedy, satyr-drama and comedy.

CHAPTER 10

1. *are satisfied*: Control is the leitmotiv of *On Horsemanship*, and an important theme in other treatises.

2. *than these*: Mercenaries, though by no means unknown in the early fifth century, were a distinctive phenomenon of Xenophon's day – this is one among several instances of 'presentism' in this dialogue, the dramatic date of which is *c*. 470. See Cartledge, *Agesilaos*, chapter 15. Xenophon himself had of course been a mercenary (see main Introduction), but his − or ostensibly Simonides' − suggestion that they might be used as a kind of police force, in country as well as town (10.4−5), went well beyond the actual practice of contemporary Greece where police forces in our sense were unknown. See W. Nippel, *Public Order in Ancient Rome* (Cambridge University Press, 1995). Perhaps here, as in *The Persian Expedition*, he was attempting to blur somewhat the stigma under which mercenary service undoubtedly laboured − not least because of its association with tyranny.

CHAPTER 11

1. *any victory . . . you preside*: For the exploitation of success in chariot-racing the *locus classicus* was Alcibiades in 415: see Introduction to *On Horsemanship*. The super-rich owners (see *Agesilaus* chapter 9 note 5) and breeders did not actually drive the chariot-teams themselves in competition, which is how women chariot and race-horse owners came to be the only women capable of winning an Olympic victory − see *Agesilaus* chapter 9 note 2.

2. *public tributes*: Hiero did actually win a chariot victory at Delphi in the Pythian Games (see chapter 1 note 1); so too did his brother Polyzalus, a lasting memorial of which is the famous bronze statue, originally part of a group, known as *The Delphi Charioteer*, still to be seen in something like its original splendour in the Delphi Museum.

3. *their advances*: There may be a conscious echo here of the scenario in Plato's *Symposium*, where Socrates, although an older man, becomes counter-culturally the object of younger men's *eros* (passionate desire) and pursuit (most famously and amusingly by Alcibiades), but not of course for his looks (he was notoriously ugly) but rather for the excellence of his moral character and teaching. Something similar is in play at *Memoirs of Socrates* 3.11. On pederasty, see also chapter 1 note 4.

4. *your life*: In other words, Hiero could cease to be tyrannical and become instead a legitimate monarch not entirely unreminiscent of Xenophon's Agesilaus.

AGESILAUS

CHAPTER I

1. *descent from Heracles*: A Spartan king was technically 'the seed of the demigod son of Zeus', i.e. Heracles (Thucydides, *History* 5.16.2); that is, the two Spartan kings, from the two royal houses of the Agiads and the Eurypontids, mythically claimed descent ultimately from Zeus via Heracles and more immediately from Agis and Eurypon, who were themselves allegedly descended from Heracles' twin great–great–great–grandsons Eurysthenes and Procles. For versions of the royal pedigrees see Herodotus 7.204 (Agiads) and 8.131.2 (Eurypontids), with Cartledge, *Sparta and Lakonia* (Routledge, 1979), Appendix 3. Agesilaus belonged to the 'junior' Eurypontid line.

2. *kingship . . . continuous existence*: This is a rare instance of Sparta's mode of government being referred to, encomiastically, as a kingship (*basileia*). Actually, there were two kings, and traditionally the two royal houses were at loggerheads (Herodotus 6.52), although, as in the case of Agesilaus and Agesipolis, some mutual appreciation was possible: see Xenophon, *A History of My Times* 5.3.20. Besides, the kings did not rule by themselves, but at most influenced the decisions taken formally by the people in assembly, mediated by the *Gerousia* or Senate, and executed by the board of five Ephors (see note 33 below).

3. *their king*: This is a highly elliptical account of a complex and – to us – obscure process, involving accusations of Leotychidas' alleged bastardy and dynastic machinations by Agesilaus' one-time pederastic lover Lysander. More, but by no means the whole story, may be found in *A History of My Times* 3.3.1–4; even more, but by no means entirely reliably, in Plutarch's *Agesilaus* 3–4 (in Penguin Plutarch, *Age of Alexander*, pp. 26–8).

4. *highest office*: For 'office' Xenophon uses *geras*, literally 'honour', equivalent to the more usual *time*. Herodotus 6.56–60 lists the *gerea*, 'privileges', hereditarily accorded to the kings of Sparta. See also chapter 5 note 1.

5. *his deeds*: The verb Xenophon uses for 'achieved', *diaprattesthai* (cf. 1.10, 8.2), had the twofold connotation of 'achieving' and 'getting done' (by others, if need be). In stressing Agesilaus' deeds, Xenophon is not merely expressing a biographer's truism but contrasting his deeds both with his words – Spartans were brought up to be so sparing of words that being 'laconic' is so named after that national characteristic – and with his image (see 11.7 for this point, attributed to Agesilaus himself).

6. *2,000 ex-Helots*: 'Ex-Helots' translates the Spartan technical term *Neodamodeis*, literally 'newly made members of the *damos*', that is Helots who had been given their freedom. Such manumission could be conferred only by the Spartan assembly, since the Helots were collectively owned slaves, or rather a sort of state-serfs. They were also Greeks, the majority of them living in Messenia rather than Laconia, and on several occasions they revolted en masse: see e.g. Thucydides 1.101 (460s) and chapter 2 note 26 below (370/369). *Neodamodeis* are first heard of in the 420s, and were used exclusively for military purposes, both as phalanx-fighters and on territorial guard duty; they seem to have been one of Sparta's responses to the dramatic fall in the number of Spartan citizen hoplites. If *A History of My Times* 3.3.6 is to be believed, even manumitted Helots were not always reliably loyal.

7. *the Greeks*: Cf. *A History of My Times* 3.4.2; the year is 396. It is an essential part of Xenophon's encomiastic purpose to represent Agesilaus as a consistent 'panhellenist' or even Persian-hater (see 7.7).

8. *the Persian . . . to Asia*: 'The Persian' here stands for the Persian empire as incarnated in the person of Great King Xerxes who had led the massive invasion of the Greek mainland in 480 described by Herodotus; 'Asia' was Greek shorthand for the Persian empire, which at its peak extended from the Aegean to the Punjab (see Cawkwell's Introduction to the Penguin *Persian Expedition*). Agesilaus in response represented himself none too modestly as a second Agamemnon conducting a second Trojan War (*A History of My Times* 3.4.3–4, 3.5.5).

9. *cost of the war . . . not the Greeks*: For the success of Agesilaus' plundering strategy (one of the few militarily successful strategies he employed), see 1.16, 34. Sparta's attention to military detail was such that there was even an office of the *laphuropolai* or 'booty-sellers' (see 1.18).

10. *to people's minds*: Allusive reference to Xenophon's own ideological 'panhellenism', on which 'fashionable and sentimental folly' see Cawkwell's Introduction to *A History of My Times*, pp. 39–41.

11. *his achievements*: Of 396–394, related at greater length in *A History of My Times*.

12. *to him*: Xenophon had clashed personally with Tissaphernes, satrap or viceroy of much of the westernmost part of the Persian empire, in 401. Technically, Tissaphernes was satrap of Lydia, with his capital at Sardis and personal domain further south in Caria. The Greek cities of Ionia such as Miletus and Ephesus fell under his control. Xenophon was only too pleased to dwell on his sacrilege.

13. *the bargain*: 'Three months' was a realistic figure given the size of the Persian empire and the difficulty of communications: see Cawkwell's Introduction to *Persian Expedition*.

14. *friendship . . . large numbers of people*: Elsewhere (e.g. *A History of My Times*

4.1.40), but not in an encomium (e.g. 11.3), Xenophon might allow a hint that Agesilaus' interpretation of the duties of friendship transgressed the bounds of justice.

15. *prisoners-of-war . . . punished*: See 7.6.

16. *taken off somewhere*: This is one of those relatively rare references in Greek literature to slave dealing, which, although – or because – it was indispensable to a slave-based society, was widely censured as a dirty business.

17. *Pharnabazus . . . Phrygia*: Pharnabazus was the other western Asiatic satrap besides Tissaphernes (1.10 and note 12), based in Dascylium in Hellespontine Phrygia. In *A History of My Times* 4.1.29–41 Xenophon gives a version of a formal interview between Pharnabazus and Agesilaus, from which Xenophon allows Pharnabazus (in contrast to his treatment of Tissaphernes) to come off by no means badly.

18. *die in one's place*: Xenophon's sarcasm is transparent, as befits a proud (former) cavalryman; compare his disparaging remarks on the Spartan cavalry of 371, where a similar separation between owner and rider was in operation (*A History of My Times* 6.4.11).

19. *effective unit*: Whether he was aware of it or not, Agesilaus was in this following the Persians' own mode of recruitment.

20. *the following spring*: Spring 395. 1.25–8 to some extent repeats, or is repeated by (depending on which one thinks was written first), *A History of My Times* 3.4.16–19.

21. *light infantry units*: 'Light infantry' translates *peltastai*, named after their *pelte* or light wickerwork shield (for the heavy hoplite shield see chapter 2 note 10). These were a Thracian type of warrior in origin, more mobile than hoplite phalangites, and introduced to Greek warfare ever more centrally during the Peloponnesian War; the most spectacular *peltast* success was achieved by mercenary *peltasts* under the command of the Athenian Iphicrates in 390 at Lechaeum near Corinth, where they destroyed most of a Spartan hoplite regiment (*A History of My Times* 4.5.7–18).

22. *target pillar*: For the desirability of offering prizes as a stimulus to competitive excellence, compare *Hiero* 9.3–4.

23. *workshop of war*: The same striking phrase is used at *A History of My Times* 3.4.17 (translated as 'one great armament factory'), and was quoted by Scipio in Polybius 10.20.7.

24. *Artemis*: The patron deity of Ephesus, to whom was soon to be dedicated a temple that would be ranked among the Seven Wonders of the ancient world. See also *On Hunting*, chapter 1 note 1.

25. *showing reverence . . . good hopes*: Here, in a nutshell, we find Xenophon's personal credo.

26. *right time to join battle, if possible*: Cf. *Cavalry Commander* 8.10–11. Great emphasis is placed by Xenophon on hitting the *kairos*, or right time, a practical principle that was to be elevated into a moral virtue by Stoic philosophical theory.

27. *a sacrifice*: Offering a pre-battle sacrifice was a universal Greek custom, but the Spartans typically practised it with unusual assiduity and respect: one commander delayed an assault on a town for four days because of a succession of unfavourable sacrifices (*A History of My Times* 3.1.17).

28. *enemy's property*: Xenophon's account here of the Battle of Sardis, Summer 395, differs slightly from that in *A History of My Times* 3.4.20–24, but irreconcilably from that given in Diodorus 14.80, which is clearly derived ultimately from the near-contemporary 'Oxyrhynchus Historian' (identity uncertain, perhaps the Athenian Cratippus) chapters 11–12: see Cawkwell's Appendix to *A History of My Times*, pp. 405–6.

29. *liberators . . . of arms*: Liberation propaganda was deeply embedded in official Spartan rhetoric, from the Persian Wars through the Peloponnesian War to the present Asiatic campaign of Agesilaus; the reality of the Spartan empire for those Greeks and non-Greeks supposedly liberated from Athens' and Persia's rule was rather different.

30. *the eye*: Xenophon perpetrates the standard Greek misunderstanding of the Persian social-political ritual of *proskunesis*, the kowtow, as an act of religious worship. Treating a man as a god was conventionally deemed by the Greeks an act of gross *hybris*, yet Lysander of Sparta appears to have received divine worship in his lifetime (d. 395) from his fanatical oligarchic supporters on the island of Samos. Lysander's, however, is the only possible such case before the lifetime worship of Alexander the Great.

31. *his booty*: At *A History of My Times* 4.3.21 Xenophon reports the figure dedicated as 'no less than 100 talents'. (A fortune of three to four talents made a contemporary Athenian the equivalent of a millionaire.) Dedications like this made Apollo's sanctuary at Delphi an unparalleled treasure house – and a too tempting source of loot, as the Phocians were to show in the so-called Third Sacred War (356–346).

32. *invaded Greece*: See Cawkwell's properly sobering note to *A History of My Times* 4.1.41. This is a classic instance of 'Panhellenist big talk'.

33. *Ephors' office . . . five of them*: The formal balance of power between the Spartan kings and the Ephorate is summed up in a ritual: 'there is a monthly exchange of oaths, ephors acting for the city, a king on his own behalf. The king's oath is to rule according to the city's established laws, while that of the city is to keep the king's position unshaken so long as he abides by his oath' (*Spartan Society*, chapter 14, in Penguin *Plutarch on Sparta*, p. 183). Kings who alienated the Ephors, or a majority of them, might find themselves tried and even deposed, but Agesilaus was careful always to humour, even flatter them, and thereby acquired unusual influence.

34. *one another*: Cf. his intervention at Thespiae in 377, *A History of My Times* 5.4.55; contrast his divisive intervention at Phleious (see Introduction).

CHAPTER 2

1. *cavalry . . . gradually to withdraw*: Even the best cavalry, and the Thessalian was the best in Greece outside Macedon (see Introduction to *Cavalry Commander*), could not normally stand up to a well-drilled hoplite phalanx.

2. *Thebes . . . Locrian peoples*: The first four of these constituted the Quadruple Alliance formed with Persian diplomatic and financial backing to resist Sparta's hegemony in Greece. From 395 until the conclusion of the King's Peace (or Peace of Antalcidas) in 386, they and their allies waged and ultimately lost the Corinthian War. The Aenianians, and the Ozolian (western) and Opuntian (eastern) Locrians (see *A History of My Times* 4.2.17), were peoples of central Greece. The island of Euboea, off the eastern coast of Attica and Boeotia, was a valuable addition, since its relations with Athens had often not been cordial.

3. *wholeheartedly to fighting the enemy*: Xenophon too anticipated Napoleon in his – surely correct – estimation of the crucial importance of the morale factor in warfare. Compare his laudation of Agesilaus' half-brother Teleutias at *A History of My Times* 5.1.4 – a passage which is also highly revealing of Xenophon's conception of historiography.

4. *the most remarkable battle of modern times*: Precisely the same is said at *A History of My Times* 4.3.16. What seems to have made it unique for Xenophon is that 'it was a double battle, a sort of knock-out championship for military excellence' (Cawkwell's note to *A History of My Times*, p. 204).

5. *the Orchomenians*: The great rivals of Thebes for control of the Boeotian confederacy; it suited Sparta's divide-and-rule imperial policy perfectly to keep the two major Boeotian cities at odds with each other. In 364 Thebes, then at the height of its power, destroyed Orchomenus utterly. Agesilaus, for personal as well as policy reasons, had a peculiar aversion to Thebes, which Xenophon entirely shared (*A History of My Times* 4.2.18, 6.5.24, 7.5.12, with Cawkwell's Introduction, pp. 36–7).

6. *a stade*: A *stadion* (whence our 'stadium') was the rough equivalent of a furlong (220 yards) or 200 metres. The *stadion* sprint was the earliest and for long the sole event at the Olympics, where the track as laid out in the fourth century measured just over 192 m.

7. *three plethra*: A *plethron* was both a square measure and a measure of length, here the latter: 100 Greek feet. Herippidas and his men were thus doing the equivalent of a 100-metre dash, but with the handicap of equipment weighing perhaps 30 kilograms or 60–70 lbs.

8. *Cyreians*: These mercenaries were so called because they had been recruited originally in 402/1 by Cyrus the Younger of Persia, pretender to the throne occupied by his older full brother known to the Greeks as Artaxerxes II. A version of their story is told in *The Persian Expedition*; Xenophon was still one of their number at this battle of Coroneia in 394 and therefore fighting against his own native city (see main Introduction).

9. *mercenary troops*: Presumably with Xenophon himself to the fore among them.

10. *they pushed*: The mass manoeuvre known as the *othismos* decided which of the two hoplite lines would break. The large round hoplite shield, normally about a metre wide, was made basically of wood, encircled by a rim of bronze; it was held rigidly on the hoplite's left arm (regardless of whether he was naturally left-handed) by means of a shieldband (*porpax*) and gripped on the inside of the rim by a flexible handle (*antilabe*).

11. *the gods*: 'The gods' here translates the abstract phrase *to theion*, literally 'the divine'. For Xenophon's own intense religiosity, see main Introduction.

12. *the polemarch*: In technical Spartan parlance the polemarch was the commander of a *mora*, or regiment; cf. *Hiero*, chapter 9 note 2 above.

13. *the god . . . their pipes*: 'The god' is Apollo; the 'pipes' were *auloi*, a reed instrument something like a modern oboe.

14. *rejected supreme power . . . in Sparta*: Xenophon's Agesilaus, like his fictional Cyrus (the Great) in the *Cyropaedia*, is a legitimate king, utterly unlike the archetypal tyrant or non-responsible despot Hiero of Syracuse.

15. *Subsequently*: Actually an interval of almost three years (391).

16. *the war*: That is, the ongoing Corinthian War – see note 2 above. What modern scholars refer to as the Union of Corinth and Argos, Xenophon, who entirely endorses Agesilaus' viewpoint, represents as the take-over of the former by the latter. The precise legal position is uncertain, although technically it would seem most likely that the two cities concluded an isopolity or 'equal citizenship' agreement, whereby citizens of each would be entitled to enjoy the citizen rights of the other when present in that city. The geopolitical consequences, on the other hand, are entirely clear, marking a strategic disaster for Sparta, whose policy in the Peloponnese depended on isolating Argos from its Peloponnesian League alliance.

17. *port of Lechaeum*: Corinth had two harbours, one on the Saronic Gulf, the other, Lechaeum, on the Corinthian Gulf; the 'Long Walls' connecting

Corinth to Lechaeum were a small-scale imitation of the Long Walls linking the city of Athens to its port city of Peiraeus, which had been destroyed in 404 but recently rebuilt with Persian financial aid.

18. *the Hyacinthia*: All Sparta's major annual religious festivals – the Carnea, Gymnopaediae and Hyacinthia – were devoted to Apollo, whose special 'hymn of praise' was known in Greek as the Paean. The Hyacinthia were celebrated at Amyclae, a settlement just a short way south of Sparta town itself but politically counting as a constituent part of the city (*A History of My Times* 4.5.11).

19. *four nations too*: The Argives in question here are not the famous Argives of the north-east Peloponnese (see note 16 above) but the Amphilochian Argives of north-west Greece.

20. *the enemy*: The Quadruple Alliance (note 2 above).

21. *later than this*: 381–379.

22. *other grounds*: See main Introduction.

23. *their opponents*: The action has now moved forward to 378. Thebes has been liberated from a Spartan garrison and has instituted a moderate, for the moment pro-Athenian, democracy. The Spartan garrisoning of Thebes in 382, defended if not instigated by Agesilaus in order to buttress a rabidly pro-Spartan oligarchic junta, was an act of sacrilege, as even Xenophon cannot refrain from emphasizing in his non-encomiastic work (*A History of My Times* 5.4.1) (see main Introduction); here he prefers to stress the revenge butchery carried out by the anti-Spartans.

24. *Agesilaus' leadership*: Xenophon's *sphalmata*, 'setbacks', is a pretty gross euphemism for defeats that included the decisive Theban victory at Leuctra in 371 (see main Introduction). As with the occupation of Thebes (preceding note), Agesilaus is – questionably, to say the least – exonerated by Xenophon from any direct blame.

25. *and Euboea*: This is the first invasion of Laconia since that of the Dorians (if indeed 'invasion' is the right word for the latter) six or more centuries earlier. Xenophon's list of invaders at *A History of My Times* 6.5.23 differs slightly from that given here; note that since 394 (2.6) the Phocians had changed sides, and that Xenophon for once speaks accurately of 'Boeotians' (including presumably Orchomenus) not 'Thebans'.

26. *at Leuctra*: In *A History of My Times* (6.5.29) Xenophon preferred to dwell on the 'slaves' – that is Helots – who remained loyal to Sparta, rather than those who revolted (see Cawkwell's notes to *A History of My Times* 6.5.52, 7.1.27). The 'dependent towns' were known technically as *Perioeci*, or 'Dwellers round about'; those in revolt here were in northern Laconia, athwart the invasion routes. At Leuctra Sparta lost some 400 citizens out of a total citizen body previously exceeding, though not by much, 1,000, so Xenophon's 'at least halved' is something of an exaggeration.

27. *get the better of anyone*: One reason why Sparta had not built a city wall (and did not do so until the late third century) was the separate existence of Amyclae (note 18 above); another was its inaccessibility, both geographically and – thanks to the normally secure cordon provided by the *Perioeci* – geopolitically.

28. *raise money*: The Greek translated 'to raise money' is *porizein*, the verbal form of *poroi*, translated later as *Ways and Means*. By 370 Agesilaus was 75 or thereabouts.

29. *and withdrew*: Agesilaus was here seeking to exploit the revolts of various of Persia's western satraps, including Autophradates and Ariobarzanes, from Artaxerxes II. Cotys was king of the non-Greek Odrysians of Thrace, whom Xenophon had encountered in his mercenary days (*Persian Expedition* 7.2; see also *On Horsemanship* 8.6).

30. *powers of persuasion*: Mausolus (or Maussollus), eponym of the mausoleum, ruled Caria as satrap or under-satrap between 377 and 353. Unlike most satraps, Mausolus was not a Persian but a native Carian.

31. *homeward journey*: Tachos at any rate later ruled Egypt, or Lower Egypt, one of several 'pharaohs' to reign during its long (404–342) period of revolt from Persia.

32. *relinquish Messene*: Artaxerxes had found Sparta the most convenient Greek state to deal with following the conclusion of the King's Peace of 386 (named after him). But Leuctra and Sparta's subsequent troubles encouraged him to switch from supporting Sparta to dealing with the Greeks through Thebes – hence the King's demand that the Spartans 'relinquish' Messene, that is cease from their irredentist campaign to regain control of the newly liberated and refounded city of their ex-Helot 'slaves'.

33. *a great deal of money*: The pharaoh to emerge from this internal struggle was Nectanebis II, who – according to Plutarch (*Agesilaus* 40.1) – heaped Agesilaus with substantial 'gifts' for himself and 230 silver talents for the Spartan war-chest.

CHAPTER 3

1. *Cotys*: Or Otys, or Thys, or Thyus, or Gyes: various ancient sources give various names to the subject of this story.

2. *personal assurances*: The Greek *dexiomata* signifies that agreements involving such assurances were sealed by the shaking of right hands; actual models of right hands in bronze might be exchanged as material *sumbola* ('tokens') of the agreement.

3. *dealings with him*: See chapter 1 note 17.

CHAPTER 4

1. *a favour*: Cf. *The Dinner-party* 8.36 (in Penguin *Conversations of Socrates*).

2. *truth of this*: Naturally, Agesilaus' largesse was far from disinterested. For example, he always sent a cloak and an ox to each newly elected member of the Gerousia (Plutarch, *Agesilaus* 4.6).

CHAPTER 5

1. *conferring honour . . . wanted to*: Both kings, whatever their personal or policy differences (see chapter 1 note 2), dined together in the royal 'mess' (technically *suskanion*, or common tent). The royal 'honour of double portions at meals' (*Spartan Society* 14, in Penguin *Plutarch on Sparta*) applied to the evening meal, daily attendance at which was compulsory for all Spartans (except when back late from hunting or conducting a sacrifice: Plutarch, *Lycurgus* 12, in *Plutarch on Sparta*).

2. *ordinary citizens*: Cf. *Cyropaedia* 8.2.4.

3. *a kiss*: Xenophon is probably gilding the lily a bit here – at any rate, one form of *proskunesis* (see chapter 1 note 30) involved the blowing of a kiss, rather than the planting of it on the lips or cheek of one's lover. But see also *Cyropaedia* 1.4.27.

4. *two gods*: In Sparta the brothers Castor and Polydeuces (Latin Pollux), also known as the Dioscuri or Tyndaridae, were worshipped as gods (as was their sister Helen). Images of them were carried by the Spartans on campaign as good-luck tokens (Herodotus 5.75). For the sake of realism, Xenophon preserves the Spartans' Doric dialect form of the word for 'gods' (*sio*).

5. *to gold*: The anecdote caught the imagination of later writers, not only Plutarch (*Agesilaus* 11.9, *Moralia* 209d–e) but also the late rhetoricians Maximus of Tyre and Philostratus. Good looks and speed were notoriously not the strong points of the congenitally lame Agesilaus, but for endurance he would have been hard to beat.

6. *enemies do*: Cf. *The Persian Expedition* 2.6.28.

7. *he does*: Cf. *Memoirs of Socrates* 1.1.11.

CHAPTER 6

1. *visible signs . . . of the fighting*: For his many battle scars see 2.13.

2. *go through uncontested*: The Greek *akoniti* meant literally 'without dust', a technical term derived from the distinctly dust-ridden competitions in wrestling and pancration (all-in wrestling combined with boxing and judo) and extended to other athletic contests.

3. *unswerving*: *Aprophasistos* is picked up again significantly in the summation at 11.13. It occurs also in *Cavalry Commander* 2.9.

4. *maidens in its orderliness*: A Greek maiden was not supposed to do anything to catch a man's eye; moreover, the way one walked was, according to Greek physiognomic notions, an index of one's moral character. Maidenly deportment was supposedly inculcated in Spartan boys by the educational regime prescribed by Lycurgus (*Spartan Society* 5.3, in Penguin *Plutarch on Sparta*).

CHAPTER 7

1. *old age as an excuse*: Not quite true – see *A History of My Times* 5.4.13 (Agesilaus, then aged about 66, cried off from leading a campaign in 378).

2. *coup . . . the laws*: How, indeed – except that in about 400, within a year of Agesilaus' accession, one Cinadon did attempt a coup (or so Xenophon reports at *A History of My Times* 3.3.4–11).

3. *a catastrophe*: This alleged principled 'panhellenism' of Agesilaus is of course just so much bunkum and balderdash – see chapter 1 note 32; for his – and Xenophon's – enmity towards the entirely Greek Thebes, see chapter 2 note 5. Xenophon's unconventional application of *philhellen*, 'supporter of Greece', to a Greek rather than a non-Greek is also nothing but a rhetorical flourish.

4. *the whole Persian army*: The Battle of the Nemea River (394) is described at *A History of My Times* 4.2.9–23, where there is no mention of Agesilaus' distress on hearing the news at 4.3.1–2.

5. *the Persians*: Compare and contrast Thucydides 4.80.4, where the Spartans have no compunction in 'annihilating' some 2,000 Helots (in about 424).

6. *harassing the Persians in any way he could*: The implied chronology is at best misleading: Agesilaus sailed for Asia in 396, and the 'war against other Greeks', which in *A History of My Times* 3.5.1–2 Xenophon ascribes to Persian bribery, began only in 395. The apologetic trumpeting of his alleged Persia-hatred is

designed to exonerate Agesilaus from the responsibility he surely bore for the conclusion and – especially – the exploitation of the King's Peace in 386.

CHAPTER 8

1. *my friendship*: Cf. Plutarch *Moralia* 213d–e. The supposed occasion was some time after the conclusion of the King's Peace; again, the purpose of the story is apologetic.

2. *return home*: Aristodemus was great-great-grandson of Heracles (see chapter 1 note 1). The local Spartan version of the 'Return of the Descendants of Heracles' myth portrayed Aristodemus as leader when the Heraclids (re)occupied Sparta. 'Lycurgus' is said to have forbidden the use of any tool apart from a saw in the making of doors, to discourage 'extravagance' (Plutarch, *Lycurgus* 13, in Penguin *Plutarch on Sparta*).

3. *daughter . . . public cart*: A pupil of Aristotle, Dicaearchus, tried but failed to discover the daughter's name; Plutarch himself discovered in Sparta's archives that Agesilaus had had two daughters, named Eupolia and Proauga (*Agesilaus* 19.10). Travel to Amyclae in the 'public cart' was for a religious purpose, to participate in the Hyacinthia festival (2.17).

4. *and fear*: Xenophon has strayed rather far from the virtue of 'charm' (8.1) and back to financial honesty (4.1).

CHAPTER 9

1. *their way*: For a revealing vignette of Agesilaus at work, see *A History of My Times* 5.4.28; cf. Plutarch, *Agesilaus* 4.5.

2. *of wealth*: Cynisca ('Puppy') was probably Agesilaus' full sister. Xenophon significantly under-reports her achievement: in 396, she was the first woman ever to win the four-horse chariot-race at Olympia, and moreover won it again at the next games of 392. Pausanias 3.15.1, 5.111.5 (Penguin *Guide to Greece*, vol. 2, pp. 50, 231–2) mentions her commemorative dedication at Olympia and the hero-shrine to her at Sparta.

3. *his renown . . . there is*: Similar words and sentiments are found at *Hiero* 11.5–8, especially 11.7; cf. 4.6 and Herodotus 5.111. Contrast *Cyropaedia* 2.3.7–15.

CHAPTER 10

1. *lament*: It is in fact mainly an encomium (e.g. chapter 1 note 7) liberally laced with apologia (e.g. chapter 7 note 6).

CHAPTER 11

1. *taken refuge*: According to Thucydides (*History* 1.128), the pious Spartans had explained the great earthquake and subsequent Helot revolt of the 460s as divine retribution for their having 'raised up some helot suppliants from the altar of Poseidon, and taken them away and killed them'.

2. *a favour*: Cf. *Cyropaedia* 1.27, 4.5.29–33.

3. *second kind*: For Agesilaus' concern with his posthumous reputation see 9.7; but without encomia such as Xenophon's how could he have been sure of leaving to posterity 'memorials of his character' (cf. 11.16)? There is surely implied Xenophontic self-reference too in 10.1 (household management) and 11.4 (praise reveals the character of the praiser).

4. *invariably . . . good sense rather than foolish risks*: 'Invariably'? But see 2.12.

5. *ageing process*: This is perhaps an implied defence of not just Agesilaus but Spartan gerontocracy more generally; Aristotle (*Politics* 1270b35ff.) challenged the ascription of virtue to members of the Spartan Gerousia and pointed out that the mind as well as the body becomes senile.

6. *his fatherland*: Agesilaus died aged about 84 in north Africa; his body, embalmed in wax, was brought back to Sparta for the uniquely lavish funeral ('of a grandeur that seemed to go beyond what a mere man could claim or expect', was how Xenophon in *A History of My Times* 3.3.1 described that of Agis II, Agesilaus' half-brother and Eurypontid predecessor) accorded to Spartan kings. The posthumous benefaction is the 'great deal of money' already mentioned (2.31). See also chapter 2 note 33.

HOW TO BE A GOOD CAVALRY COMMANDER

CHAPTER 1

1. *the gods*: On the indispensability of sacrifice, and the need on occasion for a commander to sacrifice repeatedly, sometimes for several days, until a favourable omen was received, see *Agesilaus* chapter 1 note 27.

2. *carry on*: 1,000 was the official full complement of the Athenian *hippeis* (Cavalry); that it was not easy to maintain is implied by 9.3 and 9.5. It was apparently the duty of tribally appointed 'Cataloguers' to list men qualified but not yet enrolled: Aristotelian *Constitution of the Athenians* (*Ath. Pol.*) 49.2, with the expert *Commentary* by P. J. Rhodes (Oxford University Press, 1981, corr. reprint, 1993). Spence, pp. 287–315 (see Further Reading) lists known Athenian cavalrymen between *c*. 500 and 300.

3. *rough ground*: The Greeks did not shoe their horses, and ground that was *hippasimos*, suitable for cavalry horses, was rare in Greece (cf. 8.13), not least in Attica (see Herodotus 5.63.4).

4. *javelin from horseback*: The difficulty of javelin-throwing from horseback without the benefit of stirrups needs no underlining; cf. *On Horsemanship* 8.10–11, 12.12–13.

5. *tribal regiments*: The ten tribal regiments (2.2) were each commanded by a Phylarch. Note that, like the two Hipparchs (Cavalry Commanders), they were elected, not appointed through the chance of the lot. See further *Ath. Pol.* 61.4–5.

6. *the cavalry*: The Council of 500, 50 men selected annually by lot from each of the ten Athenian civic tribes, was Athens' principal administrative body. Among its many functions two were relevant to the administration of the cavalry: (i) the conduct of *dokimasiai* or examinations to check the credentials of those appointed to an office or military function; and (ii) the distribution of public stipends (*misthos*) of various kinds, including certainly a fodder grant for cavalrymen's horses (*Ath. Pol.* 49.1) and possibly pay when on active service (see note 11 below). Hoards of lead tablets have been recovered from the Athenian Agora recording the colour, brand and value of cavalrymen's horses, the latter possibly because the state would repay the value of a horse killed in action.

7. *just notes*: In a sense the whole treatise is a *hypomnema* or *aide-mémoire*, but here and at 3.1 the author uses the term to disclaim comprehensiveness. At 9.1 he generously allows that just a 'few readings' of the treatise will suffice.

8. *their qualification*: For this double requirement of health and wealth (cf. 9.5), see also *Ath. Pol.* 49.2. Wealth was required because the cavalryman had to provide his own horse, but see note 6 above for provision from central funds thereafter. Legal procedure might be necessary in case a man's eligibility (see notes 2 and 6 above) were disputed.

9. *horse's vicious behaviour . . . ineffective too*: Cf. *On Horsemanship* 3.7–11.

10. *weight*: An Attic mina weighed 436.6 grams. See also *On Horsemanship* 4.4–5 for slightly more detailed directions.

11. *of war*: If the 1,000 cavalrymen were all on active service and paid 4 obols a day, that would yield the figure of 40 talents per annum (1 talent = 6,000 drachmas; 1 drachma = 6 obols), but that equation is by no means certain. One alternative would be to assume a daily stipend of one drachma per man, with the consequence that in the mid-360s (if that is the date of this treatise) the cavalry was seriously under-strength at only 650 men, owing perhaps to recruitment difficulties. On the cost of cavalry service at Athens, see Spence, pp. 272–86.

12. *practice yourself*: These scouts (*prodromoi*) were a special body of light-armed cavalry, the successors apparently to the fifth-century horse-archers (*hippotoxotai*): *Ath. Pol.* 49.1, with Rhodes, *Commentary*, pp. 565–6, cf. pp. 303–4.

13. *throughout Athens*: Xenophon, like Agesilaus (see e.g. *A History of My Times* 3.4.16), was a great believer in the merits of competition; see also 1.21 and 3.5. The following remark about the quality of judges is probably a veiled jibe at Athens' democratic method of selecting judges for the theatrical competitions at the Great Dionysia, by lot on a totally random basis.

CHAPTER 2

1. *something done*: Cf. Thucydides' account (5.66.4) of the Spartan chain-of-command at the Battle of Mantinea in 418, stressing the merit of an army consisting almost entirely of officers.

CHAPTER 3

1. *as possible*: The Academy and Lyceum were public gymnasia or exercise-grounds, sacred respectively to the hero Academus and to Apollo Lyceius ('Wolfish'). They are more famous for being the sites of respectively Plato's and Aristotle's philosophical schools or institutes of higher learning. Their positions in relation to the Agora (next note) are neatly shown in a reconstructed drawing by Candace H. Smith in A. A. Long and D. N. Sedley, *The Hellenistic Philosophers*, vol. 1 (Cambridge University Press, 1987), p. 4. The Hippodrome was probably in the Peiraeus area. The reference to 'Phalerum', which does not recur, may well be spurious.

2. *city square*: The Athenian Agora has been the subject of intensive exploration and excavation by the American School of Classical Studies since 1931; the specifically topographical volumes of the School's Agora Series (Princeton University Press) are 3 (R. E. Wycherley, 1957) and 14 (H. A. Thompson and Wycherley, 1972). The Herms were located on the north side of the Agora; many or most were deliberately smashed one ill-omened night in 415 as the Athenian armada was about to sail for Sicily (Thucydides 6.27). The number of shrines and statues was by now very large, including hero shrines such as the Leocoreum, honorific statues of the two Tyrannicides (see *Hiero* chapter 5 note 3) and the Stoa (portico) of Demeter and Core referred to here as the Eleusinium.

3. *their wishes*: Nostalgia is not of course peculiar to Xenophon, but the endings of both *Spartan Society* and *Cyropaedia* are extended meditations on the decline of Sparta and Persia from their supposed golden eras, and Xenophon is likely to have shared the hankering of his slightly older contemporary Isocrates for a less or rather a non-democratic order.

CHAPTER 4

1. *critical moment*: The author of an extant contemporary treatise on siegecraft, Aeneas, was especially interested in espionage and various modes of cryptic communication (D. Whitehead, *Aineieas the Tactician: How to Survive under Siege* [Oxford University Press, 1990], especially chapter 31). The author may be the politically conservative Aeneas of Stymphalus in Arcadia mentioned by Xenophon at *A History of My Times* 7.3.1, and it would not be odd if he and Xenophon were personally known to each other or if either had written his treatise in knowledge of the other's.

2. *trick I have just mentioned*: Xenophon is remarkably interested in ambushes, a convenient list of references to which in Greek literature has been collated in W. K. Pritchett, *The Greek State at War*, vol. 2 (University of California Press, 1974), chapter 9.

CHAPTER 5

1. *fake spears*: Grooms (*hippokomoi*), like the hoplites' batmen, were typically slaves. An Attic drinking cup from the early fifth century, attributed to the painter Onesimus (itself a slave name), depicts on the interior an African groom sighting along his curry comb for hairs after currying the horse (J. Ober and C. W. Hedrick, *The Birth of Democracy* [American School of Classical Studies at Athens and National Archives, Washington, D.C., Exhibition Catalogue, 1993], p. 141, fig. 23.2).

2. *out of sight*: 'The enemy will not know (*a*) the number of files when posted one behind another, nor (*b*) the depth of the line when the files have wheeled' (Marchant, Loeb edition, p. 269 n. 1).

3. *ability to deceive . . . work on it yourself*: Ruse or cunning intelligence (*metis*) had always been an admired, but also a morally questionable, quality, as exemplified paradigmatically by Odysseus 'of the many wiles' (*polumetis*). Traditional hoplite warfare by and large did not lend itself to deception or even surprise. What we seem to see in this treatise, however, as in Xenophon's accounts of Agesilaus' career, are an increasing use and increasingly positive valuation of deception (*apate*) of all kinds (cf. chapter 4 note 2).

4. *on foot*: Infantry mixed with cavalry had a technical name, *hamippoi*; they were not original to the fourth century, and Xenophon refrains from mentioning that they were a Theban invention and speciality (Thucydides 5.57; *A History of My Times* 7.5.23−4). For Athenian *hamippoi* see *Ath. Pol.* 49.1, with Rhodes, *Commentary*, p. 566; Spence, pp. 58−9, pl. 10.

5. *the god*: Here and elsewhere (6.1, 7.3, 7.14, 9.8) Xenophon uses the masculine singular, *ho theos*, without necessarily having any one male god in mind. The characteristically religious note had been struck in the very first sentence of the treatise, recurs throughout and is explicitly sounded again right at the end.

CHAPTER 6

1. *his will*: The craftsman (*cheirotechnes*) was not a figure of high status in aristocratic Greek eyes, but that did not stop either Xenophon or, more famously, Plato from using craft analogies to illustrate or point their philosophical or didactic theses. The particular craft Xenophon has in mind here is probably that of the bronze statuary who moulded (our 'plastic' comes from the Greek verb *plassein*) clay and plaster and wax − cf. *Memoirs of Socrates* 3.10, in Penguin *Conversations of Socrates*.

2. *his men*: *A History of My Times* 4.5.4 (Agesilaus sharing fire in 390) is a classic illustration.

CHAPTER 7

1. *foot-soldiers*: This is a reference to the Boeotians, and more especially the hated (by Xenophon: see next note) Thebans; see 'Oxyrhynchus Historian', chapter 11 (the status quo in 395).

2. *are just as proud . . . as Boeotians*: For Xenophon's own hostility to Thebes, see *Agesilaus* chapter 2 note 5. Athenian pride of lineage was celebrated notably in the Epitaphios or Funeral Oration pronounced over the year's war-dead (e.g. Thucydides 2.35−46).

3. *city walls*: Xenophon follows Thucydides in underestimating the offensive elements (including annual raids across the border against Megara) in Athens' Peloponnesian War strategy by land. But the cavalry was certainly relatively little used, and least of all for offence.

4. *of marauders*: Plundering (*leisteia*) was something for which cavalry were particularly well equipped; the economic as well as military importance of plundering was not lost on contemporaries: see Y. Garlan, *Guerre et économie en Grèce ancienne* (Maspéro, 1989); and *Agesilaus* chapter 1 note 31.

CHAPTER 8

1. *women against men*: The Greek for the sort of courage, bravery or pugnacity required in combat was *andreia*, literally 'manliness'. A favourite Greek military insult from Homer onwards was to deride the enemy as 'womanish'.

2. *flying . . . long to be able to do*: This is a rather revealing personal interjection. Would-be high flyers among ancient Greek mortals had of course the awful warning of Icarus to contemplate; but what Xenophon is in effect saying is that riding, or more specifically cavalry training, gave him the sort of divine pleasure that other Greeks derived from sexual intercourse, for which a regular Greek phrase was *ta Aphrodisia*, 'the things of Aphrodite'.

3. *with prosperity*: At the so-called 'crown' games (see *Hiero* chapter 1 note 1) prizes were purely symbolic tokens (an olive-wreath crown at the Olympics, etc.), but at all the many times more numerous local games value-prizes (e.g. olive oil at Athens, bronze cauldrons at Argos) were awarded. Xenophon, for the sake of his rhetorical point, collapses the distinction between token-prize and value-prize boxing-matches.

4. *with intelligence*: Xenophon was ever the elitist, a spokesman for, as well as to, the supposedly intelligent (*phronimoi*) few.

5. *to resist*: True shock cavalry tactics in Greek warfare, however, had to await the discovery − or use − of stirrups.

6. *unexpected fright*: In this Xenophon was at one with Thucydides, who also placed great emphasis on tales of the unexpected (*to aprosdoketon*). For the morale factor in Xenophon, see note to *Agesilaus* chapter 2 note 3.

CHAPTER 9

1. *seen through*: The same point is vigorously urged in the peroration of *Ways and Means* 6.2–3.

2. *of enthusiasm*: This remark sits awkwardly with his disparagement elsewhere of Spartan cavalry: see *Agesilaus* chapter 1 note 18.

3. *large estates*: The legal status and welfare of Athenian orphans were the peculiar responsibility of the annual eponymous archon (*Ath. Pol.*, Rhodes, *Commentary*, pp. 629–36). War-orphans constituted a special, and particularly prestigious, subcategory.

4. *resident aliens*: Resident aliens (*metoikoi*, or metics) were a quite numerous category of the Athenian population, concentrated inevitably in the Peiraeus area (see further *Ways and Means* chapter 2 note 2). Their status was emphatically second class, marked as such by the requirement to pay a monthly poll-tax. But they had some privileges as well as disabilities compared with non-resident foreigners and of course slaves. If they were of sufficient means, they were already required to serve as hoplites, and some of the poorest among them no doubt served voluntarily as trireme oarsmen. Xenophon in arguing for their recruitment to the cavalry was ranking military effectiveness above the strict maintenance of social boundaries. See generally D. Whitehead, *The Ideology of the Athenian Metic* (Cambridge Philological Society, 1977).

5. *the time*: Presumably Xenophon has in mind exiles from the enemy city, as at *A History of My Times* 5.3.17 (Agesilaus and the oligarchic exiles from Phleious in the late 380s); cf. *A History of My Times* 7.2.4, where Xenophon mentions in dispatches the loyalty to Sparta of the Phleiasian cavalry.

6. *in danger*: Compare *On Horsemanship* 11.13.

7. *dreams*: The treatise began implicitly with divination by extispicy, that is examination of the entrails of sacrificial animals: see chapter 1 note 1. Xenophon here adds the other three main forms of divination practised by the Greeks; cf. *Memoirs of Socrates* 1.1.3. The most famous oracular shrine was of course Delphi; the most famous site for 'incubation' (sleeping overnight in a shrine in order to dream divinely sent dreams) the sanctuary of Asclepius at Epidaurus (see *On Hunting* chapter 1 note 4); at Dodona in north-west Greece one mode of divination was by interpreting the cooing of the doves, but avispicy normally took the form of observing the flight of birds.

ON HORSEMANSHIP

The translator gratefully acknowledges the help of Sally Gilbert, Briar Maxwell and especially Wendy Price towards understanding some of the equine and equestrian points in this treatise.

CHAPTER I

1. *with him*: A 'Simon' is invoked in Aristophanes' *Knights* (line 242); the chorus that gives that comedy its name represented the Athenian cavalry, and according to one ancient commentator, this Simon was then one of its two Hipparchs, or cavalry commanders (see e.g. *Cavalry Commander* chapter 1 note 5). If so, he may be the author of the treatise mentioned here and at 11.6, part of which survives: see D. Whitehead, *Aineias the Tactician: How to Survive under Siege* (Oxford University Press, 1990), p. 35 n. 101. For the Eleusinium, see *Cavalry Commander* chapter 3 note 2.

2. *a war-horse*: As the author will shortly make explicit (3.7), he is talking throughout this treatise about horses for war, rather than for work or leisure (for the contrast, see e.g. *Agesilaus* 9.6). Horses apparently cost more to buy than houses.

3. *the frog*: The author's word here (and at 4.5, 6.2) is actually *chelidon*, 'swallow'. Presumably this is because of the V-shape of the horse's frog and of the swallow's tail. Later Greek writers, however, do use *batrachos*, the Greek for 'frog', for this spongy tissue under the horse's hoof.

4. *the pin*: What the author calls the 'pin' or brooch (*perone*) is probably the deep flexor tendon at the back of the lower leg, which is the shape of an ancient Greek fibula (similar to a modern safety pin). As the author implies, if the circulation to this part of the leg is blocked off, the horse may suffer from navicular disease, which in turn can lead to lameness.

5. *better appearance*: The ideal shape and proportions for a nude male statue (the so-called *kouros* type) were thought to have been attained by the fifth-century Argive sculptor Polycleitus in his figure named *Kanon* ('Standard'); he also wrote a treatise of that title. See also *Memoirs of Socrates* 3.10.

6. *horse's shoulders*: Another point for the modern reader to bear in mind is that the Greek rider did without stirrups and saddle (see next note; at most he might use a saddle-cloth, 7.5).

7. *double spine*: The so-called double spine made the saddle-less horse more comfortable to sit on and thus earned the praise of many ancient writers (e.g.

Virgil, *Georgics* 3.87). Rather than protruding, the spinal column in a thus favoured horse rests as it were in a slight valley.

8. *the belly*: Today, we would say that such a horse has a good girth.

9. *broad line*: Looking at a standing horse tail-on, you should be able to draw an imaginary line straight down from the centre of its rump to its hoof, on both sides. These two lines should be parallel and, as the author says, form a 'broad line' between them. This indicates that the horse is not bandy-legged, cow-hocked or sickle-hocked.

CHAPTER 2

1. *public standing*: This truism gives special point to the story that Alexander the Great himself broke the horse he named Bucephalas ('Ox-Head'), and after whom he named a city on the banks of the Hydaspes (Jhelum) (Plutarch, *Alexander* 6, 32, 44, 61).

2. *breaking in colts*: Whether or not Xenophon was the author of the present treatise, this passage refers to topics treated at length by Xenophon in *Memoirs of Socrates*, *The Estate-manager* and elsewhere.

3. *notes . . . be paid*: For 'notes', *hypomnemata*, see *Cavalry Commander* chapter 1 note 7. The practice of employing written contracts was on the increase in the fourth century.

4. *groom . . . from distress*: On grooms, see *Cavalry Commander* chapter 5 note 1.

CHAPTER 3

1. *buying such a horse*: Xenophon sold a favourite horse for 50 darics at Lampsacus, 'a fancy price for a fancy horse' (Cawkwell's note to *The Persian Expedition* p. 349 n. 11). For more normal horse-prices at Athens, see Spence, pp. 274–80.

2. *the 'chain'*: A figure-of-eight exercise; see also 7.13.

3. *of slopes*: The same recommendations are made at *Cavalry Commander* 8.1–3; cf. *Estate-manager* 11.17.

CHAPTER 4

1. *his storeroom*: Presumably in both cases the intruders were rats or other rodents. The storeroom (*tamieion*) gets a mention in an interesting comment on Athenian economy preserved in the Aristotelian *Oeconomica* 1344b33: 'The Attic system of economy is also useful; for they sell their produce and buy what they want, and thus there is not the need of a storehouse in the smaller establishments.' Masters of horses kept only larger establishments.

2. *properly treated*: Human medicine was by now a specialist craft-skill (*techne*), but there were no schools of equine medicine to compare with the centres on Cos and at Cnidus, and the earliest known Greek technical veterinary treatise belongs to the first century BC. The experienced horseman might have found it cheaper to train one of his existing slaves than to buy a ready trained groom.

3. *a mina in weight*: An Attic mina weighed 436.6 grams. See also *Cavalry Commander* 1.16.

4. *horse's mouth*: At *The Dinner-party* 1.7 Xenophon refers to pre-sympotic unguents, presumably perfumed. These and other olive-oil based emollients for after-exercise anointment were readily available for purchase in the Athenian Agora.

CHAPTER 5

1. *the horse*: What the author might have added is that such manure could then have been used as a vital agricultural fertilizer.

2. *being mated*: This amusing piece of fallacious folklore stands in sharp contrast to the 'scientific' stance generally adopted by the author. Cf. the discussion of boars' tusks at *On Hunting* 10.17.

CHAPTER 6

1. *Persian fashion*: Normally, a Greek would mount the horse unaided, by jumping on, or by getting the horse to crouch first, or from a convenient platform. 'Persian fashion' (also at *Cavalry Commander* 1.17) meant mounting with the assistance of a groom who pushed upwards from the rider's foot or knee.

2. *regret later*: At *A History of My Times* 5.3.7 Xenophon utters the general principle in the most forceful way: 'One ought not to punish even a slave in anger.'

CHAPTER 7

1. *the cavesson*: See Morgan, note 39.
2. *bunched-up clothing*: Cavalrymen favoured the *chlamys*, a cloak originating from the specialist cavalry country of Thessaly, worn over a *chiton*, a wool tunic of varying length: see for these and other items of clothing, Spence, pp. 324–9 (Glossary).
3. *naturally leads . . . the left*: This is true when a horse is bridled and ridden, but not when it is left to its own devices.

CHAPTER 8

1. *repeating myself*: See 3.7 and note (if Xenophon is considered the author of the present treatise).
2. *Odrysians*: See *Agesilaus* chapter 2 note 29.
3. *same ground*: See *Cavalry Commander* 1.18.
4. *wild animals*: See Introduction to *On Hunting*. The Greek huntsman rode to the hunt, but – despite the impression given here – hunted on foot.

CHAPTER 9

1. *rough ones*: On smooth and rough bits, see next chapter.
2. *high-spirited*: See also *Cavalry Commander* 1.14–15. High spirits were presumably less unacceptable in a racehorse.

CHAPTER 10

1. *two bits*: For an extensive description of actual examples see Marchant, pp. xxxiii–xxxiv, and Morgan.
2. *compression or tension*: Some ancient bits 'act mainly by the direct pull on the bars of the mouth, and others . . . compress the horse's jaw . . . when the reins are pulled' (J. K. Anderson, 'Notes on some points in Xenophon's *Peri Hippikês*', *Journal of Hellenic Studies*, 80 [1960], p. 7).

3. *never enjoyable*: 'Nothing in excess' was one of the three maxims with universal Greek application inscribed on the fourth-century temple of Apollo at Delphi.

4. *of turns*: See 7.17.

5. *full of spirit*: The author's rampant anthropomorphism extends to making the horse in the image of his own good self. See also 11.6.

CHAPTER 11

1. *the horses*: The Parthenon frieze springs instantly to mind: Spence, pp. 267–71 (Appendix 3).

2. *smart one*: Here our present treatise lines up alongside the *Cavalry Commander* (explicitly referred to at 12.14).

3. *supernatural intervention*: The author uses here the abstract phrase *to daimonion*, referring to the supernatural or divine generally (cf. *A History of My Times* 7.5.12), rather than a phrase involving the word 'gods' (as at 12.11).

CHAPTER 12

1. *on horseback*: See for further detailed discussion Spence, pp. 34–120 ('The combat potential of the *Hippeis*').

2. *too tight . . . of armour*: The same point is made about a hoplite's body armour in *Memoirs of Socrates* 3.10.

3. *wearer's vision*: A Thessalian coin depicts both the Boeotian helmet and a gorget (J. K. Anderson, 'Notes on some points in Xenophon's *Peri Hippikês*', *Journal of Hellenic Studies* 80 [1960], p. 8).

4. *carry too*: It appears that at Athens uniformity of offensive weapons was not imposed by the commanders or the Council: some cavalrymen were equipped with the javelins the author here recommends, some with the cane-shafted spear (here *doru kamakinon*; normally *kamax*), some with a combination of both: Spence, p. 54.

ON HUNTING

CHAPTER I

1. *Artemis*: The prolix proem is perhaps a trifle over-anxious to establish hunting's divine pedigree, but to begin and end (13.18) with Artemis, chaste and fearsome patroness of the art (surnamed Agrotera, 'the Huntress', at 6.13), was nothing if not diplomatic. The number of easily available handbooks or dictionaries of Greek myths and mythology is legion, but few bring out the myths' subtle multivalence and contextual plasticity. A shining exception is Y. Bonnefoy and W. Doniger (eds.), *Greek and Egyptian Mythologies* (University of Chicago Press, 1991), and on Artemis, see P. Ellinger, pp. 145–9.

2. *noble pursuits from him*: The note of nobility is sounded at the outset and swells to a diapason in the concluding chapter.

3. *widely celebrated*: If our author is to be believed, Cheiron the centaur (man-horse) ran a veritable stable of thoroughbred pupils; many of them had already received lyric praise from Pindar. See A. Schnapp, 'Centaurs', in Bonnefoy and Doniger, *Mythologies*, pp. 151–2.

4. *Asclepius . . . as a god*: Asclepius was worshipped both as a hero and as a god – see Bruit-Zaidman and Schmitt-Pantel, pp. 128–32, and J. Carlier in Bonnefoy and Doniger, *Mythologies*, pp. 149–51. His most famous shrine was that at Epidaurus in the north-east Peloponnese, where the priests competed successfully – and lucratively – with the relatively new breed of 'scientific' doctors. See also *Cavalry Commander* chapter 9 note 7.

5. *Atalanta*: In Bonnefoy and Doniger, *Mythologies*, Atalanta appears, of course, in Schnapp's article on 'Heroes and Myths of Hunting in Ancient Greece' (p. 121), but also, and no less relevantly, in M. Detienne's on 'The Powers of Marriage in Greece' (p. 96). See chapter 13 note 7.

6. *no need . . . to speak of it*: This is perhaps a conscious touch of humour, since Homer's Nestor was not backward in coming forward to sing his own praises, at Nestorian length.

7. *against Thebes*: Amphiaraus was one of the original 'Seven Against Thebes', commemorated notably by Aeschylus in his extant tragedy of that name (467); he was also, like Asclepius, worshipped as a superhuman power of healing by incubation at Oropus on the Athenian-Boeotian border.

8. *Telamon Hesione*: The so-called 'state' (*polis*) of Periboea was Megara, although her father Alcathous, son of Pelops and Hippodameia, was originally from Elis. Hesione, sister of Priam king of Troy, was given to Telamon after

Troy's fall to be his slave, the common fate of war-captives in the real Greek world.

9. *forgot the goddess*: Meleager's father was Oeneus, king of Calydon; the goddess was Artemis. What Oeneus forgot to do was make a first-fruits offering to her, alone of all the immortal gods (see *Iliad* 9.537). Meleager's misfortune was to fall out fatally with his relatives after successfully killing the Calydonian boar; in one version of the myth he was killed by Oeneus himself.

10. *city's territory*: Theseus had by Thucydides' time (2.15) become the reputed founder of Athens as a polity occupying the territory of Attica: see N. Loraux in Bonnefoy and Doniger, *Mythologies*, pp. 41–2.

11. *death . . . as a blessed man*: Euripides offers a rather less sunny version of Hippolytus' demise in *Hippolytus* of 428 (his second tragedy of that title). See Ellinger, 'Artemis' in Bonnefoy and Doniger, *Mythologies*, pp. 148–9.

12. *bad men*: The 'two men' were respectively Odysseus and Diomedes (see 1.13), who were clearly more to the author's taste than Achilles (1.16). The sophist Gorgias of Leontini in Sicily (*c.* 480–375) wrote for Palamedes a typically 'sophistical' self-defence, in which he represented himself as one of Greece's major benefactors (M. Gagarin and P. Woodruff (eds.), *Early Greek Political Thought from Homer to the Sophists* [Cambridge University Press, 1995], pp. 195–202).

13. *Castor and Polydeuces . . . now immortal*: They were worshipped as gods, under the title of the Dioscuri, near Sparta (see *Agesilaus* chapter 5 note 4). For Castor's interest in hunting, see also 3.1.

14. *and warriors*: Curiously, the author fails to mention the Homeric version (*Iliad* 2.731), according to which Machaon and Podaleirius were sons of Asclepius (in Homer a Thessalian hero) and skilled physicians to the Achaean (Greek) army at Troy.

15. *'the devoted son'*: Antilochus' father was Nestor; 'devoted son' translates the epithet 'Philopator', which was later to be used as a title of the fourth Ptolemy, a member of the Graeco-Macedonian dynasty of Egypt (reigned 221–204).

16. *Greece invincible*: Hellas ('Greece'), even as late as the notional time of Achilles, was not yet a usable concept; this is Xenophon's – or Xenophontic – 'Panhellenist big talk' (see *Agesilaus* chapter 1 notes 10 and 32).

17. *education in general*: Paideia, 'education' (literally of *paides*, 'children'), was the general framework within which the technical treatises, both the philosophical and the more directly pragmatic, of Xenophon – as of his contemporaries Isocrates, Plato and Aristotle – were framed. But few *paides* would have been in a position to read them for themselves; this is a rare instance of a direct address to 'young men' (*neoi*). See further main Introduction and next note.

CHAPTER 2

1. *just out of childhood*: Greek lacked a vocabulary of adolescence; a male passed from being a 'child' (*pais*), which included the stage of being a 'lad' (*meirakion*), to the status of 'young man' (*neos*; cf. 12.6, 12.7). At an intermediate stage between childhood and adulthood he might be designated *ephebos*, 'on the threshold of adulthood'. Not long after Xenophon's death, probably, Athens for the first time formalized the *ephebeia* into a compulsory 'national service' for eighteen- and nineteen-year-olds, at least for those of hoplite status or above; Xenophon would surely have approved.

2. *speak Greek*: Typically, therefore, it is envisaged that the net-keeper would be a barbarian slave; cf. 6.18. Ability to speak Greek was a criterion of admission to initiation in the Eleusinian Mysteries, which did not forbid on principle the joint participation of masters and Greek-speaking slaves.

3. *Phasian or Carthaginian flax*: Phasis was in Colchis at the far eastern end of the Black Sea (in modern Georgia), and conventionally constituted the easternmost limit of the Greek *oecumene* (the westernmost being marked by the Pillars of Hercules or Straits of Gibraltar). Flax (*linon*) of presumably the wrong type or quality was grown much closer to home, e.g. in Messenia. See also 10.2.

4. *avoid snags*: Those interested in the finer points are referred to Delebecque, *Chasse*, which also contains ingenious illustrations.

CHAPTER 3

1. *hounds*: The author refers to them throughout in the feminine gender. See also chapter 7 note 1.

CHAPTER 4

1. *thin ears*: The ideal type of Greek hunting hound seems to have been akin to our fox-terrier; cf. 3.5.

CHAPTER 5

1. *moon . . . obscures them*: Had Shakespeare written 'Fear no more the heat of the moon', we would have been surprised – but not so, apparently, the Greeks. See e.g. Plutarch, *Moralia* 658b–d.

2. *bodies are relaxed*: Cf. perhaps 4.6, where the good hound does not abandon the chase apparently because she retains a keen sense of smell even in the heat of the day. There may be an allusion to some physiological theory of smell, such as that of Aristotle's pupil Theophrastus, according to which scents can be detected only if the appropriate bodily pores or channels are tight enough to keep the air inside the body in proportion with the scent-bearing outer air.

3. *the goddess's care*: Artemis. For the quasi-religious scruple see note 7 below.

4. *sacred islands*: The author probably has in mind especially Delos, which was the birthplace of and sacred to both Apollo and his sister Artemis.

5. *eyes bulge outwards*: In *The Dinner-party* 5.4 (Penguin *Conversations of Socrates*) Socrates is allowed to claim without contradiction that his eyes, because they are bulging and therefore see sideways as well as straight ahead, are 'more beautiful' than his interlocutor's in the sense that they are better constructed for the particular function, sight, for which humans possess eyes.

6. *his passions*: For a similar rhetorically expressed point, see *Cavalry Commander* chapter 8 note 2.

7. *normal practice*: The Greek *nomos* could mean a formal law, but the author specifies none, so the alternative meaning of 'custom' or 'tradition' seems preferable. The author's scruple against hunting through all sorts of crops (contrast 12.6) is probably no more strictly religious than the taboo on hunting leverets (5.14); but springs and streams, inhabited by or identified with nymphs, sprites and even gods, might have been avoided by hunters for properly religious reasons. See also chapter 6 note 1.

8. *days when hunting is forbidden*: The tabooed days were religious festivals.

CHAPTER 6

1. *After praying . . . Artemis the Huntress*: For the tithe consecrated to Artemis by Xenophon and his fellow hunters at Scillous, see Introduction.

2. *hit it*: The author, despite 2.2, had omitted to mention that the slave net-keeper (see chapter 2 note 2) might carry a club, an interesting partial exception to the rule that slaves were not permitted offensive weapons.

CHAPTER 7

1. *best season . . . develop in*: For the breeding of hounds, see 3.1. Up to 7.6 the assumption is that hounds for hunting are female; the adjectival phrase translated 'physically well-formed' at 7.7 reverts once again to the feminine gender.

2. *discipline*: The word translated here as discipline, *kosmos*, meant at its root 'order', and by extension, because it was assumed that the workings of the universe were ordered and orderly, the cosmos. Because orderliness was considered becoming, *kosmos* could also mean adornment, whence our 'cosmetics'. Emphasis is again placed on 'due order' (the adverbial *kosmios*) at 10.8.

CHAPTER 9

1. *hard work*: Anderson, *Hunting*, p. 49, expressed the wish that 'this chapter was not Xenophon's work', contrasting its opening injunction to hunt fawns with the earlier injunction to spare young leverets (5.14). 'Indian' hounds could be a distinct breed specially imported in the author's day from the Indian subcontinent (or Tibet?), or more generically hounds known or thought to have originated somewhere in the Far East. Herodotus 1.192.4 (four large villages of Babylonia were exempted from all other tribute in return for looking after the huge numbers of Indian hounds belonging to the Persian Great King) makes the latter more likely.

2. *this makes it set off*: Had the author perhaps seen a fawn trembling in fear before bolting and assumed that it was cold? For the connection between shivering and physiological contraction, see the Hippocratic treatise *Places in Man*, chapter 9.

3. *spikes . . . into it*: The scenario we envisage (the text being, as often, less than transparently clear) is as follows: the purpose of the wooden spikes is to give way, so that when the deer steps in the trap, they yield sufficiently to let its foot in; then, when the deer tries to set off, its foot becomes impaled on the metal spikes.

4. *esparto*: The plant may be Spanish broom (*genista*, whence 'Plantagenet') rather than the grass now called esparto (*stipa tenuissima*). Some have seen a connection between *spartos* and the town Sparta.

CHAPTER 10

1. *Indian . . . and traps*: Indian hounds – see 9.1; Laconian – 3.5; Locrian – *Agesilaus* chapter 2 note 2. Anderson, *Hunting*, p. 53 rightly comments that the 'admirable description' in 10.1–18 'requires little in the way of either interpretation or commentary'.

2. *a spear*: A hoplite's spear, that is, made from *cornus mas*.

3. *for deer*: See 9.11–16.

4. *right hand*: The author, in common with Greek practice generally, did not recognize the 'natural southpaw'. Plato (*Laws* 794d–795d) entered a solitary and unheeded protest in favour of ambidexterity.

5. *wrestling stance*: The allusion to wrestling invokes another characteristically upper-class leisure activity with its own elaborated codes, rituals and protocols.

6. *by victory*: Overcoming the boar is compared to winning a military victory; for another such comparison, to different effect, see 13.12.

7. *to hunt*: Now it is the human hunters who must show 'courage' or 'spirit', *eupsukhia*; for the hounds, see 4.6.

8. *the pike*: This summarizes 10.4.

CHAPTER 11

1. *Pangaeum . . . Macedon*: It is interesting that the author should have included the Pangaeum district, in Chalcidice and so well within the Greek sphere, as a 'foreign land' (*xene chora*) roamed by exotic fauna. Note that one of the cantons of Macedonia was named Lyncestis, 'lynx-land'.

CHAPTER 12

1. *practical aspects of hunting*: Here begins the politico-philosophical epilogue, which some have attributed to a different hand from the preceding practicalities.

2. *hunting animals*: Actually, hoplite infantry militiamen and *a fortiori* the even wealthier cavalrymen had slave attendants to carry their equipment for them off the battlefield. This remark would seem to apply with greater force to mercenaries.

3. *prime . . . condition success is never far off*: The author is claiming that hunting completed the hoplite warrior's armoury, by adding extra fitness and flexibility.

There were competitions for *euexia* ('fitness') at several local agonistic festivals, apparently akin to the *euandria* ('manly excellence') contest at the Panathenaic Games (*Memoirs of Socrates* 3.3.12), but what exactly they involved is unclear: D. G. Kyle in J. Neils (ed.), *Goddess and Polis: The Panathenaic Festival in Ancient Athens* (Princeton University Press, 1992), pp. 206–7 n. 102.

4. *not deprive . . . of their game*: This passage implies a distinction between professional huntsmen and the enthusiastic amateurs to whom the (rest of the) treatise is directed. Among hoplites, the Spartans were unique for their skill in night-movements.

5. *undertake any other honourable occupation they like*: Provided, that is, they have the leisure to pursue them – which, it is understood, such elite young men will.

6. *their own*: If the treatise is indeed a fourth-century work, this passage could be seen as a contribution to the important debate over the proper political relationship between the public and the private spheres. Rather than emphasizing the priority of the public over the private, as a democrat would, the author first counters the accusation that hunting involves neglect of private affairs and then affirms the thesis developed at length in The *Estate-manager* that the private and the public are not only compatible but mutually reinforcing and beneficial.

7. *needs protection*: The author displays an odd – but perhaps quintessentially Xenophontic – combination of a pre-scientific belief in straightforward retribution for evildoers with a Socratic despisal of all pleasure, especially bodily.

8. *qualities a good man should have*: Xenophon's *Agesilaus* discourses upon the qualities comprising 'perfect goodness'.

9. *as I mentioned*: See 1.3.

10. *by him*: This casual insertion of a reference to a pederastic relationship speaks worlds for the author's social purview and pedagogic frame of reference. See *Hiero* chapter 1 note 4. For pederasty's supposed pedagogic function, see Xenophon, *Spartan Society* 2 (Penguin *Plutarch on Sparta*). As noted in the Introduction, a hare was a typical love-gift from pederastic lover to desired beloved.

CHAPTER 13

1. *sophists . . . exactly the opposite*: On the sophists, see main Introduction. On this author's hostile attitude towards them, see Introduction to this treatise; it is interesting that he should think of their teaching as being given in written not oral form. The teachability of virtue was a cardinal point of opposition between Plato's Socrates and the sophist Protagoras of Abdera as represented in the Platonic dialogue named after him.

2. *are offensive*: Whether or not this treatise, or this portion of it, is by Xenophon, here is the keynote of Xenophon's moral pedagogy in all the treatises included in this selection – they are designed to teach serious and socially useful lessons in virtue in a practical way.

3. *people who really know . . . professional deceivers*: This may be intended as an allusive plural referring specifically to Socrates, who – at least as he is represented by Plato – claimed to 'know' in a special way.

4. *men's fortunes*: In addition to all their other crimes, sophists commit the ultimate sin – the abuse of hunting. There may well be an implied contrast here with the pedagogic practice of Socrates, who taught free of formal charge (*Memoirs of Socrates* 1.2.7–8).

5. *of piety*: The treatise (or epilogue) climaxes in a fresh exhortation to piety, which leads on to the two concluding paragraphs, which in turn refer the reader back to the introduction: a neat piece of ring-composition.

6. *watching it*: See chapter 1. For the inspiration allegedly due to being overseen, see 12.20. See also *The Estate-manager* 12.20 and 21.10–11.

7. *Procris*: Procris was married to Cephalus (see 1.2) and shared her husband's enthusiasm for hunting. Atalanta (chapter 1 note 5) was so devoted to hunting that she resolved to remain unmarried, like Artemis, unless a suitor could beat her at the footrace; no one could – until Meilanion slowed her down by dropping golden apples, given him by Aphrodite, to tempt her.

WAYS AND MEANS

CHAPTER I

1. *the allied cities*: The allies in question are those of the so-called Second Athenian Sea-League, formed in 378 on the basis of mutual hostility to Sparta; within half a dozen years, the number of allies had reached seventy-five, but within the same span Athens was seen to have broken the anti-imperialist guarantees with which she had encouraged allies to join (see chapter 5 note 7). The Social (Allied) War of 357–355 put an end to the League as a viable alliance – and was a major contributory cause of Athens' public penury at the time of the treatise's writing. Some modern scholars are of the view that not only *Ways and Means* but also *A History of My Times*, which probably reached its final form around the time that the former was being contemplated or drafted (see chapter 4 note 18 and chapter 5 note 19), were motivated by

Xenophon's determinedly anti-imperialist moral stance, but see chapter 5 notes 4 and 8.

2. *anywhere else*: Xenophon's paean here and in 1.5 yields to none in patriotic fervour, but it does conflict rather sharply with the general and not unjustified perception (e.g. Thucydides 2.2; Plato, *Critias* 111) that Attica was not exceptionally blessed by nature, a defect which was compensated for by commerce seconded by imperial power (e.g. Thucydides 2.38). See P. Garnsey, *Famine and Food Supply in the Graeco-Roman World* (Cambridge University Press, 1988), Part III. Praise of 'the gods' is partly conventional, partly Xenophontic — and almost superstitious.

3. *supply of stone*: The most famous and expensive marble, used lavishly on the Acropolis, was from Mount Pentelicum; but Mount Hymettus also yielded fine marble, and workable local limestone (*poros*) abounded: see R. E. Wycherley, *The Stones of Athens* (Princeton University Press, 1978).

4. *silver ore . . . or sea*: On Attic silver, see chapter 4. After Laureium, the nearest substantial deposits of the ore were in the Mount Pangaeum district of Chalcidice (also a source of exotic huntable fauna, see *On Hunting* 11.1); these constituted a major part of the economic basis of the rise of Philip of Macedon (reigned 359–336).

5. *Athens . . . centre of Greece and . . . inhabited world*: More encomiastic hyperbole, so far as Athens was concerned; Aristotle (*Politics* 1327b29–30) saw Greece as at the centre of the *oecumene*, but most Greeks would automatically have identified Delphi, not Athens, as the centre of Greece.

6. *pivot of a circle*: Cf. Isocrates 4.42 on the economic centrality of Peiraeus. By 'Greece' here is meant not just mainland Greece, the southern extension of the Balkan peninsula, but the entire Greek world from Phasis to the Pillars of Heracles (see *On Hunting* chapter 2 note 3).

7. *most states have non-Greeks on their borders . . . non-Greek lands*: 'Most states' is numerically accurate – Xenophon is here taking an enlarged view of the Greek world with its well over 1,000 states.

CHAPTER 2

1. *into consideration*: Xenophon's primary interest here is in raising revenue and extracting other public services from the perhaps 10,000 or more Greek and non-Greek metics (cf. 4.40–1); but in other contexts (see *Cavalry Commander* chapter 9 note 4) he could take a more generous view of these otherwise under-privileged residents of Athens and Attica (especially Peiraeus).

2. *resident alien's tax*: Metics are attested under a variety of titles in over seventy

Greek cities. At Athens adult males were required to pay a *metoikion* (metic poll tax) of one drachma a month, independent women metics half that amount.

3. *and households*: Most metics were probably below hoplite status, so Xenophon's proposal to exempt metics from the obligation to serve as hoplites would benefit only a minority. Allowing the wealthiest metics to join the cavalry (see note 5 below) would measurably enhance the social status of only that privileged few. Most Greek metics at Athens were what we would now call 'economic migrants', attracted by Athens' superior economic opportunities, and therefore technically free to return to their places of birth (and, if Greeks, citizenship) at any time; a few, however, were political refugees. For the non-Greek metics, see next note.

4. *resident aliens come from*: Among the non-Greek metics, some were traders, like the Egyptians and Phoenicians who were given permission to establish religious sanctuaries to Ammon and Astarte respectively in the Peiraeus; others were ex-slaves, including skilled men such as bankers, liberated privately by their Athenian masters but not normally granted Athenian citizenship (see chapter 4 note 10). The latter might be wealthy enough – and sufficiently rooted – to be required to serve as hoplites. Xenophon's complaint about the non-Athenianness of the Athenian army might have been better addressed to Athens' increasing reliance on mercenaries.

5. *to serve in the cavalry*: This had been advocated by Xenophon already in *Cavalry Commander* 9.6, without effect.

6. *live in Athens*: Ownership of real estate at Athens was an exclusive right of citizens. Exceptionally, an individual metic might be granted *enktesis*, that is the privilege of owning land and/or a house. Xenophon's proposal to extend the privilege more widely was put into effect elsewhere, but the Athenians, jealous of their democratic privileges, resolutely kept the barrier between metic and citizen status high. By 'Athens' here Xenophon must mean the city of Athens within the walls (destroyed in 404, rebuilt in the late 390s), which was less densely and less regularly inhabited than Peiraeus (newly laid out in the fifth century to the plan of Hippodamus of Miletus).

7. *the custodians of orphans*: *Orphanophylakes* are otherwise unattested: see *Ath. Pol.*, Rhodes, *Commentary*, p. 633. See also *Cavalry Commander* chapter 9 note 3.

CHAPTER 3

1. *complete safety*: The allusive plural refers specifically to the harbour, or rather three harbours, of Peiraeus, of which the specially developed commercial harbour of Cantharus is particularly in Xenophon's mind (see also note 3 below). Despite its enormous length of coastline, good harbours were in short supply in Aegean Greece, though ancient merchantmen with their shallow draught could be simply beached rather than docked if necessary.

2. *purchase price*: Ancient coinage was not fiduciary but worth what the metal composing it weighed. All coins were issued by a central validating authority, and Athenian (or Attic) coinage was especially highly valued for its guaranteed purity – so highly indeed that in Egypt in Xenophon's day Attic coins were both overstruck (and re-used) and imitated. See C. Howgego, *Ancient History from Coins* (Routledge, 1995).

3. *Peiraeus Emporium . . . resolution of disputes*: 'Emporium' was the technical term for the commercial, as opposed to the military, part of the Peiraeus. Xenophon's 'Controllers' are probably what Demosthenes and other sources call the 'Overseers' of the Emporium. Rather than Xenophon's favourite system of differential competitive reward, the Athenians introduced special courts on an equal basis for all comers so that commercial lawsuits could be settled with particular dispatch.

4. *prospect of prestige . . . flock to Athens*: Xenophon emphasizes moral as well as material incentives, appealing to the honour syndrome that dominated the Greek civic value-system.

5. *considerate legislation*: See chapter 4 note 19.

6. *Hegesileos' command*: The wealthiest one-fifth to one-third of Athenians qualified for payment of 'war-tax' (*eisphora*), a system first introduced in the fifth century, but reorganized at the time of the foundation of the Second Sea-League (see chapter 1 note 1). Lysistratus' command was in 364/3; Hegesileos' in 363/2.

7. *recover their money . . . in part*: Eisphorai (see previous note) might also be raised exceptionally for naval expeditions, but the Athenian navy was ordinarily financed by means of a different system known as 'liturgies', or (literally) 'public works': a handful of the richest Athenians, numbering perhaps only 400, were required on a rotating basis to make themselves responsible for the outfitting and upkeep of a trireme war-ship (built at state expense, and docked at Peiraeus) for one year; the trierarch (as the trireme liturgist was known) was technically also in command of the ship, but he might and probably usually would delegate the captaincy; technically, too, the state was supposed to pay the crew's wages, but in practice the trierarch often found himself making up shortfalls. Nevertheless, a generous and successful trierarch did stand to win great kudos and honour. See generally V. Gabrielsen, *Financing the Athenian Fleet* (Johns Hopkins University Press, 1994).

8. *two minas*: There were 60 minas in a talent, and it is estimated that a fortune of 3–4 talents would have put an Athenian into the 'super-tax' liturgical

bracket (see previous note). 'Most Athenian citizens', however, were poor, unable to afford an outlay of even 1 mina (100 drachmas), and only too pleased to receive the daily wage of 3 obols (½ drachma) that was paid for serving as a juror in the People's Court. Xenophon is therefore addressing here only the seriously wealthy, the sort of people who had sufficient spare capital to make 'bottomry' loans, that is lend money (at very high rates of interest) to long-distance sea traders. To them, the potential 5+ mina-payers, he must talk in terms of investment and guaranteed return to make his proposed scheme seem attractive.

9. *human institutions*: Cf. *Memoirs of Socrates* 1.4.16 (Penguin *Conversations of Socrates*); also Isocrates 8 ('On the Peace').120 (probably written about the same time as *Ways and Means*).

10. *share in this bounty*: There was no such 'register of eternal benefactors', except in the fertile imagination of Xenophon, who seems to have modelled it on the grant of citizenship to foreigners that was made to the grantee and his legitimate male descendants in perpetuity. In Xenophon's lifetime such exceptional grants were made to among others Euagoras (a king), Dionysius I (a tyrant) and Orontes (a Persian satrap): see M. Osborne, *Naturalization in Athens* (Royal Belgian Academy, 1981–3).

11. *in general*: This idea of instituting a merchant marine is out of the same mould as Xenophon's later suggestion about Athens' investing publicly in mine-slaves: neither was taken up in practice, partly for technical reasons but mainly because they offended against the Athenians' entrenched notions of what it was proper for the state to do economically, and what should be left to private enterprise. The state did, on the other hand, lease out immovable, especially sacred, property, and did farm certain taxes: see 4.19 below; and *Ath. Pol.* 47.

CHAPTER 4

1. *first undertaken*: Archaeological evidence from the Laureium district of south-eastern Attica indicates that mining had occurred there as early as the sixteenth century BC, but the period of intense working, which depended on a suitable labour force and sufficient labour supply, did not begin before the sixth century, or even the early fifth. In the final phase of the Peloponnesian War (413–404), and for over three decades afterwards, there seems to have been a trough in working the mines, so that Xenophon's treatise coincided with a rising wave of renewed exploitation (see note 16 below). On this and many other aspects, see R. J. Hopper, *Trade and Industry in Classical Greece* (Thames & Hudson, 1979), pp. 170–89.

2. *for a while*: Xenophon would seem to be referring to the period down to 413 (see previous note), 'before the Deceleian affair' (4.25); see 4.14−15 for examples of intense investment.

3. *new entrepreneurs*: Xenophon may have in mind Hesiod's famous passage in *Works and Days* about the good Strife that encourages 'potter to be angry with potter and carpenter with carpenter' (line 25) in the interests of economic self-improvement. His point would be that so abundant is mining wealth that economic advantage accrues even without expenditure of anger.

4. *workers*: Such *ergatai* could in principle be either hired or owned, free or slave, but Xenophon is likely to have had slaves in mind chiefly here; only very occasionally do we hear of a concession being worked purely with free familial labour.

5. *more people turn to this line of work*: Mining, that is, contradicts the 'normal' laws of supply and demand, as illustrated for instance in 4.36. See also 4.25 for the alleged inexhaustibility of the supply.

6. *burying . . . to use*: There is a pun in the Greek, in that one both digs the ground in order to extract the silver and then digs the processed silver (in the form of coins) into the ground in order to hoard it. Such seemingly miserly hoarding was actually quite normal, given the general lack of secure investment outlets apart from landownership and farming.

7. *of silver*: Ph. Gauthier (whose excellent *Commentaire* is presumed throughout), p. 131, rightly distinguishes between the generally received idea, which Xenophon shared, that gold varied in value whereas the value of silver remained fixed, and the historical fact that gold on occasion depreciated. So far as the latter goes, it appears that, apart from a few blips caused by the introduction to Greece of Persian gold by mercenaries, the ratio of the price of gold to that of silver at Athens remained pretty constant at 12:1 from the late fifth century down to the time of this treatise.

8. *same conditions as citizens*: Mining was, legally speaking, a free-for-all, open to all foreigners whether resident or non-resident, as well as to citizens. Contrast land-ownership, where only a handful of specially privileged metic foreigners were granted equality of access with citizens (see chapter 2 note 6).

9. *plain . . . to see even today*: Similarly, at *The Estate-manager* 15.10−11 and elsewhere, Xenophon has Ischomachus claim that even the technical aspects of agriculture are obvious.

10. *Sosias . . . Hipponicus*: Sosias was most probably an ex-slave metic; perhaps he had served when a slave as a sort of accountant to a mining entrepreneur like Nicias, or maybe he had even himself worked in the mining area, presumably in the washeries or other ancillary services on the surface rather than in the lethal shafts below ground. Nicias was the famous conservative politician and failed general, who died in Sicily in 413, and of whom Plutarch wrote a Life (see Penguin Plutarch, *The Rise and Fall of Athens*, pp. 207–43). Hipponicus belonged to a distinguished political family, closely connected with Pericles. Philemonides (15) is not otherwise certainly attested.

11. *Athenian citizen*: This rather unclear passage is probably to be taken with 3.9–10 and interpreted as part of Xenophon's grand scheme to raise such a centrally deposited capital sum as eventually to provide every Athenian, rich or poor, with a daily allowance of three obols. The slaves would be as it were the working ingredient of this capital project, ensuring by their labour that the required surplus income of three obols per head was generated.

12. *exporting them*: Demosthenes accused his great rival and enemy Aeschines of having a father who was a branded slave and worked as public checker (*dokimastes*) in the Athenian mint. The accusation was of course false, but the public *dokimastes* would have been a familiar sight in the Athenian Agora and in Peiraeus (*Ath. Pol.*, Rhodes, *Commentary*, pp. 574, 576). Xenophon here proposes to extend the branding system to his new, publicly owned mine-slaves.

13. *their minds*: Here Xenophon does seem to be indulging in special pleading, verging indeed on the utopian.

14. *the Deceleian affair will verify*: The Spartans occupied and garrisoned the Athenian deme of Deceleia from 413 to 404 (see especially Thucydides 7.27–8). Any reader old enough to remember slave prices as they were before the affair would have to have been at least 75. Specifically, the fiscal reference could be either to the farmed tax levied on the sale of slaves or to the two per cent payable in the Peiraeus on slaves as merchandise entering or leaving Attica or to both.

15. *the silver*: The silver was extracted from argentiferous lead by cupellation (see note 22 below); it no longer exists in its primitive state in workable quantities, and modern mining interest has been concerned primarily with the extraction of cadmium and manganese, although the ancient slagheaps have been to a lesser extent reworked for the lead.

16. *restarted there*: The extant records of the ten *Poletai* ('Sellers'), the board of Athenian officials responsible for leasing the mining concessions (the state claimed ownership of all subsoil resources), would seem to confirm that after a long gap mining began again in earnest only in the 360s.

17. *worry . . . itself demands*: The implied fear is of servile insurrection, which actually is not known to have occurred at the Laureium mines until the very end of the second century BC. On the other hand, many thousands of mine-slaves took advantage of the Spartan occupation of Deceleia (see note 14 above) to run away (Thucydides 7.27.5). Contrast the known Helot

insurrections (*Agesilaus* chapter 1 note 6); and for fear of slave violence more generally, see *Hiero* chapter 4 note 1.

18. *the recent war*: On the identification of this war (cf. 5.12) hangs the secure dating of the treatise; internal and external evidence conspires, if not quite to prove, at least to make it extremely probable that Xenophon was referring to the Social War (357–355; see Gauthier, *Commentaire*, pp. 4–6, and Introduction).

19. *market rents*: Here we have the original 'peace dividend'; see further chapter 5 note 1. On 'looking after the resident aliens' see chapter 2 note 1.

20. *the enemy*: Xenophon's suggestion that the Athenians should deploy the public slaves not only in the fleet but in the land army is remarkable enough; that he should apparently also advocate that they be 'well-tended', is even more so, since it was normally – and normatively – the case that slaves were required to 'tend' (*therapeuein*; a standard word for slave was *therapon*) their masters. Perhaps his idealized Spartanism has got the better of his judgement here.

21. *besieged instead*: Chastened by their humiliating experience during the Peloponnesian War, the Athenians of Xenophon's day put a lot more effort into the land defence, both fixed and mobile, of the territory of Attica: see, with differing emphases and explanations, J. Ober, *Fortress Attica* (Brill, 1985), and M. Munn, *The Defense of Attica* (University of California Press, 1993).

22. *kilns*: The kilns were used for fusing the ore. There are fewer mentions of them in the extant mining-leases than of the ore-washeries, and only some of them were state property.

23. *plots . . . about Athens*: Xenophon's *choroi* ('plots') are to be distinguished from the *oikopeda* ('property') of *Memoirs of Socrates* 2.6 (Penguin *Conversations of Socrates*). On land in Athens, see chapter 2 note 6.

24. *effective*: Obedience, discipline, military effectiveness: here is Xenophon's holy trinity – or grail – as a didactic writer.

25. *maintenance due to each of these tasks*: Xenophon is apparently referring to some kind of ephebic training, though no comprehensive state-run programme is certainly attested before the mid-330s (see *On Hunting* chapter 2 note 1).

CHAPTER 5

1. *Custodians of the Peace*: Xenophon is here responding to the widespread longing among fourth-century Greeks for a 'new world order'; unfortunately, that yearning advanced no further than the concept of a general or Common

Peace, which in practice had to be imposed on the Greeks by an outside power (Persia) and was anyhow honoured more in the breach.

2. *held to be*: Xenophon's choice of words (*eudaimon*, literally 'well-favoured by the gods') leaves it ambiguous whether he has chiefly in mind the city's moral or its economic welfare. Possibly the former, since, as noted in the Introduction, after chapter 4 Xenophon reverts to being a moral-political theorist rather than a fiscal reformer.

3. *sacred or secular*: Strictly, the Greeks did not have our notion of 'the secular', only that of the more or less sacred; but although the Greek adjectives *hiera* and *hosia* can both mean 'sacred' in other contexts, here some such contrast as 'sacred or secular' is intended. Xenophon's tolerance of sophists here is perhaps surprising, at any rate in contrast to the diatribe against them that we find in *On Hunting* 13. On works of quality, see also *Hiero* 1.11.

4. *helping Greece*: On Xenophon's supposed 'panhellenism', see *Agesilaus* chapter 1 notes 10 and 32, and *On Hunting* chapter 1 note 16; on his anti-imperialism, see chapter 1 note 1 above. It is surprising to see him adopting here the Athenians' fifth-century propaganda line in defence of their empire that their revolted allies and of course Sparta no less vigorously repudiated.

5. *free will*: This is a reference to the foundation of the Second Sea-League; see also chapter 1 note 1.

6. *well served by Athens*: Athens had been supportive of those Thebans who ejected the occupying Spartan garrison in 379/8 (see *Agesilaus* chapter 2 note 23); soon after, in the summer of 378, Thebes, despite being virtually landlocked, became one of the six founder-members of the Athenians' naval alliance.

7. *well treated by us*: The defeat of Sparta by Thebes at Leuctra in 371 so disrupted the diplomatic concordat of 378 (see previous note) that in 369 Athens allied with Sparta against a newly hegemonic Thebes.

8. *recovering our control*: Xenophon's 'current situation of chaos in Greece' echoes the concluding sentence of his *A History of My Times* (7.5.27), the terminal date of which was summer 362. The Greek word translated as 'recovering our control', *anaktasthai*, means literally 'regain possession of' – which seems hardly innocent of imperialist overtones, or compatible with 'a complete end to war' (5.10).

9. *the Phocians*: Some scholars have tried – misguidedly – to use this reference to date the treatise to 346, interpreting the 'war' of 4.40 and 5.12 as the so-called Third Sacred War of 356–346. The latter, in which the Athenians in fact allied with the Phocians against Philip of Macedon, was fought in part, but only in part, for the autonomy – or rather the control – of the sacred site of Delphi.

10. *everyone's prayers*: The official ritual formulae of prayers in the Athenian Assembly (which met four times a month) included prayers for the 'safety' (*soteria*) of Athens.

11. *projects of their own choice*: Since Athens failed to keep the requisite records, it would in fact have been technically impossible for anyone to conduct the exercise Xenophon airily recommends with any mathematical precision. But this is anyhow mere rhetoric, dare one say mere sophistry, contradicted by the evidence of the eyes. True, 'the war' (that is, the Social War) had been financially devastating; but compare and contrast Athens' situation in the previous century. The Acropolis building programme of the fifth century, which was publicly paid for, was indeed significantly carried out during peacetime in the 440s and 430s when the funds were temporarily not needed to make war; but had Athens not devoted itself to war making in the previous thirty years, on the whole very successfully and lucratively, those funds would not have been there to be used in the first place.

12. *support their cause*: Cf. *Memoirs of Socrates* 2.6.27 (Penguin *Conversations of Socrates*), *Cyropaedia* 1.5.13 and Isocrates 8.138−9.

CHAPTER 6

1. *doing things*: Here speaks Xenophon the radical conservative, appealing to tradition (*ta patria*, literally 'the things of the fathers' or 'the ancestral things') under the banner of far-reaching innovation. In other words, trying to have his cake and eat it too.

2. *the gods*: Xenophon adopts the regular formula for a state's consultation of Zeus at his oracular shrine at Dodona, and of his son Apollo at his at Delphi. Consultation of Delphi was almost second nature, for all Greek states; Dodona, however, was to find increasing favour with Athens in the period 350−320, as Delphi fell under the control of Macedon (see chapter 5 note 9).

3. *the state*: Xenophon typically ends, as he had begun (1.3), with the gods − but by comparison with some other treatises, for example the *Cavalry Commander*, the gods have been conspicuous here rather by their absence.

TEXTUAL NOTES

I have translated Marchant's Oxford Classical Text, except at the following points.

HIERO THE TYRANT

2.14 Reading οἱ σὺν ταῖς πόλεσι with Erbse.

6.6 Reading δέ τοι with Denniston.

11.2 The OCT reading κόσμου is presumably a misprint for κόσμον.

11.7 Reading σὺ ἔσῃ ὁ instead of κηρυχθήσῃ, with Galliano.

11.13 There is a lacuna in the received text, which must have contained some such sentiment.

AGESILAUS

1.6 Reading οὐκέτι instead of ἔτι, with Richards: Agesilaus was over 40 years old.

1.19 Retaining the MSS reading ἰόντες.

2.17 Reading κατὰ Τενέαν instead of κατὰ τὰ στενά, with Köppen *ad Hellenica* 4.4.19.

2.20 A sentence or two seems to be missing, perhaps describing Agesilaus' decision to help the Achaeans and his arrival in Acarnania. However, the campaign is also covered in Xenophon's *Hellenica* 4.6.

2.20 Retaining τοῖς ψιλοῖς with the MSS.

2.22 Reading Λακωνιζόντων, Cartledge.

2.26 Reading οὐκ ἂν ἀλόγως with Marchant in the Loeb.

2.27 There is a short lacuna in the text, which probably contained something along these lines.

3.2 A short lacuna in the text probably contained something like this.

3.4 Retaining the MSS readings δισχιλίους and τετρακισχιλίους.

5.1 Reading μανίας and then ἀργίας with Athenaeus 613c.

6.4 Some text is missing. In his *Life of Agesilaus*, at 4.1, Plutarch paraphrases the sentence: 'Xenophon says that Agesilaus' obedience to his fatherland won him a great deal of power, enough to do as he pleased.'

11.14 Reading μεγάλης καὶ καλῆς ἐφιέμενσς <δόξης, εἰ καὶ μή> with Marchant in the Loeb.

HOW TO BE A GOOD CAVALRY COMMANDER

1.13 Reading τούς γε μὴν <βλάκας> ὄντας ἵππους with Delebecque.

1.24 Retaining καί with the MSS.

2.7 Reading ὅπως with the MSS.

4.3 A short lacuna in the text must originally have contained a Greek word meaning something like this.

4.10 Reading κρυπτὰς τάς with Delebecque.

5.10 Reading ὀλίγους <λίθους> τ' ἔχοντες with Delebecque.

6.3 Reading ὑδάτων with the MSS.

7.9 Reading ἐπί τε λείαν instead of ἐπιμελείᾳ, with Pierleoni.

7.14 There is a lacuna in the transmitted Greek text, which must originally have been filled with something like this.

8.3 Reading πτηνά with Harrison.

8.14 Reading ἐξ ἀπόρων with Erbse.

8.23 Retaining the MSS reading ἐκ τῶν ἀναστροφῶν.

9.5 Reading τοῖς καθίστασι τὸ ἱππικόν, Waterfield.

ON HORSEMANSHIP

1.9 Retaining the MSS reading ἢ σκληραὶ ἢ ἑτέραι.

1.13 Reading αὐτὸν τὸν ἵππον with MSS AO.

4.2 Retaining μή with the MSS; cf. Anderson in *Journal of Hellenic Studies* 80 (1960).

4.3 Reading δεῖ δέ, ὡς μὲν μὴ ᾖ ὑγρά, εἶναι with Marchant in the Loeb, and also omitting both the forthcoming lacunas marked in the OCT.

4.5 Reading ἀνάγκη γάρ, Waterfield.

5.5 Reading ἀναστήσαντα with Delebecque.

6.1 Omitting τὰ πρόσθεν, added by Marchant in the OCT.

6.8 Reading πέσαι instead of ποιῆσαι, with Pierleoni.

6.14 Adopting with some confidence Marchant's hesitant conjecture σὺν ἵππῳ.

7.1 Reading ἵππον ὡς ἀναβησόμενον with Delebecque.

7.8 Reading <τὰς> ἡνίας with Hermann.

7.11 Reading τῷ ἐπιρραβδοφορεῖν with Stephanus.

7.11 Retaining ἀναβαίνοι with the MSS.

9.4 Omitting, with Cobet, the entirely superfluous sentence εἰδέναι . . . ἐξεργάζεται.

9.8 Reading καί ποτε τοῦ, Waterfield.

10.2 Reading δινεύειν with Pollack.

10.10 Reading ὑγρότερόν ἐστιν with Delebecque.

11.7 The comma after μέχρι in the OCT is surely a misprint and should precede it.

11.9 Retaining the readings of MSS AB.

11.11 Retaining the clause found in the MSS but deleted by Schneider.

12.1 Reading ἱκανὸν φέρειν with Erbse.

12.4 Retaining καὶ τά with the MSS.

12.7 Omitting τῷ with the MSS.

12.8 Retaining παραπλευριδίοις with the MSS.

ON HUNTING

1.8 Reading ἀεὶ ζώντων with Delebecque.

1.9 Retaining ἐβουλεύετο with the MSS.

1.11 There is a misprint in the OCT, which has no iota subscript on σοφία, and should have a colon or a comma after this word, not a full stop.

1.17 Reading ὧν with some MSS.

2.1 Reading τιμὴν ἔχοντα with Loewenklau.

2.1 Another misprint in the OCT: ὠφελείας for ὠφελείας.

2.7 Reading τῶν τῶν ἀρκύων with Delebecque.

2.9 Reading <τὰ> δίκτυα ἕνεκα θήρας with Delebecque.

3.1 Reading καθαράς instead of μάλιστα, with some MSS.

3.3 Reading ἀφιστάμεναι τοῦ ἡλίου with Delebecque.

3.5 Reading καταπατοῦσι with Rühl.

4.1 Punctuating after ἄσαρκα with Pollux and the MSS.

4.3 Reading <ποιησάμενοι>, Waterfield.

5.3 Reading <ἐκ>τῆς γῆς, as conjectured by Marchant.

5.7 There is no need for the OCT's inserted ποιῶν.

5.12 Reading τοῖς νεογνοῖς instead of τῆς νυκτός, with Delebecque.

5.15 Reading ἐκ τῶν ἔργων ἄνω τ' ἐν ὅσοις ὁρμῇ ἔχονται αὐτῶν εἰς τὰ ἀργὰ σιμά with Delebecque.

5.17 Reading διωγμούς instead of δρόμους, with Delebecque.

5.30 Omitting Marchant's addition, gleaned from Pollux.

6.6 A word or two has dropped out of the text – presumably something like φραττεῖτο.

6.8 Transposing ἐν δὲ ταῖς . . . ταχύ to §11, as indicated below.

6.10 Reading προσιέσθω instead of προθείτω, with Delebecque.

6.10 Reading ἑώρακεν ἢ οὐ κατεῖδε with MSS BM.

6.11 Taking in the transposed sentence from 6.8.

6.15 Reading προφορούμενα with Pierleoni.

6.18 Reading δὲ κινουμένῳ instead of δ' ἐκεῖνον, with Delebecque.

6.20 Reading εὖ κύνες, εὖ ᾧ κύνες with the MSS.

6.21 Retaining προσχῶσι with the MSS.

7.1 Reading ἡ ἀνάγκη αὐτὰς ἔχει, Waterfield.

7.9 Omitting Marchant's unacknowledged addition in the OCT.

7.9 Reading ἕως ἂν θέλωσι (Delebecque) <εἶναι πρὸς> τῷ ἴχνει (Waterfield).

7.12 Omitting Gesner's inserted μή.

8.2 Omitting Marchant's inserted ῥήγνυσι.

8.3–4 Reading ἀπὸ δὲ τῶν τοιούτων ἐπειδὰν φανῇ with MS A, and therefore punctuating with a full stop after ἀεί.

9.2 Reading <καὶ> τὰς κύνας, Waterfield.

9.4 Reading οἱ instead of οἵ, with Delebecque.

10.2 Reading ἱκανοί with MS A.

10.5 Reading ἰχνευούσῃ with Schneider.

10.7 Reading συνέχονται γὰρ (MSS) ἐν τοῖς λίνοις (Delebecque).

10.12 Omitting τήν before ἀπό, Waterfield.

11.4 Reading ὑπερορᾶν, Waterfield.

12.5 Reading εὐεξίᾳ with the MSS.

12.11 Reading πρόοιντο instead of ἀργοῖτο, with the MSS.

12.17 Reading ἀμείνους δέ with Stobaeus.

13.10 Reading τῶν ἀστῶν with Schneider.

13.11 Omitting the second τῶν ἰδιωτῶν, Cartledge.

WAYS AND MEANS

3.8 Reading κατεσκευασμένας with Bake.

4.37 Reading αἱρώμεθα and moving ἡμῖν to after καλῶς, Waterfield.

4.51 Reading ξύμφημι with the MSS.

4.52 Retaining πλείω with the MSS.

5.1 Retaining πυκνοτέραν with the MSS.

5.2 Reading ὡς ἐμοὶ δοκεῖ (Castalio) παραλόγως σκοποῦσιν (Loewenklau).

INDEX

Visit Penguin on the Internet
and browse at your leisure

- preview sample extracts of our forthcoming books
- read about your favourite authors
- investigate over 10,000 titles
- enter one of our literary quizzes
- win some fantastic prizes in our competitions
- e-mail us with your comments and book reviews
- instantly order any Penguin book

and masses more!

'To be recommended without reservation ... a rich and rewarding on-line experience' – Internet Magazine

www.penguin.co.uk

READ MORE IN PENGUIN

In every corner of the world, on every subject under the sun, Penguin represents quality and variety – the very best in publishing today.

For complete information about books available from Penguin – including Puffins, Penguin Classics and Arkana – and how to order them, write to us at the appropriate address below. Please note that for copyright reasons the selection of books varies from country to country.

In the United Kingdom: Please write to *Dept. EP, Penguin Books Ltd, Bath Road, Harmondsworth, West Drayton, Middlesex UB7 0DA*

In the United States: Please write to *Consumer Sales, Penguin USA, P.O. Box 999, Dept. 17109, Bergenfield, New Jersey 07621-0120*. VISA and MasterCard holders call 1-800-253-6476 to order Penguin titles

In Canada: Please write to *Penguin Books Canada Ltd, 10 Alcorn Avenue, Suite 300, Toronto, Ontario M4V 3B2*

In Australia: Please write to *Penguin Books Australia Ltd, P.O. Box 257, Ringwood, Victoria 3134*

In New Zealand: Please write to *Penguin Books (NZ) Ltd, Private Bag 102902, North Shore Mail Centre, Auckland 10*

In India: Please write to *Penguin Books India Pvt Ltd, 706 Eros Apartments, 56 Nehru Place, New Delhi 110 019*

In the Netherlands: Please write to *Penguin Books Netherlands bv, Postbus 3507, NL-1001 AH Amsterdam*

In Germany: Please write to *Penguin Books Deutschland GmbH, Metzlerstrasse 26, 60594 Frankfurt am Main*

In Spain: Please write to *Penguin Books S. A., Bravo Murillo 19, 1° B, 28015 Madrid*

In Italy: Please write to *Penguin Italia s.r.l., Via Felice Casati 20, I–20124 Milano*

In France: Please write to *Penguin France S. A., 17 rue Lejeune, F–31000 Toulouse*

In Japan: Please write to *Penguin Books Japan, Ishikiribashi Building, 2–5–4, Suido, Bunkyo-ku, Tokyo 112*

In South Africa: Please write to *Longman Penguin Southern Africa (Pty) Ltd, Private Bag X08, Bertsham 2013*

PENGUIN AUDIOBOOKS

A Quality of Writing That Speaks for Itself

Penguin Books has always led the field in quality publishing. Now you can listen at leisure to your favourite books, read to you by familiar voices from radio, stage and screen. Penguin Audiobooks are produced to an excellent standard, and abridgements are always faithful to the original texts. From thrillers to classic literature, biography to humour, with a wealth of titles in between, Penguin Audiobooks offer you quality, entertainment and the chance to rediscover the pleasure of listening.

You can order Penguin Audiobooks through Penguin Direct by telephoning (0181) 899 4036. The lines are open 24 hours every day. Ask for Penguin Direct, quoting your credit card details.

A selection of Penguin Audiobooks, published or forthcoming:

Little Women by Louisa May Alcott, read by Kate Harper

Emma by Jane Austen, read by Fiona Shaw

Pride and Prejudice by Jane Austen, read by Geraldine McEwan

Beowulf translated by Michael Alexander, read by David Rintoul

Agnes Grey by Anne Brontë, read by Juliet Stevenson

Jane Eyre by Charlotte Brontë, read by Juliet Stevenson

The Professor by Charlotte Brontë, read by Juliet Stevenson

Wuthering Heights by Emily Brontë, read by Juliet Stevenson

The Woman in White by Wilkie Collins, read by Nigel Anthony and Susan Jameson

Nostromo by Joseph Conrad, read by Michael Pennington

Tales from the Thousand and One Nights, read by Souad Faress and Raad Rawi

Robinson Crusoe by Daniel Defoe, read by Tom Baker

David Copperfield by Charles Dickens, read by Nathaniel Parker

The Pickwick Papers by Charles Dickens, read by Dinsdale Landen

Bleak House by Charles Dickens, read by Beatie Edney and Ronald Pickup

PENGUIN AUDIOBOOKS

READ MORE IN PENGUIN

A CHOICE OF CLASSICS

Aeschylus	**The Oresteian Trilogy**
	Prometheus Bound/The Suppliants/Seven against Thebes/The Persians
Aesop	**Fables**
Ammianus Marcellinus	**The Later Roman Empire (AD 354–378)**
Apollonius of Rhodes	**The Voyage of Argo**
Apuleius	**The Golden Ass**
Aristophanes	**The Knights/Peace/The Birds/The Assemblywomen/Wealth**
	Lysistrata/The Acharnians/The Clouds
	The Wasps/The Poet and the Women/ The Frogs
Aristotle	**The Art of Rhetoric**
	The Athenian Constitution
	De Anima
	Ethics
	Poetics
Arrian	**The Campaigns of Alexander**
Marcus Aurelius	**Meditations**
Boethius	**The Consolation of Philosophy**
Caesar	**The Civil War**
	The Conquest of Gaul
Catullus	**Poems**
Cicero	**Murder Trials**
	The Nature of the Gods
	On the Good Life
	Selected Letters
	Selected Political Speeches
	Selected Works
Euripides	**Alcestis/Iphigenia in Tauris/Hippolytus**
	The Bacchae/Ion/The Women of Troy/ Helen
	Medea/Hecabe/Electra/Heracles
	Orestes and Other Plays

READ MORE IN PENGUIN

A CHOICE OF CLASSICS

Hesiod/Theognis	**Theogony/Works and Days/Elegies**
Hippocrates	**Hippocratic Writings**
Homer	**The Iliad**
	The Odyssey
Horace	**Complete Odes and Epodes**
Horace/Persius	**Satires and Epistles**
Juvenal	**The Sixteen Satires**
Livy	**The Early History of Rome**
	Rome and Italy
	Rome and the Mediterranean
	The War with Hannibal
Lucretius	**On the Nature of the Universe**
Martial	**Epigrams**
Ovid	**The Erotic Poems**
	Heroides
	Metamorphoses
	The Poems of Exile
Pausanias	**Guide to Greece** (in two volumes)
Petronius/Seneca	**The Satyricon/The Apocolocyntosis**
Pindar	**The Odes**
Plato	**Early Socratic Dialogues**
	Gorgias
	The Last Days of Socrates (Euthyphro/ The Apology/Crito/Phaedo)
	The Laws
	Phaedrus and **Letters VII and VIII**
	Philebus
	Protagoras/Meno
	The Republic
	The Symposium
	Theaetetus
	Timaeus/Critias

READ MORE IN PENGUIN

A CHOICE OF CLASSICS

Plautus	**The Pot of Gold and Other Plays**
	The Rope and Other Plays
Pliny	**The Letters of the Younger Pliny**
Pliny the Elder	**Natural History**
Plotinus	**The Enneads**
Plutarch	**The Age of Alexander** (Nine Greek Lives)
	The Fall of the Roman Republic (Six Lives)
	The Makers of Rome (Nine Lives)
	Plutarch on Sparta
	The Rise and Fall of Athens (Nine Greek Lives)
Polybius	**The Rise of the Roman Empire**
Procopius	**The Secret History**
Propertius	**The Poems**
Quintus Curtius Rufus	**The History of Alexander**
Sallust	**The Jugurthine War/The Conspiracy of Cataline**
Seneca	**Four Tragedies/Octavia**
	Letters from a Stoic
Sophocles	**Electra/Women of Trachis/Philoctetes/Ajax**
	The Theban Plays
Suetonius	**The Twelve Caesars**
Tacitus	**The Agricola/The Germania**
	The Annals of Imperial Rome
	The Histories
Terence	**The Comedies (The Girl from Andros/The Self-Tormentor/The Eunuch/Phormio/The Mother-in-Law/The Brothers)**
Thucydides	**History of the Peloponnesian War**
Virgil	**The Aeneid**
	The Eclogues
	The Georgics
Xenophon	**Conversations of Socrates**
	A History of My Times
	The Persian Expedition